MICHELE!
ALL OF THE
AND CHALLENGE IS
CREATIN' THE MOST
BEAUTIFUL VERSION OF
YOU. KEEP LEADING WITH
YOUR HEART.!!

NOBODY
CAN SAVE ME

LOVE AND STRENGTH
TO YOU. ALWAYS.

MICHELE!

ALL of THE PAIN, STRESS
AND CHALLENGE IS
CREATIN' THE MOST
BEAUTIFUL VERSION of
YOU. KEEP LEADING WITH
YOUR HEART?!

LOVE AND STRENGTH
TO YOU. ALWAYS.

MATT RUNNALLS

NOBODY
CAN SAVE ME

REDEFINING MENTAL HEALTH
WITH HOPE AND ACTION

First published in 2021 by Dean Publishing
PO Box 119
Mt. Macedon, Victoria, 3441
Australia
deanpublishing.com

Copyright © Matt Runnalls

Cataloguing-in-Publication Data
National Library of Australia
Title: Nobody Can Save Me — Redefining Mental Health With Hope And Action
Edition: 1st edn
ISBN: 978-1-925452-43-3
Category: Self-help/Memoir/Mental health

The stories in this book reflect the author's recollection of events. Some names, locations, and identifying characteristics have been changed to protect the privacy of those depicted. Dialogue and some encounters or experiences have been recreated from the author's memory.

This book deals with mental health. While the author has taken great lengths to ensure the subject matter is dealt with in a compassionate and truthful manner, it may be troubling for some readers. Discretion is advised.

The information provided in this book is designed to provide helpful information on the subjects discussed. This book is not meant to be used, nor should it be used, to diagnose or treat any physical, emotional or psychological medical condition. For diagnosis or treatment of any medical problem, consult your own physician. The publisher and author are not responsible for any specific health or psychological needs that may require medical supervision and are not liable for any damages or negative consequences from any treatment, action, application or preparation, to any person reading or following the information in this book. References are provided for informational purposes only and do not constitute endorsement of any websites or other sources. Neither the publisher nor the individual author(s) shall be liable for any physical, psychological, emotional, financial, or commercial damages, including, but not limited to, special, incidental, consequential or other damages. Our views and rights are the same: You are responsible for your own choices, actions, and results.

DEDICATION

Aurora, you gifted me another opportunity
at life because you saw something in me that
I couldn't see in myself, and you wanted me
to be here to recognize it.

This book is a testimony to my rediscovery
of hope visible in your kindness.

The same potential you saw in me, is now
what I am able to see in everyone else.

I am able to love bigger because of you.

You taught me what it looks like
to love and be loved.

You taught me to value self,
as imperfectly perfect as we all are.

Aurora Alexander (passed away 30/5/21)
Out of sight but always close to my mind.

Matt is sharing more in his INTERACTIVE book.

See exclusive downloads, videos, audios and photos.

DOWNLOAD it for free at
deanpublishing.com/nobodycansaveme

CONTENTS

PREFACE

FROM ONE BELIEVER IN RECOVERY TO ANOTHER, *I HEAR YOU*

I am no stranger to the darkness.

Every day I remember the beautiful faces of the ten friends I have lost to suicide. My heart aches for them and their families left behind. My heart aches that I was nearly next.

Every day I am grateful that I am still here, grateful that some beautiful hearts saw something in me that I couldn't see in myself back then. Every day I am grateful that my destructive thoughts no longer become my actions.

Every day when my eyes open, my heart beats stubbornly, my feet hit the ground and I breathe that fresh air, I know I am the lucky one, still here, able to talk about living.

HEAR THIS:
If you are lost and broken and feel like you can't take the pain anymore, I promise you it is making an incredible YOU!

The most beautiful people have been through the most adversity; the toughest roads create the most remarkable human beings.

That feeling of shame, that fear of being judged by others, that belief that you're a burden on people, is NOT true.

The unbearable emotional pain you're experiencing, will be your gift to a better life. Life's challenges and setbacks are what make you *"you,"* and we need *you.*

All that stress, confusion and frustration threatening to overwhelm you is creating a more beautiful version of YOU every day, alive and learning!

You do not have **to do** anything to make yourself accepted, you do not have to bring anything to the table to be accepted, just show up as your weird, crazy, stupid self; whatever your true self is. Whatever you are feeling *is worth feeling* for a wonderful purpose and those feelings will show you the path to lightness! Know that it exists waiting for you to find it.

I promise you there is hope, healing and recovery. Know this as Truth:

You are Worthy (yes, YOU!)
You were Not Made to Fit In
You Belong

You are Beautiful:
Not because you are perfect but because **You Are Not**.
You are Unique and I love that!

Put your hand on your heart.
Feel that?
That's your reason as to why you can, why you will.
I believe in that every moment. Even as you are reading these words I am sitting somewhere thinking of you and what you're going through.

ARE YOU WORRIED ABOUT SOMEONE?

For those people wishing for something better for their loved-one wondering why they can't connect with them, I implore you to see them and hear them for their true self that is often buried deep down beneath the fear of judgment from telling the truth.

Think about the people closest to you and how much you love them. Have you told them today? Have you made them feel it today? The difference between how much we care and how much we *show* it is the difference that this world is aching for. A human being is wired for connection, love and belonging.

For the caregivers reading this story, it's about learning to connect to the emotion of someone's story, acknowledging someone's pain and letting them feel it without judgment or shame. The circumstances don't matter, simply showing them you've felt pain too and feel empathy for their pain can reignite connection and hope that their pain does not define them, it's building them into a beautiful person with a unique and remarkable life to lead.

Instead of judging, marginalizing and shaming people, we need to rewire that connection, love, acceptance and belonging back into people's lives. The hardest part is helping people understand just when and how their words and actions can have such a negative effect, even on those they love.

As family, caregivers, teachers or mentors in every setting, facing this conversation is scary, it's daunting and sometimes it even feels dangerous, that you're worried about the consequences, the shame and potential fallout.

This conversation doesn't save lives directly; remember it helps our loved one to save their own life. That's the most motivating and beautiful part of something so simple we as caregivers can do.

It's our responsibility to take on this new level of consciousness, learn the words and actions to look after those around us who are struggling and who need to know we hear them and see their pain. This is the most important conversation we can all have, that of our mental well-being.

You need this conversation if you identify with any of the following:

- Do you know a teenager that is showing signs of withdrawal or anger or they just keep saying, "I'm fine?"
- Don't know about the mental health continuum or where your loved-ones sit amongst it?
- Are you unfamiliar with the idea of **Holding Space** for others?
- Don't have the time for self care amongst your own schedule?
- Are you struggling to get those closest to you to open up?
- Do you feel like you can't find good help?
- Do you feel inadequate to provide support for others?
- Did they tell you to keep it a secret, but now you're weighed down?
- You don't understand how someone's life can be so bad?
- Medication isn't working?
- Think kids are too sensitive these days?
- That it's just boys being boys?
- You don't know what it feels like so you think you can't help?
- Have no tolerance for those who do drugs?

That person you are worried about is lucky to have you. **But the truth is they can't hear you.** I want to rip open the truth behind their pain and once you hear and feel it, it will reframe how to care for someone struggling, how you can help them feel real hope and find the tools to recovery.

This conversation is not to judge you, guilt-trip or blame you. Firstly it's to say thank you for learning how to look out for someone, and to talk about new ways of supporting, connecting and empathizing with those in your care whether it's an hour a day in a classroom or if you share a relationship under the same roof. Let's get talking.

INTRODUCTION

THIS IS THE BOOK I WISH I HAD READ WHEN I WAS 15.
THE BOOK I WISH MY MATES THAT ARE GONE FOREVER HAD
READ BECAUSE MIND HEALTH IS AS IMPORTANT AS PHYSICAL HEALTH.

It's not just a story about me.

It could be the story of you or the loud mouth kid next door, or the quiet guy on your team that you don't know very well yet. It's about what we all have in common: our human need to be seen, to be heard, to be loved and to be accepted for exactly who—we—are.

The emotions that surround these needs are the wires that connect us all. This story is about what happens when those wires are cut, how frequently they are being cut and importantly what it takes to reconnect them. This book is for anyone that needs hope to rise above the pain and mess of thoughts in their head and are looking for the tools and strategies to manage those spiraling, crushing feelings.

This book is for teachers in every setting; schoolteachers, parents, bosses, coaches; mentors everywhere of any age that have the welfare of others in their hands, even for a short time because every single moment of interaction adds to a person's story about themselves.

Every forty seconds, somewhere around the world a person takes their life because they believe a story about themselves that's **NOT** true. It might be a continent away, a country away, a street away or under your very own roof. But it *is* happening and it breaks my heart.

Unfortunately it's been a frequent event in my life dating back to the age of twelve. I had no understanding of what it meant to lose someone, I had no idea how life could be so bad that suicide would be the only answer. That lack of understanding, acceptance and education around people's emotions, behaviors and feelings would be the exact ignorance that would lead to my own downward spiral several years down the track.

Over the years the ripple effect from the loss of my first friend to suicide has only grown bigger, as suicide kept blasting through my life—schoolmates, teammates, work mates and even leaders I've looked up to—and devastating the loved-ones left behind.

In many parts of the world it is still a taboo subject yet the World Health Organization acknowledges:

Suicide is a serious global public health issue. Globally, 703,000 people die by suicide every year. Suicide is among the leading causes of death worldwide, with more deaths due to suicide than to malaria, HIV/AIDS, breast cancer, or war and homicide. More than one in every 100 deaths (1.3%) in 2019 were the result of suicide.[1]

Worldwide, suicide is the fourth leading cause of death in young people aged 15–29 and the third leading cause of men in this age group. In my home country of Australia, it is even worse with suicide being the **leading cause of death** for males between 15–44. In 2019, 3318 lives were lost and 2502 of them were male. That means in Australia:

9 beautiful people
die each day from suicide

In addition, 65,000 attempts at suicide are reported each year in Australia alone.[2] Over 10 million Australian adults are estimated to know someone who has died by suicide, and 1 in 2 young people are impacted by suicide by the time they turn 25.[3]

Further breakdown shows that living with a mood disorder is the most common medical condition associated with suicide, reported in 40.6% of all suicides. And again, 64% of suicides were found to have one or more associated psychosocial risk factors identified.[4]

I was in the second highest demographic of suicide possible in my country, behind Aboriginal and Torres Strait Islander people, whose risk and rate of suicide is often found to be twice that of non-indigenous Australians.[5]

Many advocates and professionals around the world have said that suicide, when associated with mental ill health, is 100% preventable. Whether that is true or not I cannot prove, however the very possibility compels our efforts to always help, support and vigorously treat every individual as though it is true. That's what matters to me.

It all starts by changing the stories people believe about themselves. It's about understanding how those stories are formed and why they are accepted as "truth." It's about what we can do differently every time we interact with a person.

It's about recognizing the importance of how we spend each minute we have and how these choices affect our brain health. It is the realization that life isn't easy, that there is pain in it for everybody, pain that builds you into an incredible soul, creating a life well-lived, experiencing the beautiful breadth of human emotion.

It's about the knowledge and acceptance to know that when we put the time into ourselves and align with who we truly are, our minds become free and life becomes simple.

I believe with the array of skills I have equipped myself with and present in this book, I have helped to save my life and gone on to change the lives of others through the sharing of this knowledge.

This knowledge is not new or revolutionary. It has been around for thousands of years, resurfaced, spat out, ignored, picked up again and run with and hopefully now, implemented. When we put more work into our minds the same way we do our bodies, we can become more resilient, better versions of ourselves, finding our true value, our self worth, our belonging and purpose. Without those four things life can be pretty miserable.

For many years, my life operated on the core beliefs that I was worthless, a failure and a burden on every single person I came in contact with. I can't know what you're going through right now but I know well the pain of battling those debilitating thoughts every minute. I do know what it feels like to hit rock bottom, to claw your way back up, only to fall even harder, too close to that one way cliff.

I know what it's like to have a long-running, day-to-day battle with a brain disorder, bipolar. I know grief too well, having lost ten friends to suicide (yes, ten) over 13 years and I have stood next to the abyss of death four times, my feet balancing on the precipice without knowing which way I would fall.

It's taken me many years and tireless work and effort to be able to consistently find myself in the right place on my mental health continuum, a place I thoroughly deserve to be. I am impatient to spoil the surprise and show you the heart of the fire that drives me today. I want to shout out the miracle that your pain can be your savior that can shower you in hope. But why would you believe me if I didn't share my own tangled, agonizing mess that I went through?

I don't tell it because my story is any better than yours; it isn't. I don't tell it for my own self-service. I still feel a hell of a lot of shame for it. I've hurt a lot of beautiful people through it. I don't need anybody to feel sorry for me or cry for me, but simply to open up your hearts as you sift through this journey, for yourself or to help someone else.

I am not afraid anymore, and I don't want anyone else to be.

HOPE AND AN ACTION PLAN

Society may have told you that mental illness is to suffer, that depression means you are weak and the only option is to take antidepressant medication to keep the pain and the fog in your mind at bay. **I am here to tell you that all of this is not true.** Pain has a phenomenal purpose in your life.

This book will show you the scars of how I learned this; it will show you the adversities that have empowered me to have this conversation with you. **I don't have a degree that hangs on the wall behind me; take what you need from my story and ignore what you don't.** My learnings are not a replacement for professional advice. They are just that, learnings; from someone who is obsessed with finding a more optimistic and hopeful path for anyone needing one, like I did.

My involuntary "degree" that allows me do what I do today, has taken much longer to obtain, has cost me the lives of beautiful people around me that I can never pay off and helped me overcome a narrative about myself that wasn't true at all and nearly cost me my life.

CHANGE YOUR WORLD – TIP #1

Education is not just found in books and degrees.
It's about widening your knowledge through all the
adversities, the punches, and the experiences that
often provide the real truth about life

I have had years and years of work, research and learnings from some of the most experienced and well-recognized thought-leaders in the field of mind and behavioral health from right across the world. From their individual stories of recovery and finding amazing beauty in life, I determined the similarities between their well-being tools and strategies and how they could benefit me too. Best of all they are available to everyone looking for better health and well-being in their life. I have gathered a collection of common themes and approaches to life that are proven to dramatically change your outcomes. It has become a repertoire of consistent tools learned from all those remarkable souls who showed me that if they could recover, I could too!

The tools and strategies I have collected (but are not new) have often been overlooked, undervalued or in my opinion, withheld by the western medical fraternity. They are techniques that we have always possessed unlimited amounts of but commonly forget to embody. There are countless different tools so when you don't connect with one, there will be another to choose from. Many of them are natural extensions of understanding the balance of chemicals and hormones within our bodies' biological functions and how they are affected by certain lifestyle choices we make.

I have two clear objectives for sharing my story. Firstly, to help anyone in pain recognize themselves somewhere along in this story and for them to know with absolute certainty, **that their story isn't over, that their future is fucking unstoppable**. My own self-worth was shattered during my transition to adulthood by unexpected ridicule, abuse and the painful disregard I experienced in my trade apprenticeship. This began eight years of my life—prime years—spiraling out of control under the weight of the negative narrative playing in my head all day, before I found real help, support and natural ways to maintain my mental health.

This is the urgent, life-changing knowledge that is not being given to our young people, not being taught in the foundational periods of adolescence and early adulthood that could arm people so much better as they transition into adulthood. This transition does not simply happen upon turning 18; it takes many years of learning and support to develop the countless psychological and emotional skills we need to thrive as adults.

My other objective is to help society's teachers and caregivers recognize someone in their care that is struggling somewhere along this lonely road. To help them to see the signs because believe me, once you look back after the worst has happened, you'll see the signs of struggle were there like flashing neon lights that somehow we ignored. To help them see how the smallest word or gesture given from a place of compassion, can be the catalyst to ignite hope in a person's life. Acknowledging their pain and struggle awakens the power of human connection in them. They say that **Hope isn't an action plan, but it sure is the start of one**.

"MAN CAN LIVE ABOUT FORTY DAYS WITHOUT FOOD, ABOUT THREE DAYS WITHOUT WATER, ABOUT EIGHT MINUTES WITHOUT AIR...BUT ONLY FOR ONE SECOND WITHOUT HOPE."
HAL LINDSEY

How powerful are the well-timed words of a compassionate teacher to a student in pain, those words and gestures could be the catalyst to help them see their own worth and value and hope for a very different future.

CHANGE YOUR WORLD – TIP #2

The right words, in the right order, at the right time,
to the right people, may just be the difference
in them choosing to be here tomorrow.

CHANGE YOUR WORLD

The reality is you won't wake up one day and you're suddenly better; your pain, mistakes and doubts gone. What is possible is to **Change Your World** through putting powerful ideas into mental and physical action minute-by-minute, day-by-day.

I've stepped in shit, I've burnt bridges, I've caused myself pain, I've won awards, I've had sporting success, been dumped, fallen in love, broken bones, been broke, lost my job, met amazing people, spoken in front of thousands, made big mistakes, tried to fix them, while other mistakes I made again and again.

After I suffered or triumphed through each of these lessons, not long afterwards I'd inevitably realize the crucial lesson I needed at the time, and understood I needed to remember it going forward in life. These lessons have built up a philosophy for me around the power to **Change Your World**.

**Change Your World is about engaging with yourself,
engaging with others and the world around you from
a place of love and inspiration.**

As you read through the book, look out for these **Change Your World** Tips. They are my shortcuts to get to the heart of living well, they don't get rid of all the shit but help you to understand it all has a purpose.

My life today is full of drive and passion as I ride through the natural highs and lows that life brings, as well managing the luminous gift of my bipolar condition. Only because I am so far down this road, can I reflect on the building blocks of my story in the hope that others arrive at this place of light and love so much sooner.

My journey is far from over, I have recovered from the darkness but I am not healed, am not superhuman like some suggest or possess magic in what I do or say. I will be forever learning and finding ways to support myself and others to live a life that we might not have thought possible. Writing this in itself has allowed me to look deeper in that mirror of my life and feel even more. It's all beautiful stuff ... just give it time.

My experiences herein and the stories of the amazing people I have met since my journey began, will speak directly to your heart and not your head. Logic and reasoning are not necessarily felt or found on the mental health continuum but love, warmth, care and connection are. The lessons were awkward, hard and disillusioning at times, shedding light on many of society's assumptions and cultural habits that many do not want to hear yet but the truth is they are damaging lives and do not serve us well; it is time to evolve from the past.

I want to raise our awareness of those deep cultural habits that can both create an identity and destroy it. We must talk about the challenges and trials of adolescence and early adulthood and show the incredible value of mistakes and failure in building our character, one that can bend with life's struggles but not break. Developing minds need boundaries and discipline to build their place of belonging and purpose in the world. It's important each child knows that discipline comes from a place of care, not hate or power. Help our children hear your "why" even when there are consequences.

From here on in my story gets uncomfortable, ugly and might challenge your own sense of responsibility and behaviors. I can't apologize for that, it's something I had to acknowledge too; my own part in mine and other's stories.

It was my rediscovery of hope visible in the kindness of others and advocates and leaders in the community and around the world that showed me it was possible. That's all I want, not to tell you what to do but for you to know it's absolutely possible.

I have returned from the pain of the disconnected. Waking up every day and feeling like shit is not a way of life. You can wake up and know that you belong and you are loved for exactly who—you—are and it is *incredible*.

You can wake up faced with any adversity, knowing that you can tap into the strength of who you are and you will overcome it. And that too, is incredible.

 CHANGE YOUR WORLD – TIP #3

The potential for every butterfly lives within the caterpillar. It is the same for the human condition.
The caterpillar evolves from releasing gas, the same way it takes a little bit of shit to become fucking beautiful.

From one believer in recovery to another ... let me show you.

PART 1:

THE UNCOMFORTABLE TRUTH

Before we begin, I want to put the spotlight on two important facts. Firstly is to express my boundless love and gratitude for the unwavering support, love, kindness and compassion from the best parents anyone could ever ask for: my mum Louise and my dad Andrew, from day one until this very moment they have backed me at every hurdle. Where I would be without them isn't worth contemplating.

Secondly, what I'm about to tell you comes with the strongest of provisos. This story could have been very different had I been prepared with the skill set to tackle the emotional and psychological trials that I encountered as a young adult new to their working life.

Like so many young Australians, I was at the mercy of many of our subliminal cultural beliefs and behaviors that run deep in this country about masculine expectations, and the "harmless" jokes and initiations made through the disguise of larrikinism. The directive to "man up" when faced with new emotions and situations is the most powerful way to disconnect a young man from identifying, controlling and expressing the truth of who he is and what he's going through in a positive and proactive way.

Without having an emotional foundation of self-worth and value, the messages I received from significant "role models" at the time, delivered me the most soul-destroying period of my life.

And like for so many others, it did not have to be this way.

It began innocently enough: ideal childhood, amazing parents, good student in primary school who loved all forms of sport. In high school I was the athletic kid with an easy confidence, fun-loving nature and cheeky comment for everyone.

I was also the kid exiled to the hallway for much of the day for not being able to sit still. I was labeled a distraction to the class. Chances are you remember a guy like that from your school days. A guy who struggled to focus but no one bothered to delve any deeper into why this was or why he couldn't fit in to the one-size-fits-all system. That was me. So I scraped through Year 11, thinking how much better the real world would surely be.

What I found was a path to destruction.

My optimism soon turned to confusion, fear, and a growing belief in my own worthlessness. From being that sportsman at school who excelled on the cricket pitch, receiving praise as he moved through the ranks, my decline after leaving school came as a sudden blow.

The flipside to my sporting disguise was a lingering, subliminal feeling that I had failed as more than just a student; that the teachers' claims that I was the headache kid who would never amount to anything were true.

I didn't understand until much later, that years of hearing those disapproving comments and the physical forms of exclusion from the class (that I deflected with bravado, laughter and more bad behavior at the time) had in fact slowly been eroding my armor of youthful confidence. Those words and actions from several teachers had created a crack that was about to rip wide open under the toxic conditions that I encountered starting out in the world.

I had been excited to get a plumber's apprenticeship; or rather I was excited at the prospect of escaping school to work and become independent. My parents had only agreed that I could leave school early if I promised to complete the apprenticeship; the security of a trade certificate made a reassuring future for their son. I was happy enough to learn a trade if it meant embarking on a hopeful future so I made them a promise that I would absolutely finish my plumbers' apprenticeship no matter what it took.

It became a promise that would nearly kill me.

Despite my enthusiasm to forge my way in the adult world and leave the futility of high school behind me, in no way was I prepared for the shock of being an apprentice on a construction site in Australia in 2010. It was out of the frying pan and into the fire. While I enjoyed the novelty of my first month's pay and was open to learning from experienced tradesmen, soon enough I was finding each workday tougher and tougher to get through.

I could deal with the verbal corrections and discipline from making mistakes, and even the smaller deceptions of not being paid on time and working unpaid overtime, but I was unprepared for the disrespect, the bullying, the mocking, the vulnerable target I became for the mental (and later physical) abuse. I suffered these poisonous environments with two different bosses in four years, each with their own particular specialty of put down, derision and ridicule.

I'd walk into work each morning and say, "Hello" to the boss who would look up and just scowl at me without a word in reply. If I made a mistake I was mocked in front of anyone who was within distance. It might start out as scorn from not being able to start a motor on the first go, or not being able to tie off the ropes on the work vehicle perfectly within the first few minutes, the boss shot straight and loud with disdain, "Didn't you go to Scouts as a kid? Didn't your fucking dad teach you anything?" The condescending tones would eventually lead to the next humiliating scene and gradually these defeats began to eat away at my sense of self, my self worth and my personality was quashed from anxiety.

I didn't know how to respond to the onslaught, my usual cheeky personality had no place, and my boss didn't understand humor, only anger. My fear of being yelled at or made fun of with scathing tones intensified so I swallowed every word yelled at me. It was so confusing; from being the outgoing jovial guy with my mates in school to feeling wholly rejected and patronized in my first workplace.

At first I thought it was part and parcel of the real world. I thought this must be what bosses looked like for everyone. I was ready to shut up and just get on with the job to try and impress my boss. I thought if I told anyone what was happening, they would just say, "Welcome to the real world Matt!"

The workdays got longer and the breaks got shorter. It was repetitive work without any camaraderie or warmth that drained me each day. I had no energy left at night to do anything out of work, no time or energy for football training, catching up with friends was all gone, replaced by the relentless, soulless work. I saw other apprentices sometimes who had fun work stories to tell and they bounced around with energy after work and I wondered how they did it.

Finally one day about a year into it, I heard that another local plumber was looking for a worker so I spontaneously gave him a call. It was all quick and easy and I started working for him soon after. Now I admit I had heard he could be tough to work for but I figured it couldn't be worse than what I had already experienced—could it?

As they say, it's better the devil you know.

This opportunity quickly nosedived into another battlefield every day: a battlefield that I often tried to hide from as the rebukes turned physical. It started out with the humiliation of being threatened with tools, then fists, being shirt-fronted and finally hit with objects. Any mistake could lead to being swiped at with the head of a shovel, being pushed, chested or slapped over the head.

I had found another toxic, traumatic environment that was unraveling my self-confidence and blocking out all the light from my mind. Even though I wasn't scared of the physical pain of being hurt—a throwback to growing up with a competitive older brother—walking on eggshells, frightened of making the wrong decision or making a mistake swelled the anxiety within.

If I asked for help with equipment or had a question in regards to the job, I was told I was, "a privileged, private-bloody-school-kid with a sheltered upbringing." From the moment I opened my eyes in the morning, I felt anxiety building in the pit of my stomach wondering what would happen that day. The emotional abuse fed into a nagging feeling that I'd been hiding deep down since school, that I was a failure. Even the smallest of tasks became a challenge as I became caught up in this destructive narrative.

I still remember being on a job site in a little country town near where I grew up. All day I was emotionally battered and threatened, but I stood and copped it, I didn't mouth back or retaliate. I was always extremely anxious whenever my boss was on site but I just wanted to keep my job. I had to keep my promise to my parents at all costs.

On this particular day, the owner of the house we were renovating approached me as I was packing up and asked, "Does your dad always treat you like that?"

I quickly corrected her, "That's not my dad."

She was shocked, "The only reason I haven't called the police and Work Safe is because I assumed he was your father. But I will be ringing your apprenticeship management right now."

I panicked at the thought and asked her not to, "Please don't, it's okay— I'll handle it," I assured her. But I never did bring it up with anyone for fear of the repercussions. I lived in a small town, everyone knew my boss, and everyone knew me. If I lost this job word would spread fast that I couldn't take it, that I wasn't reliable, jumping from boss to boss; who else would want to give me a go?

For the first time all I could see, all I could feel was that I was worthless, a failure and a burden, that I wasn't good enough. Even when I did something right, I looked for the weakness in it. I started to question whether I was soft and weak. Was I a defect of humanity? Did I need fixing?

Would others react differently to this treatment, or was it just me that couldn't take it?

 CHANGE YOUR WORLD — TIP #4

Who is putting logs on your fire and who is pissing on it?
You're a product of your environment; so rid yourself
of the masquerade friends, people who cannot see
your value. Don't continue to hold space for toxic
people that cause you discomfort and pain when
good ones are queuing up to get in.

The situation dragged on for many months unraveling one day when I was unfairly dismissed over a trailer incident. The first day I ever stood eye to eye with the boss as a 2nd year apprentice and demanded, "Don't treat me like shit, I won't put up with it!" I was shirt fronted, screamed at and threatened. He said, "Good, fuck off then!" The whole sorry mess ended up going to the Fair Work court and a lot of damning information against my boss came out in the hearing. Yet somehow the judge simply ruled that he should reinstate me!

What?! That wasn't what I had wanted at all! It felt like a death sentence and I just couldn't go back. When the judge asked me if I had any final words for my boss before his ruling, I simply said, "I just hope that your daughter never grows up and experiences a boss like you."

I have since learned that subsequent apprentices to the same man did achieve a small victory when the court finally blacklisted him against taking on apprentices; however he was still free to hire sub-contractors. So I despair at the thought that any other young man or woman could have suffered such degenerate role modeling as I did.

Battling my apprenticeship wasn't the only thing that was going on in my life, but it played an enormous role in losing a lot of who I was and affecting the traits that people had loved about me. I lost a lot of stability in my mind and my moods suffered and even though I tried to hide all of the emotional struggle, people around me suffered too. To this day, I miss many aspects of the old Matt and often wonder what life would look like if the young, bubbly, energetic Matt hadn't been emotionally abused out of me. It was a big price to pay to grow up; an unnecessary price.

Over the years since then people have said to me, "Why did you stay so long? No one held a gun to your head, you put yourself through that shit for so long because you were too stupid to get out of it." Quite simply, my promise to my parents to finish my apprenticeship was absolute. I couldn't recognize at the time that it was costing me my well-being.

I used to tell my parents, "This apprenticeship will be the death of me," and then collapse into my bedroom at the end of each day, quiet and withdrawn. They assumed I'd had a tough day plumbing, which was par for the course; plumbing is a tough physical job. But they were words with a hidden meaning; they were me screaming out for help.

Every time I built up the courage to explain what was wrong and how I felt, the old-school mentality of never complaining held firm; that if I quit again, I was weak and unreliable. Half the time I was so consumed by the pain and fog of how I was feeling, I didn't have the brain space or strength to contemplate making any other decisions; I was just trying to cope, to survive.

My paycheck was a little bit of security to hang onto that I desperately needed. Mum and Dad weren't to know or understand the exact depths of how I was feeling. I battled negative, self-loathing thoughts all day and I spent many nights tucked up in bed imagining how to put an end to this pain.

How did I go from a fun, confident and energetic young guy to an emotional wreck by the age of twenty?

I am not alone in this experience. Some recover from mistreatment, some do not, some won't live to see out the completion of their apprenticeship and that is a cold, hard truth that may hurt many of you to know. Some of the mates I've lost did not make it because of the mistreatment and pressures of those initial years transitioning into the real world and working life.

I'm not going to lay blame on any individuals for the way in which I came crashing down, as I truly believe the real problem lies in the lack of education about mental health through our early years and not on any individual for the way in which they treated me.

The simple truth is, if I had had the skills back then to understand and articulate what I was experiencing I could have talked about it, and become knowledgeable and resilient enough to go and seek out more professional options. I wouldn't have had to struggle the way I did and the way in which people treated me could have been managed much easier. Sharing this lesson with people in all stages of their own journey is a passion that drives me every day.

 CHANGE YOUR WORLD – TIP #5

Our well-being is innate, meaning that it belongs to us and no one else. No "one" and no "thing" can give it to us or take it away.

The idea is not to believe we can prevent bullying, we can educate of course but ultimately we cannot control the way in which others are and behave to us, they may well be victims of their own stories, their own conditioning. The one thing we can control is the way in which we learn to show up resiliently in the face of any adversity with an extensive toolkit to draw upon.

But in my early years I had no knowledge of any of this.

JAKE

Along with the struggles of my 2nd year apprenticeship, another tragedy happened in May of 2011. I received a call one night that rocked me to the core. I learned my good mate Jake had taken his own life at the age of 19. His passing stunned the entire community; Jake was a very popular kid, always carrying a smile and indulging in humor and cheek. I hadn't known the depths of his struggle. In fact not many had; he had battled alone for too long.

In truth, I doubt that we would have had the required skills at that age to help him even if we had known of the crisis state his mind was in. Jake was the third and closest friend I had lost to suicide at the time.*

Along with the shock and pain of losing Jake, I felt fear. Fear that suicide was a monstrous black poison that was coming for me next. It had been creeping around in the corners of my mind for a while. Losing Jake was a very confronting way of making me recognize just how severe and powerful our thoughts can be. I realized those horrible feelings I fought on a regular basis—throwing myself and my tears into my pillow at the end of a shit day of plumbing—were extremely valid: valid and insidious.

I'm not saying they were true; they were a warning to be heeded. Sometimes I would make small, ominous efforts to tidy up in my bedroom as though for the last time. I would wipe out all records of communication by deleting my old messages and inboxes on my phone: it meant less to worry about for those I would leave behind.

Losing Jake to suicide made it all so real, that I was being pushed along to be next. At the time, I had no idea why things had become so difficult for me to deal with. I was supposed to be this young, happy, carefree guy working to gain a respectable apprenticeship.

I think this is the hardest part people deal with: the misconceptions around what depression actually is. For a long time we have believed that it is when we are feeling down or sad for a period of time when something goes wrong and we can't snap out of it. I believe it is when everything in

---

* Some families have requested their loved-ones remain anonymous.

your life is going right externally and you still feel unbearable amounts of emotional confusion and pain, unbearable amounts of negative thoughts and self-doubt.

In hindsight, this pain and self-doubt stemmed from the disconnection I felt from everyone. I wanted to be loved, to love, to be seen, heard, felt and got for who I was[†] but the criticisms and damaging experiences overrode any chance of feeling any connection that I was searching for. I suppressed all those needs in order to try and fit in, to conform.

There is a hard lesson to learn here. I did have people in my life that told me they loved me but what they were saying wasn't working. Their words didn't change the inner dialogue that had been entrenched in me from my apprenticeship. Outwardly, my life appeared pretty perfect so that only added to my runaway thoughts that I shouldn't complain. What right did I have to whinge about anything in my seemingly ideal life? So I stayed silent, suppressing emotion and bottling it further and further down because of my "perfect" life. It was exhausting carrying this around and took even more effort to keep hidden.

Life had become one shit day after the next; creating a cycle of shit feelings so that I woke up already feeling defeated each morning. The more I tried to put a reason on it or point the finger, the more exhausting it was and the harder it became to think about. I felt lost, without any knowledge there were tools out there that could help me and give me hope.

There were no conversations about the health of your mind back then, there were only a few limited, stigmatizing labels that people threw around in derogatory tones as they scoffed at the "selfishness" of the people we lost. My teeth would grit in anger whenever I heard those ignorant words spoken with disdain by so many people around me.

Despite my anxiety over this attitude at the time, losing Jake was and still is the reason I am able to pen these thoughts. The grief of his passing triggered a deep, primal sensation of fear that I was going to be next. Only out of sheer dread and constant worry about being the next

---

† My mentor Heather Yelland's words.

"statistic" did I reach out and seek the professional help and support I desperately needed. It was far from easy.

Mum and I were shopping for a suit to wear to Jake's funeral. Endless questions about Jake swirled around my head, feeding off the shame of my own pain and confusion that I was battling. I like to think Jake leant me the courage to finally turn and ask Mum casually, "How would Jake have known if he was struggling?"

Mum wasn't silly; I think she knew this was a huge question from me so she replied just as casually but carefully, "Oh, I think he would have had to go to a GP, they would go through a series of tests or questions that would form a diagnosis."

Her answer instantly made me break out in a hot sweat. Was I struggling the same way Jake had been? Would a test show me something that I already knew deep down? My throat choked up, then my stomach twisted. I rushed off to the bathroom to be sick. I felt swamped at the thought of what I had to do; the next step was overwhelming yet I knew I had to get off this road.

 CHANGE YOUR WORLD – TIP #6

It might take years of dissecting the stories you
have come to believe about yourself, but you will
walk the rest of your steps on this journey knowing
that everything exists with good reason.
Acceptance is the solid foundation on which we rebuild.

This was the first step I took in acknowledging my mental health challenges and reaching out because I knew I couldn't continue on safely without help. It was nowhere near the full answer, I hadn't even hit bottom yet as you'll see, but it was some kind of start to understanding the journey. An awkward start considering Mum was a pharmacy assistant in our small town. In 2011, any mental diagnosis was misconceived as being a weakness and being seen with a "label" was pretty daunting.

But I knew how important this was so I had to put all those concerns aside and built up the courage to book an appointment at the clinic. As I sat in the waiting room I flicked through the mental health resources that mentioned signs and symptoms of depression and anxiety: *tick-tick-tick*. I identified with so much of what I read in that information sheet.

It was one of the hardest things I've ever done: to walk in and tell a stranger what I was feeling; my confusion, isolation and fear every day. I so appreciated that doctor's warmth and compassion in response to the emotion that came out of me, she nodded and encouraged me to talk it all out as honestly as I knew how. Soon I had left the clinic with a diagnosis of severe anxiety and depression and a prescription for Sertraline otherwise known as Zoloft, an antidepressant used to treat major depressive disorders.

The only instruction or information I received was to take two tablets each morning and if I felt any worse on any given day to take another half. While I felt like the weight of the world had been lifted off my shoulders that day by talking to someone about it for the first time in depth, I also now realize how demoralizing this experience was and it saddens me that other people are still receiving the same treatment today.

It felt like I was told, "When it gets worse just drown it, when it gets worse just numb it, when it gets worse just run from it, when it gets worse just avoid it." I see it every day in my line of work and it breaks my heart. Being told to increase a dosage if feelings persist is not a message filled with hope. A diagnosis is not filled with hope.

"You need your pain. It is a message, and we must listen to the message. All these depressed and anxious people, all over the world—they are giving us a message. They are telling us something has gone wrong with the way we live. We need to stop trying to muffle or silence or pathologize that pain. Instead, we need to listen to it, and honor it. It is only when we listen to our pain that we can follow it back to its source—and only there, when we can see its true causes, can we begin to overcome it."

JOHANN HARI (LOST CONNECTIONS)[1]

The only other bit of information that the GP shared with me that day was that my brain was lacking in serotonin, apparently this was critical to me feeling my best. The reasoning for the prescription was apparently to help produce serotonin where my brain failed to provide it. I had been informed that I was living with a chemical imbalance of the brain. This was my first basic understanding of the "malfunction" I was supposedly living with. I believed I was broken and needed fixing. I was forced to believe that medication was the only fix.

Yet the research I uncovered did not support this. For example:

The cause of mental disorders such as depression remains unknown. However, the idea that chemical imbalances cause depression is vigorously promoted by pharmaceutical companies and the psychiatric profession at large.[2]

This is why for many years society's understanding of mental disorders has been falsely shaped, and has therefore found justification in using medication as a first response to any mind and behavioral challenge, which can be incredibly harmful. There is often no chemical imbalance evidently found to begin with, but when treating mental illness with psychiatric drugs, we throw a spanner into the mechanics of our human condition, our neural pathway, which can create the abnormality.[3]

In other words people believe they have a diagnosis and so gain a prescription—believing they are doing the right thing—believing they have a chemical imbalance in their brain, which from research is highly questionable. The research actually suggests taking medication as a first resort can create this "abnormality" that they didn't have to begin with. This is a powerful realignment of some entrenched societal notions.

Back then I took my set of instructions and was ushered out the GP's office but not once was my environment, surroundings, lifestyle habits or behaviors even asked about. Not once did this person, before giving me medication, ask me if any traumatic events had happened in my life, if I had any family or financial troubles; **they did not know anything about me**.

Imagine giving someone something that can alter their brain's function without even knowing anything about them, I could have even had an addictive personality. It was as if I was handed the prescription as a band-aid, without attempting to address the cause behind the diagnosis. There was no follow-up appointment, no referral to a psychologist. **Most worrying of all, there was no mention of other alternative therapies or actions I could be doing to help myself.**

Upon getting home, my head down in confusion, Mum asked me, "How did you go?" I simply handed her the prescription. She instantly looked worried, "Do you think this is necessary? Is there something else we can do before we try this?" It is only now much later down the track that I understand that Mum, who spends her life behind a dispensary in pharmacies, knew more than I did.

If I had the opportunity to turn the dial back and answer her, I would confidently say, "No" or at least request more information. Mum knew about the side effects; I didn't. She felt she was at least in a position to monitor any side effects I might have, so she left it up to me to go ahead with medication or not. This was my mum's way of making me feel heard and my experiences valued rather than saying, "No" to medication and making me feel like what I was going through wasn't severe.

But all I could hear were the doctor's words, "You should start to feel better soon Matt," and that was enough for me to believe these tablets would make everything go away.

CHANGE YOUR WORLD – TIP #7

Before we go any further repeat after me:

"I'm going to create a beautiful life for myself and those around me, no matter the effort it takes, no matter the darkness, I'm going to continue to show up in my light. I am not a broken machine that needs fixing. I am a beautiful human being that has emotional needs that must be met."

ONE SET MENU

For too long we have been given a single limited menu when dealing with mental health: get professional help and/or go on medication. That menu leads us to believe that we are doing the right thing, without asking questions, without understanding what we are putting into our body and the effects it may have. I don't say this as a deterrent from medication; it has helped to save some people's lives in some regard.

I say this because it is my mission to ensure that people **understand what else exists for them** and to make better informed judgments for their mind and physical health based on the countless choices that actually exist, compared to the two limited options that society tells us to choose from.

If society and our communities were familiar with the information and truths, there would be more focus on how to use these drugs safely and there would be more focus on alternative therapies that don't rely on medication or finding pathways that minimize our use of them. We would not walk out of our first emotional challenge with a prescription and no fall protection for it.

It is vital that we support any medication prescription with information from all other evidence-based methods, such as cognitive behavioral therapy, bibliotherapy, strength-based tools, diet and lifestyle changes, holistic measures ... the list goes on.

When I first started taking the medication prescribed to me, I distinctly recall feeling like I was on the "mend" or certainly "improving." I couldn't have known then that I was experiencing a placebo effect from the relief of thinking I was being "fixed." This temporary improvement is quite a common experience for many people that occurs within the first 30–90 days of taking antidepressants.[4]

I thought I was doing so much better that I actually came off the medication because of a misplaced belief in my recovery. For many people the placebo wears off and within the first few months they have fallen backwards because they believe the narrative the same way I did: that I had improved and I didn't need them any longer: only to come crashing back, harder than before. Yet, I had not actually done anything to improve my situation other than taking medication, so how could my self assessment of being "fixed" be remotely true?

Let me expand on an incredibly important concept regarding taking antidepressants. As mentioned above, the placebo effect refers to a person's *belief* in the benefit of treatment that produces a positive result, rather than the efficacy of the treatment itself.[5]

Irving Kirsch Ph.D., of Harvard Medical School, has been fascinated by the placebo effect for the whole of his career. When he set out to measure the placebo effect in depression back in 1998, he and a former graduate student, Guy Sapirstein went on to inadvertently expose the incredible misconceptions behind the largely unquestioned effectiveness of antidepressants.

In 2014 Kirsch published a review article on their original meta-analysis (a study of multiple studies) entitled *Antidepressants and the Placebo Effect*.[6] This is a fascinating read for both patients and carers. Kirsch goes on to explain that out of the two test groups used in drug trials, one group that does receive the active tablet and the other that unknowingly receives the placebo, the results were astonishingly similar for both groups among numerous trials.

This tells me that antidepressants work very differently than what had been assumed. Kirsch's report shows the opposite of what I was told that day in the doctor's clinic and exposes the facts of what I now know to be true. Read for yourself:

Antidepressants have long been thought to work by fixing a chemical imbalance in the brain: serotonin. Indeed, their supposed effectiveness is the primary evidence for the chemical imbalance theory. But analyses of the published data and also the unpublished data that were hidden by drug companies reveal that most (if not all) of the benefits are due to the placebo effect.

Some antidepressants increase serotonin levels, some decrease it, and some have no effect at all on serotonin. Nevertheless, they all show the same therapeutic benefit. The effect on depression is the same. What do you call pills, the effects of which are independent of their chemical composition? I call them "placebos." [...] The serotonin theory is as close as any theory in the history of science to having been proved wrong. Instead of curing depression, popular antidepressants may induce a biological vulnerability making people more likely to become depressed in the future.[7]

It is that last sentence that needs particular attention. Kirsch is referring to the most troubling possibility in a long list of side effects associated with antidepressant use.

You see, the drug I was prescribed, Sertraline, has a black box warning: the most serious warning from the FDA (US Food and Drug Administration). This alerts prescribing doctors about the potentially serious side effects of taking the drug. It alerts the doctors perhaps, but little did I know what lay in store for me; that conversation just didn't happen.

The high doses of Sertraline that I ended up taking produced frustrating and in some cases life-threatening side effects that I still battle today. The range is staggering; agitation, irritability, shakiness, muscle tremors, loss of sex drive, fatigue and sleep insomnia. I dreaded the thought of the lights going off as it meant I was on my own for hours, just me and my spinning, erratic thoughts until morning. At its worst I could be lucky to sleep three hours over a seven-day period, dropping 5–10kgs in quick succession. Other short-term effects were fluctuating heart rate, aggressiveness, worsening of dark thoughts, and inability to hold or stomach food as well as fading away in body fats.

Through lack of appetite I became really exhausted and that's when I lost all energy for anything which only compounded my challenges, disconnecting me further from all the things I had enjoyed doing once upon a time. Later on in my journey I also developed atelectasis‡ in my lungs through taking alternative medications to Sertraline, this now requires more medication and I have been rushed to hospital twice for the first signs of a heart attack.

It's one thing to be experiencing something emotionally exhausting yourself, but having everybody else around you notice changes in you while you are dealing with these thoughts and feelings is another. I was frequently told how tired I looked, how skinny I'd become and how jittery I was and couldn't sit still. Not many people knew I was on medication to understand I was experiencing side effects. Trying to deal with these symptoms added even more shame, bias, stigma and embarrassment.

In his report, Kirsch outlines in no uncertain terms the following counsel:

Antidepressants have been linked to increases in suicidal ideation among children and young adults [...] Perhaps the most surprising health consequence of antidepressant use is one that affects people of all ages. Antidepressants increase the risk of relapse after one has recovered. People are more likely to become depressed again after treatment by antidepressants than after treatment by other means. Furthermore, the degree to which the risk of relapse increases depends on the degree to which the particular antidepressant used

---

‡ Atelectasis is a complete or partial collapse of the entire lung or area (lobe) of the lung.

changes neurotransmission in the brain. Given these health risks, antidepressants should not be used as a first-line treatment for depression.[8]

I doubt that the public, or even much of the medical community, is attentive to this fact. I believe everyone has a right to know every viewpoint behind the medication they are prescribed or prescribed to their loved-one.

It is not to persuade people away from this choice, rather to help people avoid the same errors I made for many years, years filled with misinformation and assumptions that created their own set of challenges. If you are one of the 1 in 4 people in the world that live with a diagnosed depressive disorder[9], you deserve to know as much about the condition, treatments and relevant research as any doctor or scientist.

Kirsch's research has contributed in no small part, to my ability to choose other alternatives and in turn, find and build on my own strength within. The final words of his article provide a clear perspective that gives pause to anyone weighing up their treatment options.

Fortunately, placebos are not the only alternative to antidepressant treatment. My colleagues and I have conducted a meta-analysis of various treatments for depression, including antidepressants, psychotherapy, the combination of psychotherapy and antidepressants, and "alternative" treatments, which included acupuncture and physical exercise.[10]
We found no significant differences between these treatments or within different types of psychotherapy. When different treatments are equally effective, choice should be based on risk and harm, and of all of these treatments, antidepressant drugs are the riskiest and most harmful. If they are to be used at all, it should be as a last resort, when depression is extremely severe and all other treatment alternatives have been tried and failed.[11]

I am extremely passionate about this part of my journey, even more so now after losing several of my friends to suicide within the first 30 days of taking medication handed to them in the same way it was handed to me and that breaks my heart every day.

In the last few years, I have taken great leaps in my knowledge and management of my mental health, as I have witnessed and experienced the wealth of underlying treatment methods that unbelievably are still not being shared with the people that need these options urgently.

Am I trying to deter people away from medication? Absolutely not—it is one of the many options to be explored. Am I trying to show people there are alternatives to medication that may be more suited to them, just as medication proved incompatible with me? Absolutely.

Everyone's journey and needs are unique. Each of us must learn what works and what doesn't work for ourselves. **There is no outsmarting the human condition, our physiology or biology. There is no quick fix or short cut.** Complaining about a mental health epidemic but not changing the behaviors and habits which has led us here in the first place, is a result of living in a society that provides praise and instant gratification for little to no effort. A society that has become content to handball beautiful people into the hands of sickness management as a first reaction, rather than learning about a natural health path.

You could think of it like this: do we clean out the tank of a sick fish, or do we medicate the fish and leave it swimming in dirty water?

Countless times in my field of work today, parents or community members tell me these exact words, "Matt, the medication isn't working, they are still struggling and I don't know what else to do, we've tried everything," only to find out the only thing they have tried was the one set menu that I mentioned, seeing a professional and being prescribed medication.

One of the most important elements of my work today is urging more mental health treatment education, targeted for carers and professionals in this field. A wider knowledge of treatments can only support these incredibly inspiring and compassionate specialists that choose to work on these uniquely beautiful, yet hard and sharp edges of love and life.

Remember, just because one therapist doesn't feel comfortable or connect with you, there are countless more. Not all of us wear the same pants, on the same day, the same length, pattern, color and fabric and the same goes for professional support. Not all of them are comfortable, not all of them fit and not all of them suit you. It really is about trying them on until you find the one that makes you walk taller, that hears your voice and you connect with the pathways they help open up for you.

There is often a misconception that males don't like to talk about their emotions; for me it's never been true. While I'm naturally a quiet person, I wanted nothing more than to be able to talk about what I was going through, looking for some connection and understanding. However, finding the right words to explain how I was feeling so that people understood was the most difficult part of the beginning of my journey.

Finally building up the courage and stumbling through what I wanted to tell someone, often only resulted in confusion and uneasiness from people. I could see them thinking: *Is Matt crazy? Will he do something crazy? I don't want to be close to that.*

There was so much recoil and misunderstanding of mind and behavioral health back then, that those hollow awkward conversations only added to my feelings of being lost and alone. The hard truth is, it isn't easy to hear and talk about, but it's better than losing someone to suicide—so even if I've made you uncomfortable, don't stop now.

I would personally rather sit with you to the early hours of the morning and wipe away countless tears, than to never have that opportunity again and have to wipe away the tears of thousands of people who right now— whether you can see it or feel it—love you. I promise you that.

TRAVELING SOUTH

My trials of 2011 continued. Even though I had made that first important step to face and talk about what I was battling with my doctor, I made no actual headway. It was the beginning of the rollercoaster ride of going on and off medication that I would wrestle with for six years.

So on the back of losing Jake, the sudden end of my last employment, and experiencing more frequent, dark, dangerous thoughts and a sense of worthlessness, I thought a move interstate and a fresh start was just what I needed; I had no other answers. I blamed my community, my friends, my family. I blamed everything else other than myself for how I was feeling— which was shit every single day.

I was so desperate for something to change that I moved away from all my support and everything I knew. Initially, the new job, change of scenery and the Queensland sun made things manageable. Meeting new friends distracted me for a while and enabled me to show them a happy side to me that protected people from identifying the truth of why I was new to town and what I was still experiencing each day. If I wasn't lying to fit in, I was often self medicating to numb my emotions, drinking and partying non stop to fit in with people, which only gave me a false sense of the belonging I was deeply searching for.

With hindsight, I can tell you I was battling three very powerful and limiting beliefs that had been forming over many years: the beliefs that I was worthless, a failure and a burden. The seeds of these beliefs had been planted many years before and by the time I moved to Queensland, they were growing too big to handle.

Today I can sit here and give these feelings names and explanations and put them in perspective whenever they flitter across my mind, as they still have a habit of doing. Only through years of experience and practice, have I learned they are not real: simply my own clouded thoughts, not tangible, concrete facts to live by.

At 21 years old however, a young man's brain, specifically the prefrontal cortex, the part we use to think and make decisions, is still developing and maturing (this is not fully accomplished until around 25) and these thoughts (aka stories about themselves) can create a fog that disables young men from seeing things as they really are, seeing the truth of how much they are seen, heard, loved and needed by people in their lives. And these "stories" can prevent them from *feeling* that love and connection too; the wire is effectively cut.

CHANGE YOUR WORLD – TIP #8

No one can truly understand their true beauty or recognize a sense of their own worth until it has been reflected back to them in the mirror of other caring, compassionate and loving individuals.

Young men's minds are still learning to decipher the signals their environment sends them. On the weekends those signals seemed fun and helpful for me. Drinking with my new mates and being sought out for the entertainment value my drinking gave them.

But from Monday to Friday, I felt cut off from those people who gave me my value, my propped-up sense of self-worth. I realized their care for me wasn't for the real me and that wasn't any of their fault; it was based on the false Matt that I presented to them who did crazy things that they could watch and laugh at.

This is by no means a criticism of the friends I had; they were beautiful people who have played a big part in me being able to share these moments with you. It was all coming from me as I developed severe sleep insomnia on the back of withdrawing from medication, all of which was intensified by the shame of self-medicating. None of this helped me to think clearly and fight the colossal negative emotions that were pressing on my chest all day.

When I moved to Queensland, my trade school was transferred but I lost most of the three years of modules I had completed in Victoria because of a change in standards and rules between the two states. This felt like another cruel blow below the belt. I didn't enjoy plumbing and to think I had to do more of it to fulfill my promise to my parents hurt like hell.

Trade school in Queensland was held in Mackay, hours away from the town I lived in, Gladstone. My theory studies were scheduled in month-long blocks, meaning that I would live away for big chunks of time. I didn't know anyone in Mackay and I was the "new kid" in my trade school class.

Between Mackay and Gladstone I spent time living out of my car that carted my plumbing tools, some clothing and things to get me through as I wandered around from street to street. Not one person in my life knew that this was how I was living, effectively homeless. Often going without a shower or just washing at the beach or from a public fixture. On the nights I built up enough courage, I might get lucky enough to score the mattress on the floor of one of the trade school guys in town.

I didn't have to live like this at any stage of my life; it was a choice I made to protect the people around me, from me. Many days I fielded phone calls from Mum and Dad, assuring them that I was fine, that trade school was going well and I would be completed before I knew it. I made it sound like I had no existing problems and my life was perfect. I safeguarded everyone close to me from the truth of the way I was living, for fear of coming off as—you guessed it—a failure, worthless and a burden, those gremlins skulking around in my head.

 CHANGE YOUR WORLD – TIP #9

I've built stronger relationships with people by being authentic and open about my struggle, than I ever did by pretending they didn't exist around people that claim they have their shit together.
In a world full of fake news, let's be the real ones.

FROM A PLACE OF LOVE

My time spent living without an address, taught me about two of the most intrinsic and powerful human conditions: apathy and empathy. One leads to hope and the other to hopelessness. A person can see someone down and out, emotionally upset, distressed, a shade of the person they once were and walk straight past them as if it's not their problem. They can only see and/or judge the *circumstances* that led to someone's sad and difficult situation, and are unable to relate to how they possibly could have fallen so far.

Empathy on the other hand is the ability to feel sensitivity to what that person is going through. Seeing their pain connects you to a time you felt pain and you want to do anything in your power to support them, to offer a hand or be there for that person. Just as you remember that's what you desperately needed in your hour, of need too. You don't need to know or understand their circumstances: you just know that they are in pain.

In my experiences in this field and travels around the world, we seem to have an uncanny knack to offer apathy when we see someone visibly struggling and can walk past and say it's not our problem. Often believing that we don't have the skill set to help, that maybe it's none of our business, or perhaps we feel scared to prompt someone with the simple question, "Are you okay? Is there something wrong?"

Unfortunately for one reason or another, many people display a lot of apathy and yet as human beings there is nothing to suggest we are born with it. We've all felt pain at some point in our life and this shared experience is the catalyst for change. Anyone can learn the power that comes from connecting—not to the circumstances of someone down and out on the street or to an addict that's lost everything they have—but connecting to the *emotion* of a person's current state of pain or crises, feeling empathy for their overwhelming feeling of hopelessness.

This is the synergy that makes every moment interacting with a loved one or stranger so powerful. The ability to sense other people's emotions, paired with the ability to imagine just what someone else might be going through, not related to the circumstance—but to the emotion.

This can feel daunting and people shy away from doing it, but if we don't do it, that person can then fall through the gaps and when it's all too late, we are left to wonder why.

I have seen too many parents writhing in pain and confusion after the terrible fact because they didn't see it coming; they hadn't been able to connect with the circumstances of their loved one's pain so they didn't connect with their pain.

Many people only look for one sign or one symptom, they say, "But they were never upset." We need to pull apart the signs and symptoms for everyone we care about, and understand that signs of struggle manifest in many ways. Is it closed doors? Are they reticent or distant? Haven't shaved or showered as regularly as usual? Stopped going to places they used to love? Haven't been playing at their usual level? Short text responses or eye contact non-existent? Or maybe it's sudden inexplicable happiness? The truth is we understand what the visible and behavioral indicators are, but we are still seeing people fall.

Whatever it is, you're more likely to figure it out if you establish a rock solid connection where they can be who they really are in front of you. Where their relationship with you provides enough comfort for them to strip back and be who they truly are rather than showing up as someone they are not, in order to protect you.

When you're pulling your hair out trying to figure out why they're struggling, or asking yourself what were they thinking (there's a big chance they *couldn't* think clearly) remember it's not the cause of the pain that matters; it's the emotion itself. The cause of the emotion is different for different people, but the *emotion* is universal and that is how we can relate and connect. Connecting to the emotion doesn't come naturally for everyone yet the interaction is simple, imperative and universal.

I call it **Holding Space** and it's a powerful way to show someone your concern is real and let them feel the comfort of your compassion.

ALLOWING OTHERS TO BE HEARD

Holding Space is a big part of my advocacy and workshops because to be honest, universally we aren't that crash hot at it yet. Holding Space has four primary actions to help people feel real comfort and hope in their conversation with you.

1. The Reflex Head Nod.

This is the nod that reassuringly goes up and down numerous times, the one that shows: *I have no idea what Matt's talking about right now but if I nod my head in the right timing, he will know I'm listening.* This gives the person speaking an indicator that what is being said is being fully acknowledged whether it is understood or not.

2. Listening.

Listening with no intent to reply, to judge, to criticize, no comparisons, no advice, no need for answers. Let them talk to you to get the thoughts, feelings and emotions off their chest without being stopped in any way. If you interpose, even with good intentions, that person may hear something that suppresses their feeling back down, again unwilling to share out of fear of judgment, even unintentional judgment.

Every time we disrupt the moment with our own response we unintentionally cut off what might have been said, had we not interrupted. Those words may never come up again. With every bit of information we receive, we can interpret and help with. We can't with information that is suppressed. As I say more than once, we are only as good as the information we have at the moment we need it; our role is to receive as much information as possible.

A simple example I heard frequently during the 2020/21 pandemic was people sharing the fact that they were struggling with the restrictions and isolation. I often heard people reply, "Me too!" And the first person's attempt at reaching out was then thwarted, they said no more. The situation went from one person struggling to two people struggling without a hint of anyone listening or helping.

3. Eye Contact is imperative.§

Not looking at your phone, not looking at the sky or random things close by. Doing these things shows: *I don't care enough about you to listen properly.*

External surroundings fall into the background as you look into their eyes. Fiddling with something while they are talking also says: *This conversation is way too difficult for me to be in.* The other person feels that recoil and that discomfort. They need to see the reflection of their own eyes in your eyes to know you hear their pain and feel empathy for them.

Even if you've never been in the same situation, eye contact says you connect with their pain. If you've never experienced cancer for example, you don't have to think therefore you're no good in that conversation. Instead, remember your own pain you have been through and think: *I can show up for this person, in the same way I needed someone to show up for me in the past.*

Eye contact can always be tapered off to prevent the other person from feeling intimidated, however it needs to be done in the right moments. Avoiding eye contact because you feel uncomfortable is the prime way to show someone that you are more worried about how you feel than the person who is trying to share.

 CHANGE YOUR WORLD – TIP #10

Stop lying in your own bubble of emotion.
Jump into the bubble of others, that's true empathy.

---

§ When culturally appropriate

4. Discipline.

The disciple to show up for that person, not just for one conversation but every single day. Not to ask one day, "Are you okay?" Then not show up for a month. It's the discipline to align our values with our behavior. So when that person in pain gets to a place where it's so dark and they can't see hope one inch in front of their eyes, a little spark says to them they need to have a conversation right now. And because you have **held that space** for them so consistently and made them feel comfortable, they will come to you to talk about it.

I know it's hard at first. But the only way we get better at our articulation is for more people to share their experiences. The only way I have become comfortable with communicating my struggles is from relating to other people's experiences they have being brave enough to share.

When we share we soon realize that we all go through similar things and it's a beautiful comfort to know this. It gives us a change of perception, from looking at something from its lowest point, when we think we're alone in it and have no view of the horizon to better places. Hearing the words of other people's struggle and story out of it; lifts us up to a higher perspective where we see hope and possibilities.

Just like the way a uniquely beautiful person in my life taught me **I don't suffer from bipolar, it is my gift.**

Their articulation opened my eyes to the beauty of emotion I get to experience and I stopped using the expression, "I suffer from ..." Society often commiserates with the people that "suffer" from a mental illness for example; the label is then entrenched and repeated.

We must reframe our mindset around what life has gifted each of us, each struggle and test that shows us both the depths and heights of human emotion. In my talks I try to give people something to emulate and take heart from. If you use the word suffering, that is what you'll feel. I advocate using different ways to describe our circumstances that people relate to and take hope from.

People often say to me, "Oh, that's not my field." But at the end of the day reframing concepts and understanding around the health of our minds is the most important thing to everyone in every field.

The only way we can change the outcomes of the real pandemic this world is going through—people dying every year by the thousands feeling alone—is to start doing it together. **The true meaning of life is living in the betterment of the person sitting next to us.**

BACK FROM THE ABYSS

By late 2012, without any of this knowledge of how to look for hope and strategies out of my mess, I was racing full speed toward a dead end, as I turned to any way possible to numb the pain for short periods. It was around this time that a new feature began manifesting in my behavior: manic episodes, invincible feelings of over-excitement, racing thoughts and actions.

One extreme moment saw me sitting comfortably on the external edge of a penthouse skyscraper with nothing between the fifty-story drop and me. I didn't want to jump off it, I just thought it was a tangible place to sit and I couldn't understand why no one wanted to join me; from my position you could see the world so much better. It looked crazy and dangerous to other people, but internally my brain's racing thoughts couldn't see the recklessness of the situation, only the benefits.

My spending habits became heightened too because I thought why would anyone need money in the bank if they probably weren't going to be here soon to spend it? Gambling and throwing money around became a symptom of something deeper.

At one time, I thought donating my whole tax return to charity was a great idea. Not because I didn't need the money—I was just scraping by myself—but because the mania had suggested it was a good idea at the time. Only to realize what I had done when I came crashing down from the high manic episode the following day. A cycle had begun which would take me many years to fully recognize and understand.

BIPOLAR IS MANY THINGS...

During a manic episode those with bipolar disorder have an inflated self-esteem, less of an urge to sleep, are more inclined to engage in risk taking behavior and are quite easily distracted, all of which lead to impulsive spending habits. For me, it was excessive generosity and impulsive shopping.

Bipolar mania is a period of mood elevation. It is generally a combination of high energy and activity, however much more complex and complicated than that. The euphoria of feeling "on top of the world" can be incredibly disruptive in my life. Those feelings of mood elevation are not always grandiose and beneficial. Sometimes that extra burst of energy doesn't show up in creativity, confidence or risk taking behavior, but rather fast moving and thought provoking scenarios.

Trying to do ten things at once, agitated and almost believing that I'm Superman, wanting for things to happen faster, but lacking the logic to know they can't. I probably am not alone in my challenge to sit still at a red light, to drive a car at the allowed speed limit or waiting "impatiently" for people to respond to my emails or messages. Not because I am rude or disrespectful or like breaking the law, but because I have an urgency to do more and the actual pace of life slows down the millions of great ideas that are bubbling over in my head.

Some days I feel untouchable, I don't need sleep, I can go multiple days without food, any objective and goal is achievable and I am living at a euphoric pace. Then there are the days that you recognize that all of the above is bullshit and as the saying goes, "What comes up, must come down." You fail to lift your head up; you don't want to talk to anyone because you are completely zapped from being so "up" for so long. Your brain fog is increasingly hard to see through and your enthusiasm and drive for life disappears.

Just as you gather yourself and begin to feel normal, you shoot into hypermania again, potentially experiencing racing thoughts and moods several times in a day or the same elevated mood for several days.

But, it doesn't have to always look like that. The easiest way I have found to explain it is that people live with three main levels of brain function: highs, lows and normality. A non-bipolar brain can consistently navigate within and around the "normality" level of brain function. For those that live the bipolar condition it can be more challenging to navigate into normality, that part of their brain function is much smaller to land on and maintain.

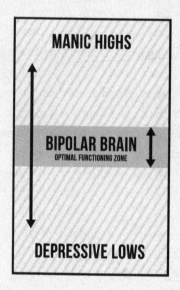 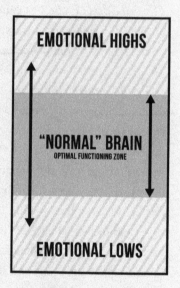

Or, I should say, **was** much smaller to land on and maintain. Through tireless work I have found the triggers that shoot me into manic highs and what spirals me into depressive lows. Regardless of your condition I believe this system to be true and relevant for everybody. It's the essence of finding knowledge of yourself and applying consistency to your lifestyle choices.

Back then I believed whole-heartedly that I was a burden on every single person I came in contact with. The thought of reaching out to my parents for help, even though I knew they would help me regardless of my situation or mistakes was nonexistent; there was no chance in hell I would put my problems on them too. I already felt like I had weighed enough people down on the journey.

I remember being content that I had made that final, irreversible decision, thinking that all this emotional pain would finally leave me. Amongst my clouded mind I could only see the relief that would result from my decision. Everyone would be better off without me. All the problems and challenges and headaches I'd given my friends and family over the years, were finished. They wouldn't have the burden of me anymore. I honestly believed nobody would even notice that I was gone.

It is confronting to think that for a short time leading up to my plans, I felt invincible. If I were no longer scared of dying, why would I carry fear or any regard for anyone else or my own personal safety? This led to multiple fights in nightclubs and toxic, violent behavior and thoughts. Each day after work my 15-minute drive home became a game to me. How long could I drive with my eyes closed? How long could I drive with no hands on the wheel? It haunts me to admit to these behaviors, but it is the honest reflection of the severity of brain pain I was experiencing and an acknowledgment of how powerful the brain is when it is working against you.

I was no longer scared of non-existence; that loss of fear has actually been one of the scariest things to this day. It wasn't real though; it was a state of mind that zeroed in on a single illusion that temporarily blocked my feelings from the millions of dimensions that actually made up my life.

This is the illness we talk about in mental illness, I was not thinking straight.

You can't when you have a thousand voices in your head and a fog that disables you from seeing an inch in front of you.

This was the blackness that surrounded me; the day I had decided would be my last. That fateful day happened to be Derby Day on the weekend of the Spring Racing Carnival in Australia. A little fact I remember because it was one of those iconic days that people from Melbourne know well. But I was far from all I knew and loved, feeling disconnected and powerfully alone in a world of pain that I couldn't take anymore. With a shaking hand I penned a final letter, I didn't want anyone to be upset, everyone would be much better off without me.

There was chaos and noise in my mind as I tried to end it all, a crescendo of competing protests of confusion at what I was actually fucking doing. Then the noise faded away to leave me with one single immense thought that sounded like it was spoken. This voice had such clarity, a message straight to my core. I don't know who it was but the message rings thick in my mind to this very day:

Matt, one day you are going to have a family,
you need to be here to see that out.

The thought of having kids saved my life that day.

I did what was necessary to bring myself back to the land of the living. This thought of having kids has been the most influential thing to happen in my life which is a bizarre thought considering I was just 20 years old.

This thought gives me energy and drive to get out of bed even when it's hard. It was no longer about "how" I was going to do it, or "what" I was going to do. From then on, it became all about "why" I am doing it: kids. It became finding the clarity for what I stand for.

Helping kids has become my everything and one day I feel destined to get to that place where I will be blessed to have my own and become a father.

I am so grateful every day that my lowest day didn't eventuate the tragic shattering way I had planned. It wasn't meant to, the same way it isn't meant to for anyone reading this.

Your destiny is to feel pain *and* exquisite joy!

The thought that saved my life is the same reason I would go on to develop a Social Emotional Learning (SEL) program in primary schools and kindergartens for young champions in Australia, *Healthier Hearts & Lighter Minds*, that helps those as young as three years old to identify, control and express their emotions in positive ways using our six core emotions in the human face: fear, anger, disgust, sadness, joy and surprise. Stripping back the layers of emotions helps kids to identify what they're going through and also understand what these baseline emotions can lead into, such as fear growing into anxiety: this is a great starting point for their emotional education.

I didn't lose my life that day however, by no means did my problems magically disappear and the thought of kids didn't eradicate the brain pain I was living in.

The weeks and months following a suicide attempt can be so much harder to deal with than the time leading up to it. The realization that you are at the very rock bottom of your life, that you are further away from being happy and living a fulfilling life than ever before, compounds the challenge of moving upwards to get there. Even though you have only one direction to go, it's like a mountain looming in front of you.

 CHANGE YOUR WORLD – TIP #11

Acceptance of the very thing that has happened to you is
the necessary starting point in the overcoming of it.
Be challenged by it, not defeated by it.

Soak up that view; take in all that led you to the bottom of that mountain. All of what you are going through right now is carving you into the beautiful person you are meant to become. That mountain is not the stumbling block, but the stepping-stone. Something better is just up ahead.

MY VERY OWN ANGELS

In 2013 I got my lucky break thanks to the compassion of one very special family in Queensland. I felt the full benefit of their humanity when they took me into their home and their lives and just kept loving me until I smiled again. By no means is the message in this to pick up the homeless off the street and house them. In an ideal world we wouldn't have to do that and those that find themselves in those situations would be adequately supported in safe means and ways.

However, thankfully I was picked up and cared for by an amazing human being, who happened to also be a single mum of five kids, yeah that's right, as if she didn't have enough to deal with and look after already without throwing someone like myself into the mix. But she did. Her name was Aurora and she was my real life version of an angel, just like her daughter Hollie, who is my best friend. They came to me in dire times to remind me of my faith in humanity and to show me there was still so much meaning left in this world for me if I could just feel connected to it.

I met Hollie one night at a party when I first moved to Queensland. Her cousin Liam (whom I had met at the football club) introduced us that night and Hollie's energy was infectious from the start. We kept in touch from then on, forging a strong friendship as she constantly included me and introduced me to everyone she knew along the way: the most important being her beautiful family. From the moment I met them, it was as if they could see a completely different person in me than I ever felt about myself. It was an immediate sense of belonging and the ideal environment to just be who I really was.

From those earlier times in Queensland to this very day I am blessed to have had Hollie's full support, even when I was hard to deal with or be around she was there for me. Most of the time I rejected her help for obvious reasons, other times I longed for it.

For some reason unknown, first Hollie and then Aurora saw something in me that I couldn't recognize in myself. No matter how poorly I behaved, how many obnoxious or inappropriate comments I made, they didn't take offense, instead they found it in them to laugh with me or at least pretend to.

Being with them gave me a bizarre, unfamiliar feeling. Even though they weren't family, I realize now that feeling was "belonging." They just seemed to "get" me and enjoyed me just as I was.

Between Hollie and Aurora, they held space for meaningful conversations, watched the old *Batman* series with me until 2am, had drinks by the yacht club, sunbaked by the pool, continuously told me off, kicking my ass for everything in between; they became family, giving me so much. We weren't always as close as we are now mainly due to my inability to appreciate what was good for me and my tendency to kick back at anything that served me well, but all those boundaries fell away when Hollie and Aurora took me in off the street to become part of the family.

Hollie had invited me over to her house for my birthday in May of 2013. As I trekked up the stairs of the two-story house to see her family, I was met with, "Surprise!" Hollie had organized some of my friends in town to be there to surprise me for my birthday. It caught me off guard, I wasn't used to identifying with anything but the idea of feeling alone; here, I could immediately see I wasn't. She had a knack of going above and beyond, even though she knew I hated the attention. Actually that might have been why she did it, we often got more satisfaction out of stirring each other up than anything else; that's our relationship.

Hollie somehow knew to call me again the next day and I remember she kept pressing me about where I was staying, as if her sixth sense as a good friend knew I wasn't in a good place. She demanded I come and stay with her and her family. I refused a million times until she said, "Stop being a fucking idiot, you're staying with us."

It wasn't like they had a spare bed or a room free; there was already Aurora plus her five kids. But Aurora met me at the house with a big pearly grin on her face; I knew she was up to something. Much like Hollie, her mum Aurora enjoyed shit-stirring me too. She said, "Come on Dixie, (Aurora only ever used my nickname) I have something to show you." Leading me downstairs to the double garage, she flicked on the lights, "Do you like your new room?"

I was gob-smacked. There was a comfy bed, fridge, mirrors, clothes hangers and the concrete floor had been carpeted. They had turned their much needed garage space into my new room; taking me in off the street, giving me somewhere to belong. "Now you're fucking stuck with us," Hollie declared. It still makes me laugh. The double garage was by far the best room in the house, I won out! To this day I don't think I've had a more luxurious setup.

It wasn't the first time this family had taken someone in, made them feel part of their tribe, it was actually pretty common practice. They loved you like their own, a modern day and real life version of *The Brady Bunch* with less blondes and better hairstyles and if anyone had Marsha's broken nose, it was usually me. The youngest was my little brother Tatey at seven years old, he often had to share a bed rotating around whichever one he fell asleep in each night, but they always made it work. There were the girls Jorja, Brydie and Hollie aged from 16 and into their 20s, and the oldest, Jay was the same age as myself: all of them became family to me.

It was no ordinary home. Each of them had their hands full and yet gifted me their time and care to get me on the path to wellness again. From May 2013 to Christmas 2013, Aurora and Hollie frequently checked in with my parents back home, reassuring them I was safe and doing well. They did everything they could to get me on my feet again. We didn't let Mum and Dad in on the extent of my troubles, it was only in the later years when I started advocating for mental health did they find out I had been homeless, and experienced and survived multiple suicide attempts. I consciously protected my parents from everything that I was ashamed of, because I loved them.

I often drove Tatey to school and picked him up. I also took great pride in making him do his homework with me each night (I knew how much it annoyed you Tatey!). Cooking with the girls (or as they would tell it, getting in their way and shit-stirring them while they tried to cook the family meal), getting my ass back into the gym with Jay or enjoying an evening drink out on the decking with Aurora. It was very special.

I believe having the responsibility of being part of this family for those months I lived there, provided me with what I now know to be the fundamental elements of the human existence. The things that allow people to get on the right track, to see the forest through the trees: the elements of love, belonging and connection. After all, "The human being only ever wants to love, be loved, to be seen, heard, felt and got for who we truly are." I think of my mentor Heather's words often because she has become a very important person in my life.

I met Heather in a very unique situation when I was applying to be part of The Growth Project where a group of not-for-profit charity leaders could be mentored by Australia's business leaders. It was that day meeting Heather and every day since, that she has always made me feel as if I could achieve anything. She wears so many hats, a mum with a knack of keeping me accountable and seeing through my bullshit but loving me unconditionally anyway, and with formal training in psychology, has taught me an incredible amount about all aspects of the human condition, the one I turn to for advice in all situations. Yet what I believe to be her actual superpower is her incredible ability to help people embrace and understand the difference we were all born to make in this world.

Heather's words about belonging are spot on and I found all of those things through Hollie, Aurora and my extended Queensland family. Never did anyone judge me for the mistakes I made, think less of me because of how I felt or behaved. They reasoned with it, listened to it and held space for all the pros and cons that came along with taking me in.

From the Aurora text archives (22/2/2014):

> *How often do you find a person that admires your little weird habits, puts up with your shit and still can say they like you at the end of the day?*

TAKING ONUS

Even with that unshakeable help, support and love I still frequently experienced thoughts of giving in and giving up. Love, belonging and connection will provide you hope and we only need a smidgen of hope to continue to tomorrow, but hope alone is not an action plan. The continual support of those around me was amazing but I failed to understand that above all else, I needed to build a mental health skill set to manage my own well-being. It was up to me.

Hope was the ability to see the light, despite the darkness.
Hope was a start, but it requires action to win the fight.

It's like being in an exam setting; the teachers have fed you the education all year but you've copied off the kid sitting next to you. Come exam day it's far stricter, the chairs are further apart and you can't skim the answers from the kid nearby, you're on your own and the teachers can't help.

You are the only one that can lift the pen to paper. That was how it was for me with my mental health and well-being, I had great support and people there to help, but I never used them. I didn't have the skill set required when I really needed it. I know I am very fortunate to have always had the love and support that every kid wishes for. However my limiting belief system that I was a burden often prevented me from using it. In many ways, I cut myself off without knowing it.

Eventually, I found myself sitting out on my savior's driveway one night, wrapped in a blanket, sobbing and suicidal, and I finally picked up the phone and called Mum. I told her, "I can't do it anymore, I don't want to wake up and feel like this." In that moment many parents would freak, panic and say something that doesn't land well. I'll never forget it was as if Mum realized that answering with the usual, "Dad and I love you," had lost its full effect. I had heard it so often that—the words bounced right off me.

There is a fundamental difference between hearing something and feeling it, and that is no discredit to my parents because it had been my decision to run away. Living so far from immediate family compounded my feelings of loneliness and disconnectedness and that was my mistake.

So this time Mum had the quick thinking mid phone call to pattern disrupt my brain. Instead of the token, "We love you Matty," she interrupted my thoughts with, "Nan rang today, she really misses you, she said she can't wait to have you home, actually we all can't wait." An image of Nan sprang to mind and connected straight to my heart. I wanted to see her; I wanted to see all of them.

CHANGE YOUR WORLD – TIP #12

Let your heart speak fluent love to other hearts.
The one language that is universally renowned
for cutting through pain and creating miracles.

I could see the sense in returning back home to my support network and those that wanted to see me smile again. The next moment I picked up my blanket, wiped away the tears and walked inside to tell Aurora and Hollie that I would return home as soon as my trade school was marked off and my plumbing apprenticeship was finished. I've always been a man of my word and I wasn't going home without the one thing I had promised Mum and Dad all those years ago, the one thing that has haunted my whole fucking life, that stupid apprenticeship that I agreed to start in 2010.

On those tough days, I felt more alone than ever before. Staying in Queensland was another stopgap in finding a real way forward. After realizing that it would be good for me to return home, I approached my boss to ask if he would sign me off on my apprenticeship. I had finally completed the trade school component as well as the minimum number of required work hours. Officially my apprenticeship would have me continue to the end of the year but in the September, I sat in his office pleading with him that I desperately needed to go home because I was struggling with my mental health. Would he agree to signing off and letting me go home? I didn't want a pay out, I didn't care about being qualified or earning more now, I didn't even care about my tools; he could have them just, "Please let me go home," I begged. He refused.

It felt like I had a gun held against my head for those last remaining months, extending the trauma of working in an environment I hated but couldn't get out of. Without the support of Hollie and her family, I believe I wouldn't have made it through.

Being loved by Aurora and her family was the solid foundation on which I returned. From homelessness and suicide attempt, to being one of the luckiest people in the world, taken in by such incredible people with the biggest hearts. Most people are fortunate if they get one family who loves them, but I've got two. My Queensland family were my lifeline that I clung on to during that period and I wouldn't be here today if it wasn't for their support holding me above water. From the bottom of my heart, thank you.

From the Aurora text archives (1/1/2016)

Well, Mr. Although I am a long way away I have had the pleasure of watching you climb mountains and I am so proud of you and where you have got yourself. So, to this amazing 2016 that we all again get to enjoy together, may our journeys not always be perfect, as we are just us. Amazing health, laughter and lots and lots of love—I love you Mr.

LABELS BELONG ON JARS

I had finally finished my apprenticeship but it had come at a huge price that was nearly my life. When did it start to unravel? How did despair become the mainstay my mind kept returning to?

In my experience and research since then, early adolescence is often a pivotal part to understanding the origins of people's self-destructive stories about themselves. Mine was no different.

Much of my inability to deal with the struggles of my apprenticeship I trace back to the unforgiving experiences I had in school, to the labels and judgments I received from several teachers at crucial developmental times, when they simply didn't know what to do with me and my unconformity that stemmed from my struggle to focus and sit still until I was kicked out of the classroom.

This is not to indulge myself in the blame game. In fact, I openly confess that I was no angel. Within weeks of starting high school my cheeky spirit and optimism had been turned into rebellion and talking back due to some pretty confusing and humiliating encounters with my teachers that I had no answers for. Out of fear came the only strategy I could think of to battle and be heard against the system.

In no way did I know how to help myself and improve the interactions and relationships with the people around me. I only knew fear of the next humiliating reprimand and so I grew ever more defiant to smother that feeling at all costs. I became a turd of a kid in high school but I still needed and longed for the same love and acceptance as those kids that ticked all the teachers' boxes.

This is my unchangeable past but knowing there are kids going through a comparable situation as mine right now, charges me with urgency to tell the story of the kids who fall through the gaps. Some of these kids will outwardly shrug it off macho style, "Who cares what the teacher thinks of me? He's an idiot anyway."

Some kids will laugh it off to become the class clown as though by choice and some will turn inwards, replaying the words against them until that is all they can see when they look in the mirror. They are going through this shit right now, their developing sense of self is clouded with confusion, pain and self-doubt but they have no idea it is not the truth.

We need to hear them; we need to see them.
They don't know yet that they are fucking
unstoppable and there is a way to find it.

More understanding is needed by teachers and mentors to look out for the kid not "fitting in," not responding to the assignment in any positive way. Questions need to be asked with more discernment and compassion about how we can reach these special kids. The adults surrounding these kids have immeasurable influence.

It starts at birth when we are totally at the mercy of the adults and cultural environments around us; this enormous influence continues for decades in some form or another. Over time these signals from our "adults" develop identity, character and sense of worth. As we move from childhood, to adolescence and then young adulthood, these default adults (we don't get to choose them) all contribute to the "story" of us.

The gift of learning by example can't be underestimated. What difference can be made if a young boy is privy to hearing vulnerable conversations from their father, **seeing conflict in the household talked through and resolved between parents**, and simply witnessing tears and pain to understand what that space looks like before we are thrust into it ourselves. To know that there is safety and security in emotion, to be confident that it is okay and necessary in fact, to bring it up to talk about or sit in the emotion and know the learnings will follow.

Later on we turn to the mentors, coaches or managers that society tells us must be respected and listened to. It could be praise from a job well done or blame for a mistake made, from these lessons young minds then swallow these words as "truth." They are a blank page, ready to start adult life based on the signals and teachings they've had and continue to receive.

SPEAK TO THE LISTENING

"EVERY DAY IN A HUNDRED SMALL WAYS, OUR CHILDREN ASK,
'DO YOU SEE ME, DO YOU HEAR ME? DO I MATTER?'
THEIR BEHAVIOR OFTEN REFLECTS OUR RESPONSE."

L.R KNOST

No kid is stupid; no student wants to fail. Before teaching success we must teach responsibility: responsibility in learning to love, which is compassion and empathy and the belief in ourselves.

Teaching comes with responsibility like no other; guiding developing minds in each moment of interaction, each moment of explanation, of praise or encouragement or reproach. Unfortunately the role of teacher is not always respected for its power; it can be undervalued, misunderstood and misused to detrimental results.

It ignites a fire inside me to help everyone in these crucial positions of education and training, to undertake them from a place of respect, love and compassion; to praise or correct from a place of respect, love and compassion. If the student knows the "why" behind the teacher's words or actions, it can help them to understand and accept the redirection and feel better for it.

Do you remember a special teacher from your younger years? Someone who took time to see and hear your young voice, who understood your passions, your challenges and your worries? A thoughtful teacher who could pull you up without shaming or embarrassing you?

These teachers leave an eternal spark in our minds; bringing hope and optimism when we remember the way they made us feel like little champions. They are natural teachers, seeing the need for total acceptance in the eyes of their young charges.

Immediately several spring to mind. That influence of teachers extends beyond any classroom I was in, and well into the rest of my journey. The teachers that educate from the heart, rather than the book will leave a bigger impression on the life of the student than any test result will have.

Everyone has the potential to become a change maker in someone's life and I want to empower this on as wide a scale as possible, reaching as many teachers and caregivers everywhere. In these stressful, modern times, I am the first to point out that many of the pitfalls are unconscious by-products of overworked teachers in overflowing classrooms. There are a ton of good teachers out there but they have to battle tighter schedules, teach more topics than ever to more students than ever, it's overwhelming for them.

For me, there was nothing in the curriculum about emotional literacy and learning to understand our needs and the psychological barriers to getting them. I also wasn't taught how to read and understand those needs in other people; people that often got things wrong too. The responsibility of this equally lies in what happens at home. Open, honest, authentic and sometimes uncomfortable conversations about what really matters in our lives.

All of this happens with greater education for ourselves. This is not designed to add guilt, but for all of us to acknowledge what we can be doing more of and the difference it would make on the world.

We have to change the culture of this topic of suicide. The only way it becomes safe and "okay" to talk about it is by taking the power away from the word we've been conditioned to not mention: suicide, suicide, suicide. The more we say it, the more open we are to understanding it and acknowledging society's pressures of trying to conform to appearances, when we are all uniquely diverse and beautiful in our struggles.

Growing up I thought there was a hard, rigid line that said adults knew everything and behaved according to universal rules that saw me fall well outside of those expectations. I was an anomaly that couldn't fit in with the behaviors and attitudes around me.

However, authority figures can be shockingly guilty of their own prejudices, ignorance and fears coming out in their harsh, insensitive relations with young people in their care. How regular are the scandals that break out in every field and industry about someone in a successful position, being brought to bear for their poor decisions and behavior? Sometimes they are criminally wrong, sometimes morally, either way someone else suffers from their actions.

STICKS AND STONES

It hasn't been easy looking so far back considering what a terrible long-term memory I have; it's way below the average person's. I listen in wonder to my family sharing funny stories from when my older brother Beau and I were kids. It's been a long, hard slog to dig deep for the memories and there's a whole stack of reasons for that whose fault lies somewhere between trauma, medication, self-medicating and too many head knocks in sport.

Nevertheless, I am grateful for my earlier, carefree years. I am one of the lucky ones, who has the most amazing parents in the world. Who gave me all the support and opportunity to do and be whatever I wanted. They gave endlessly of their love, compassion, and empathy and paired these with the accountability, boundaries and lessons that all kids innately need.

I was a happy, smart-ass, fun kid in primary school. I was voted a house captain, worked hard to get good grades with dreams to someday be as successful in the sporting community as my fearless and skillful older brother.

We had a great neighborhood and I was lucky that my best mate lived across the road. You could usually find us down the park together, at the river making bark boats to race along in the current, or wheeling and dealing our trading cards and collectables. If I wasn't with him, I was in the front yard knocking around with my brother in a high-stakes game of cricket or footy.

Through both summer and winter, we were obsessed with imitating our favorite international cricketers in the backyard or on the beach; left-handed, right-handed, spin to seamers, we were mostly outside competing with each other. On the flip side I was also happy by myself, scribbling away inside creating my own "homework" to do and asking my dad for equations and problems to solve.

I was lucky to get to tag along with my brother on the local paper run to earn a little pocket money to splurge on sweets at the Milk Bar. Most of the pamphlets never made it into the letterboxes in our rush to get that sugar hit as fast as possible. My childhood was pretty cool and I know not everybody is blessed like that. I wish I remembered more of the good stuff.

So finally there I was, an excited Year 7 student on his first day of high school. Hair spiked full of my best gel, shiny white runners and everything I needed for the day, as organized and punctual as I always was (perpetual habit by the way). There were no nerves, no anxious thoughts and feelings, just an energetic, bubbly kid who was pumped about making new friends and starting at high school, the real deal finally! The day was supposed to be one of joy, a new chapter. A chance to be back amongst a lot of my friends who were in the year level above me, having missed them for the 12 months since their graduation.

My excitement was cut short as I heard the words, "Matt Runnalls? Beau's brother? Oh great—more headaches, another handful!" The teachers seemed to have already painted a picture of me based on my bold and confident brother: a brother who'd already broken most of the rules before me. They saw my last name and judged me. They saw I couldn't sit still and judged me. They saw I could push back and judged me. I felt their prejudice from virtually day one.

The good energy and feel of life changed for me as I entered high school. I was told I was too hard to teach, too difficult and took away other students' opportunity to grow and learn. This conversation evolved into being removed from science and English class because the teacher refused to have me in the room and so I'd end up in the coordinator's office. I was constantly exposed to belittling tones, disparaging comments and an incompetence to see the struggle I had in comprehension.

It was so foreign to me, I remember feeling like high school was the hardest thing ever, but it wasn't that I was dumb. It was my inability to concentrate, sit still or focus, often remarked in discussions with my parents as, "Boys will be boys."

My classes would always start the same; my eyes front, pens lined up with neatly ruled borders. I would try to tune into the teacher's explanations, but soon I was lost, I couldn't follow their point the way they were saying it and it was all over for me.

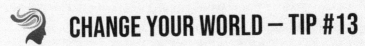

CHANGE YOUR WORLD – TIP #13

Women most fear for their safety,
while men most fear being laughed at.

The thought of raising my hand to ask a question was ridiculous as the voices in my head reminded me that I was a burden when I did that, my time was worthless and I was a failure. The idea that I would get something wrong, disabled me from sharing.

I could read a book from front to back and not be able to tell you who the main character was. The teacher could tell me the answer was on page 6 and by the time I opened the book to page 6 I forgot what I was looking for. It was hell and I didn't have the slightest idea what it was or if anybody else endured it the same way I did. Since when did learning become so difficult I wondered? I had gone from pestering my dad for extra homework at night as a primary student, to being the challenging kid in the classroom who never did his homework and was a distraction to everyone.

I would do anything to escape those feelings of failure: talking in class and fidgeting until I was removed from the classroom, or sometimes the teacher would pull me up the front to sit next to someone I felt even more uncomfortable around or the real clincher, having to sit next to the teacher facing all the students just to add more salt into my humiliation and isolation. I do not ever recall a conversation around "why" I behaved like this, or discussing practical alternatives we could try. The management technique was simply, "Don't do this again!" or "Matt, you are disruptive and stopping everyone from learning!" paired with punishment.

There was one teacher who picked up on my lack of focus and clarity, who never yelled at me, kicked me out or told me, "You will never amount to anything," as other teachers had in the past. She was my Grade 5 and 6 teacher. Having the same teacher for two years was unusual in itself, however being the intuitive teacher she was, I wonder if she took me on for a second year because she felt there were in fact ways to teach me.

For example, when the class assembled on the carpet, legs crossed, facing the front this teacher allowed me to spin a cricket ball from hand to hand. She knew I loved cricket, she knew it would occupy my hands and my mind and it would prevent me from distracting others. She probably also knew that by allowing me to do something that was so prevalent in my life, it would help me feel a sense of belonging. She was right; it worked!

I remember trying to take the same method into high school, but my ball would get confiscated and I would get sent packing from the room again, "You don't get special privileges, you can focus like the rest of the class." As though using a sensory technique to manage what we now understand to be bipolar disorder was a privilege.

I won't pretend that I wasn't a handful more often than not for the teachers but a strange cycle began around: *If they think I'm trouble; I'll make sure I am.* Not a helpful pattern I know, but forgivable in a child who looks to the teacher to show him a way out of that mindset. They kept treating me the same way expecting a different result.

School wasn't all bad all the time and I have good memories from the times and places that were filled with the right emotion. Athletics Day was one of those times. A place where I felt confident, having grown accustomed to some fierce competition with my brother in the backyard testing our strength and speed in every possible way. This was the rare day each year when I felt I could finally "do" something to feel accepted and worthy, instead of being seen as the "troubled" kid, the "rat-bag" kid, the kid who couldn't sit still, the kid who drove the teachers nuts, the kid most likely to be sent to the principal's office.

Athletics Day was a much-needed break from the isolation of a normal school day. It gave me a temporary sense of belonging that I craved. The cheers of people supporting everyone, the rare feeling of something going right for me, the acknowledgment and encouragement of people picking others up after a loss, the sense of contributing to your school house points and the connection that comes with teamwork; I loved everything about that day. The idea of being a part of something together, rather than isolated by myself. Classrooms often didn't model team environments.

> *"TEAMWORK IS THE ABILITY TO WORK TOGETHER TOWARD A COMMON VISION, THE ABILITY TO DIRECT INDIVIDUAL ACCOMPLISHMENTS TOWARD ORGANIZATIONAL OBJECTIVES. IT IS THE FUEL THAT ALLOWS COMMON PEOPLE TO ATTAIN UNCOMMON RESULTS."*
> ANDREW CARNEGIE

Many times though I found my love of sport used as leverage. I remember being told to relinquish my turn in sport so that some other kids could get a longer turn to get the hang of it or to compete. Yet somehow that didn't apply in the other classes of English and math, the smarter kids were never asked to sit tight so other kids like me could have a "longer turn" until we got the hang of it. Instead you were made to feel inadequate, shame, or encouraged to seek a tutor or stay behind during lunchtime. Bizarre theory really.

For the five years I was at high school, my report card and parent teacher interviews followed the same pattern each year: "Matt has all the potential to do really well but has frequent challenges paying attention in class and should endeavor to remove himself from distraction. If he works harder to focus, we have no doubt he can turn his results around." Some teachers' reports were even more foretelling like this one, "Although Matt endeavors to be a serious student he is unable to apply himself for more than very short time spans."

Nobody questioned why I couldn't focus; nobody cared to. If only they knew I didn't *choose* not to focus; I didn't choose to make things so much harder than they had to be.

Hidden amongst all my books that I folded up into my backpack at the end of each day, was all the emotional baggage of the words said to me in those class rooms, words that echoed in my head as I sat exiled to an empty hallway listening to the hive of learning going on in the classroom without me. Words that over time formed a deep belief about myself: a belief that I did not fit in, that I was a failure and a burden on others. A belief system that still rings thick in my mind on my bad days, to this very day.

It is the voices of these "teachers" that I hear amongst my often racing thoughts, the scar tissue I'm reminded of whenever I attempt something new that says to me, "I can't," their words are the chains that pull me back:

You'll never amount to anything Matt.

Matt, your parents must be so ashamed.

If only they could have seen the ignorance of their comments and understood what it felt like to live in an overwhelm of thoughts that clouded my judgment, focus and clarity; to sit in a fog of noises and none of them made sense. Again, this was not the outright fault of the teachers; they were operating within the paradigm of many decades of strict educational constructs that most kids could operate in, except me.

SAWUBONA: I SEE YOU

In Year 9, my parents spoiled us with a family trip to South Africa. The Australian Cricket Team was touring there and so as a family who loved watching cricket, we combined the month-long series tour to coincide with seeing all the beautiful places in Johannesburg, Durban, Port Elizabeth, Cape Town and Zimbabwe.

Without doubt that trip was one of the best things that I have ever done. Getting up at sunrise to put on the traditional pith helmet and head out on safari for the day with Dad, ticking off our list of animals that we saw in the wild. The game park was as big as Belgium, 7 hours traveling in each direction. We hoped to see each of the African animals known as the Big 5, but the jungle was so big it wasn't a certainty.

Each day was thrilling, from witnessing lion packs on the hunt, hippo's in their natural habitats, a crocodile trying to eat a giraffe to watching monkeys throwing rocks at the vultures, there was always something incredible happening. Everything about the jungle and animals was so bloody intriguing; it made me feel alive and purposeful again.

This was my type of learning environment and I soaked it all up from every perspective. One particular day we had the opportunity to hike through the jungle in an area where they had lions under conservation. When I say conservation, it was still the wild and the lions could sneak up on you at any time and if they had been hungry I wouldn't be here today! We were handed a stick and given a set of specific instructions if a lion approached, "Point this at its nose *with intent.*"

I'm not even joking! The trust we put in that guide, well, I'm not sure they would allow it these days. That's what I loved about it. These lions weren't cubs, they had enormous claws, and paws as long as the best part of my forearm, they could launch from the grass to the top of a tree in a couple of leaps. Nowhere was safe if one of them didn't like the look of you.

The lions were familiar with some of the guides and they virtually played and rolled around together at one point. I was fascinated how the guides spent their day learning and researching these magnificent cats; it really filled me with excitement and intrigue. *That was it,* I thought. *I know what I want to do.*

When I returned from Africa I put my head down to find out what it would take to work with wild animals like they did. I set my mind on doing my utmost to make this dream work, and I found out the subjects I would need to study to pursue this career. They sounded impressive, environmental science and psychology, yikes.

The dream was short-lived, not because I lost the passion for it but because I found the subject lessons extremely difficult to comprehend. Trying to process and retain 90 minutes of scientific information in my head? Forget it. The old cycle—distracted, kicked out, in trouble—began again. I scraped through the year before dropping both subjects the following year and I turned my attention back to sport as my last hope. I had no idea where else I would find meaning and purpose for myself. I felt like I wasn't good at much else or at least that was the story that was bubbling within.

The career discussions from Year 10 onwards were relentless and full of pressure. Apparently every decision I made at school carried lifelong weight or at least that was their attempt at showing adolescent support and keeping things in perspective—yeah right.

While everyone else seemed so excited by their career options, I became more certain that my way forward was to drop out. In my experience, there is still a frustrating pattern and expectation for a certain group of males at school that tells them they are only suited to look for a trade, often in the construction industry.

For all those budding builders and carpenters out there, that's great, we need them after all. Yet sometimes it still feels like this path is the last resort for some kids that don't feel like they have a place—just tell them they can be a tradie. Tell them that's what masculinity looks like and therefore off they go and do just that. I had no interest in plumbing or waking up at 5am to fix people's toilets or dig a trench in the cold and wet for $250 a week. But that's not what I focused on when I was struggling in Year 11, I saw an exit and I took it.

SAWUBONA

So many teachers have the welfare of kids in their hands for 6 or 8 hours a day but how many of them know about modern behavioral health? My sole mission isn't to help improve the education system and slam teachers, I'm pure to my cause when I see a lot of kids presenting with lifelong mental health challenges that stem from being dismissed, ignored, suppressed and undervalued throughout their most important years of education.

Instead of telling young Matt Runnalls how ashamed his parents must be of him, ask him how he's feeling that day, how are things going in his life. Can we look behind the behavior, look behind the physical and emotional scenes to see what is happening underneath?

Based on my experience, I now live by the following expectations:

- If a teacher starts telling that unruly kid he's great, he will *become* great.
- If a teacher starts telling him that he can do it, soon he *will* do it.

- If a teacher can show how important mistakes are in the learning process, kids won't swallow the mistake and allow it to define them as a failure.
- If a teacher provides the right environment, the kids will feel more confident to engage.

If we all put in the work, we can make it happen. Something as simple as knowing how long a child's brain can engage in content for, is often overlooked. I ask this question regularly in my talks and few teachers know the answer. It's actually only 20 minutes of engagement time.[12] This doesn't mean every 20 minutes you stop teaching. You have to pattern disrupt their brain to reset it.

So instead of throwing one or two hours worth of information straight at them from the front of the room, make sure you engage a different part of their brain or different physical sense at regular intervals. Flick the lights off, get them doing star jumps, tell a joke or a riddle, play intermittent music for different parts of the learning, you'll get the hang of it soon and see them jump back into the discussion refreshed and ready to go deeper into the lesson.

Each way that we choose to teach, hits different chemical reactions in the classroom. It is absolutely possible to influence students' brain chemistry. I am fortunate that through my study and learning as part of the team at Green Super Camp Australia under Heather Yelland, this enabled me to study at California State University in 2019 and learn a whole new meaning of what is possible when an educator engages in all necessary parts of the human brain.

When we are able to do this even the "challenging" students get excited and persist with their work no matter the difficulty. It enables these beautiful kids to have a sense of being seen and valued which helps them interact with the content of each lesson and not from a surface level but in a deep and meaningful way.

There are four distinct parts to the **Emotional Mind Map of Education**.

1. Serotonin: Set the Mood

Atmosphere creates excitement and comfort. A place that is fun for learning and aligned with the outcomes; a room with all the right distractions.

2. Oxytocin: Prime the Excitement

Not every student loves learning. Set clear boundaries, speak into their way of listening and build strong, positive communication and trust through positive and comforting interaction.

3. Dopamine: The Pleasure Centre

We are more receptive to learning when we aren't in repetition. Change it up, offer feedback, involve people. Learning is meant to be fun!

4. Norepinephrine: Get moving!

The same part of the brain that processes information is the same part that processes movement. Kinesthetically get involved, move around, don't get stale. Bring the energy.

I meet a lot of teachers in my advocacy role running workshops and talking at schools and sharing ways to connect with kids on different levels. In the past I have copped some criticism, not from many but from a handful of educators who seem to get defensive about listening to someone who is not a teacher. This is exhibit A of an ego that prevents us from growing and learning. If we can't appreciate and value the opinion of others, then we most likely show up like that in the classroom with our students, disregarding their thoughts and opinions. School is a place of learning, for everyone.

Regardless of my qualifications and studies, who better to learn from than someone who went through the system and fell through the cracks? From someone who knows so many others who went through similar experiences but are not here to talk about it. That's what hurts the most.

I have to make sense of my experiences and although I would want my friends to still be alive today above all else, I believe all my experiences, interactions, struggles, altercations, poor choices, unruly behavior, all happened for a significant reason. That is to get me to where I am today, a good place, a lasting place where I can find contentment and understanding while channeling my lessons to help others avoid the misunderstandings that society offers them, and find the tools that work for their own health and happiness.

CHANGE YOUR WORLD – TIP #14

What we learn with pleasure, we will never forget.
Prioritize the fun and where the education is
delivered from, and the learning will come.

CHANGING THE NARRATIVE

All these lessons were still in front of me when I returned to Victoria in late 2013. I can look back now at the turbulent years that followed as the critical learning experience they became. It was a mixed up time of hurting and learning while often still numbing any real feelings through self-medication. Each day I scrapped together whatever reason I could to continue, sometimes I couldn't find one.

Balancing on that one-way precipice for so many years has enabled me to now recognize the struggles of the 3000 people we lose to suicide in this country each year.[13] We lose them because they believe a story about themselves that's not true. For a long time I was on my way to becoming one of them.

A lot of people look at me today and see an upbeat, outspoken guy; they think I'm productive and "successful" and have even said to me, "It's easy for you to say these things Matt," as though my past is a distant speck that I no longer connect with.

The truth is, **my past is always in my pocket.** I'm not naturally resilient; I'm not made differently. I've been worried and scared probably for a longer period than I haven't. Some people think that because you've written a book, your life must be dandy. I'm not writing this book for the fun of it. I have done a hell of a lot of work to get to the place I'm in now. Writing this book has been an uncomfortable, awkward, uncompromising, unforgiving process that I knew had to be written at all costs.

If my experiences can help others in tough workplaces or school environments find the way to manage those powerful situations as they happen, to not bottle them up and suppress the emotions for years, then my purpose is clear: to battle and overcome society's ignorance around mental health and offer tools to help people speak up and stop suppressing what they're going through.

LEFT-RIGHT-ALRIGHT!

Once back in Victoria, I had a great homecoming, people seemed happy to have me back and for a time I felt like the weight of the world was off my shoulders.

The challenge was I had been so desperate to get away when I had left in 2011 that I hadn't said goodbye to a lot of people; I had basically dropped them from my life. Now that I was back, I didn't have school friends to reconnect and hang out with, I didn't really have friends from sport anymore either. I hadn't nurtured any relationships so I didn't know where I fit in.

One of my best friends from high school offered for me to live with him in Essendon, which I was so grateful for as he understood I had battled some struggles along the way, just as he had. We were a good support for each other. He even took the time to help me integrate back into life, as I once knew it, encouraging me to play competition basketball with him and holding me accountable to exercise weekly.

I had finally finished that god-forsaken apprenticeship so I was subcontracting as a plumber. There wasn't a lot of security in this, working hard for different companies on short-term jobs that often had nothing else to offer once they were finished. This didn't help with my feelings of uncertainty about what the future held. They picked you up when they required your skill set and no matter how hard you worked for them, you could be gone the next day.

I was still on and off medications for depression and was feeling angry, frustrated and helpless. Once again, I had changed my location and outwardly my circumstances but I was still battling the debilitating thoughts and self-recriminations, to the extent that I self-harmed numerous times. Sometimes it felt like my head was about to explode, the voices, thoughts and confusion seemed unstoppable. I would rock back and forth uncontrollably at the end of the bed, desperate for a stop button to the bloody thing on top of my shoulders.

Social media was one way I was noticing there were other people going through similar challenges to mine. Yet still no one was talking about it in a way that was empowering or hopeful. Instead it was rolling media feeds filled with posts telling me how awful it was to live with depression and anxiety and the complexities of it. It seemed like people used their illness across social media as a commodity, looking to find comfort when they found others who struggled like them, so they could struggle together.

I was looking for someone to show me what was possible instead. I already knew how bad it was.

One important outlet I found during this period, a sport that I had long felt drawn to but never tried, was boxing. There was a boxing club near me but my social anxieties had never let me walk through the door until finally I knew I had nothing to lose, so I dug up the courage one day to cross the threshold into a whole new world.

I saw coaches and professional fighters swinging earth-shattering punches at each other. The coach took me in with open arms. He welcomed me by putting me on a bag, giving me a skipping rope and I was away.

Tucked away in the boxing club, a short, tough looking guy—a professional boxer who turned out to be an Oceanic Pacific Champion—was working out rigorously in the lead up to one of his upcoming bouts. An extremely warm character who would go on to be my sparring and training partner for the next two years.

Amongst our initial conversation I wanted to find out why he boxed. It was the sort of place I suspected people came for reasons that would surprise most, and he replied straight up, "If I didn't have boxing I'd be dead." I asked another boxer the same question later on and his reply was even more honest, "I box to keep my head out of a noose."

Boxing is not a barbaric sport where people are lunatics that want to take it out onto the streets. From my experiences, it has been quite the opposite. It helps people learn to control their aggression; it helps people deal with emotion. It's a place of belonging and I felt that deeply. That tough little guy I met sparred with me on my first night leaving me battered and bruised and yet I couldn't wipe the grin off my face. I left the club bleeding and cut up, but I remember finding the spring in my step again, for the first time in a long time.

I had never remembered being happier than I was that night. It made me feel alive. When you're standing in a boxing ring, there's only one thought in your head; focus on the moment, look for the openings, the next punch, the counter punch. **Boxing is soaked in all manner of discipline.** Keeping your guard up (just like in life), knowing what's next, planning for the next move, being on top of your game through endless training.

I learned that through clarity, precision and focus we can find a way through anything, but most importantly that when we are knocked back, knocked down, we always have the opportunity to retrace our steps, our moves and our next decisions to make a more calculated one. We always have a choice. The way we get punched initially is not the same way we get punched the next time. We take the learnings and don't tend to make the same mistake twice, or at least not in the same scenario.

The biggest change from spending time at the boxing club was the control of my aggression in other situations. Previously heated exchanges would see me kick up a stink and I'd get into a fight, feeling like I was backed into a corner and the only way out was through confrontation. Through releasing and controlling so much energy with boxing, those same interactions would happen and all I felt was controlled, no mindless reaction.

Despite my love of playing AFL¶ (footy) and cricket, while I was doing them I was still always thinking, thinking, thinking; the inner dialogue didn't switch off. But with boxing, there was no time for thinking except: *How do I get out of this situation without being beaten up?* Or if I'm honest, it was more like: *How do I not get punched in front of other people?* I wasn't scared of the beating, I was scared of looking like a fool in front of other people, of feeling like a failure and it just made me feel so alive. I didn't realize how dead I had felt until boxing made me feel the exact opposite.

Since that day, I have always tried to spend my life living in real purpose, trying to feel alive. This doesn't have to mean something dangerous, all sorts of things make us feel alive if they activate certain parts of our brain. I transferred the discipline of learning about my instincts and preparing for things, into my skill set for handling any situation and also into my well-being plan that I use to this day. I realized that if I built a healthier relationship with everything in my life that caused me pain or discomfort, then everything in my life would be simple again. This helped me to appreciate and acknowledge the things in life that caused me pain or took me outside of my comfort zone.

Discipline will get you over the line every time. It's often what's missing in people's attempts at making changes in their lives. People can know the benefits of meditation, gratitude, compassion, exercise, nutrition etc. but they don't do it. If you have a boxing coach bearing down on you in the ring who knows you haven't kept up your end of the training, you'll regret it and never do it again. But not all of us have those people that hold us accountable and that's where **self-determination** plays a big part in driving us forward.

That's how I finally felt the truth emerging that nothing would change until I changed; the truth that nobody can save me except me. I was rewiring the story in my mind from one of "torture" to one of acknowledging and

---

¶ Australian Football League

giving credit to all the good things that had happened to me as a result of the pain, trauma and grief I'd been through. I even began to believe that perhaps I could channel what I had seen and felt, for the betterment of someone else.

POUNDING THE PAVEMENT – FINDING PURPOSE

One day in January 2015, I spotted an ad in a newspaper for a charity event raising money for mental health. The AFL player Lance Picioane was organizing a fun run for his charity Love Me Love You. He had started the charity in 2013 after many years of his own mental health challenges. I had lost four mates to suicide at this point and was aching to make a real difference. Knowing that such a prominent person from the sporting community was putting a public face to this issue was incredibly heartening to me.

At this stage in my advocacy, I had not yet found my voice due to the stigma and bias that were still prevalent around mental health issues, especially with men. I had been accustomed to staying safely behind a keyboard to voice my thoughts but now I felt like I could do something more, that awareness was starting to be found in all the right places, that perhaps it was time for action.

It was time to show people how much it meant to me and to raise money so that this organization could do something amazing as the beneficiary. So I decided to lace up the sneakers and pound the pavement to help raise both funds and awareness. It would be a 220-kilometer event over four days around Port Phillip Bay.

I increased my training, my boxing sessions and even cut alcohol out of my life for the first time. Soon I was pumping out in excess of 100 kilometers a week, wearing out my running shoes and becoming obsessed with utilizing exercise as my outlet and escape. Most especially, I loved connecting with the other members of the charity who would meet up to train every Sunday in preparation for the event. For the first time in many years, I felt like I'd met my people, people who understood what I was going through, had been through their own shit and talked about it freely, offering support the whole time. I felt incredibly at home.

This was my awakening in understanding the fundamental difference between fitting in and belonging.

Fitting in is coming to a situation and having to bring something to the table in order to fit in with people, changing your behaviors and your personality traits to feel accepted by the people. It could be nodding your head and agreeing even though you don't feel the same, it could be dressing or looking a certain way to blend in; all the things we change about ourselves so that we can find forced connectedness. Sometimes we can't know if we belong until we try different scenarios and then learn to recognize where we feel most at home.

That Sunday morning training group enabled me to feel a sense of belonging simply by showing up as my true self, flaws and all, I could be as weird and wacky as I felt (as some know me to be) and they loved all of it. They genuinely wanted to know about me, what my story was, what I'd been through and why I was so passionate about all this. They accepted me just as I was.

*"WE ALL HAVE A STORY AND THERE ISN'T ANYBODY
WE CAN'T LOVE, ONCE WE HEAR ALL OF IT."*

On the back of finding this sense of belonging and some serious training, I went into the event pretty cocky. In fact I felt like I was in the best shape of my life and so figured I could actually sign up for all four days of the 220 kilometer distance. The majority of participants signed up for much shorter distances, which were still important contributions, perhaps they would do one day, a lunch break or off and on sporadically to support the others.

Waiting at the start line on the day of the event, I slipped in my headphones to listen to my playlist, blocking out every single person. I believed that this was part of "getting in the zone"; that I had to block out external noise and distractions, so I could stay focused on the task at hand.

Forty kilometers in on the first day, I still hadn't spoken to a soul and I was bloody struggling. I didn't know what I had done wrong but I was wincing with every single step. I had trained so hard and my body was in peak physical condition but the truth was, my head wasn't. My thinking was in overdrive and I was listening to the voice in my head for hours. I felt panicked and disappointed with myself as the dark, dangerous thoughts started to take over.

There were blisters and blood all over my feet and I had almost passed out at one of the pit-stops. The pain was bearable at first but once I started to tell myself I couldn't do it, that I didn't think I could finish, I started to believe it and the pain got more extreme and more persistent. It was a downward spiral. The thought that I had people sponsoring me put me in a heavy world of anxiety.

At the next stop, I phoned Mum and blathered on about how hard it was and how badly I was doing. She cut straight to the heart of it, "Matt, have you seen how much support you have online? There are so many people behind you encouraging you to keep going. Jump on and have a look at just how many people are behind you, supporting what you're doing. And try taking out those headphones and join in with the people around you—tell *them* what you're telling me!"

Funnily enough, as much as I often hate to admit it, Mum was right. **Connecting with people made a huge difference.** Of course for someone who is riddled with social anxieties, it was initially difficult, but soon I was talking to so many amazing individuals that were there with the same goal and passion as me. Within moments of sharing a meaningful conversation with someone I had just met, my mind forgot the physical pain I was in and I found myself on top of the world.

I gradually opened up and shared some of my experiences with several other participants. Some of those people that I talked to during that day and the remaining days of the trek became some of my closest friends. I saw firsthand how our similarities far outweigh our differences and that by stepping into something that is uncomfortable to begin with, actually helps us create and feed into what the human being is wired for; contribution and connection.

We formed a little group and bounced energy off one another the whole way. Sharing laughs, stories, jokes, challenges and even traumas. Finding the emotional support and connection from people around me helped to dig deep within myself to complete the first day of the four-day journey around the Bay.

On day three, I experienced what I now know to be one of my most significant experiences of mania. Feeling confident, comfortable and sharing the experiences with others, combined with lack of sleep through soreness, my emotions became extremely heightened and produced an energy and a place within myself that was insanely different to anything I had ever felt.

The more I talked and connected with those around me, the more the pain lingering in my foot seemed to disappear, as did the fear I'd had about the distance left to go. I didn't feel exhausted anymore either: quite the opposite. I was bursting with energy and ready to tackle anything thrown in front of me. I felt invincible.

So much so that as we approached street signs, poles or park benches I would hurdle, swing or leapfrog wildly over them. My mind was telling me how easy it all was, **but I was acting like a delirious and manic six-year-old.** Beneath the mania I was experiencing, my body was aching and hurting. My mind was high but my overspent body was crashing my weight into the concrete at every step.

As the saying goes—what comes up must come down—and sure enough, soon after my exuberance I experienced the most excruciating feeling in my left ankle. Through my experiences of self-harm and struggling to identify with fear following a suicide attempt, I had developed quite a high pain threshold, to the point where if I mentioned I was hurting or injured, people never dismissed it, they believed it.

I had had a niggling feeling that I'd actually suffered a stress fracture in my foot sometime on the first day of the event. I mentioned it to the guys I was with and they encouraged me to rest, that I shouldn't continue on it. For me though, I had come too far to stop and so I removed the shoe from my swollen foot and pushed on. In doing so, my body over compensated for the pain it was experiencing and made a subtle adjustment to my running technique. This subliminal change was actually squashing and damaging my nerves in the left side of my body, from my left buttock all the way down to my left ankle. This injury would go on to play a big part in my challenges, my choices and my path over the following 18 months.

We finished the remainder of the event, over 220kms (we may have run a few extra kilometers due to a couple of wrong turns) and successfully met our immediate goals: to bring awareness and meaningful conversations across the communities we traveled through, while raising money for the implementation of important programs supporting mental health.

I was over the moon; I had met some of the most amazing people and learned more about myself, my body and my mind in those four days than I ever had previously. That charity event was the first step I took to actively support a greater awareness and understanding around mental health away from the online conversations. I never imagined the biggest platform for me to have a voice would stem from this event.

Just as I couldn't have known the hardest cross to bear was waiting for me too.

 CHANGE YOUR WORLD – TIP #15

Life, like music should not be rushed or forced.
It should be intently listened to, right to the very end.

PART 2

BE THE CHANGE

November 24th 2016: Enough is enough, something has to fucking change!

I was sitting at another funeral, the seventh mate I had lost to suicide by the age of twenty-five. This one the most shocking of all, the funeral of my 22-year-old mate Shaun. I struggled to lift my head up as I fought back tears, everyone around me broken. Too many lives were being lost to suicide and it felt like so much more could be done to prevent it. The words became so clear in my head: *That's it! This is changing, and I've got to be the one that does it!*

Remembering that phone call with the news of Shaun's death, 8:30am on a Friday morning still jolts me with pain every time. Shaun and I had made a pact to battle our demons together, day by day, left foot right foot, supporting each other. He had wanted to fight that thing in his head; he actively tried to fight every day and never used it as an excuse like many do.

I had met Shaun two years before at the football club I had joined when I moved back to Victoria from Queensland. I had cut so many ties when I had left years ago; I had little to come back to in the way of social or sporting connections. Thankfully a good friend took me down and helped me integrate into this club: a unique club that would play a huge role in the evolution of Mindfull Aus and myself as an advocate and person.

After the fog and struggle in Queensland that had involved all sorts of toxic behavior—drinking, fighting, self-medicating to avoid emotions—I had backed off the drinking when I returned and tried to clear my head a bit.

I was beginning to realize how much it helped to express what I was going through, whether it was talking to my housemate who understood from his own experiences, or posting some words online about mental health on my Facebook profile. I had just spontaneously put it out there one day when I thought: *Why the hell not? I can't feel worse anyway.* The responses I got to those early posts were amazing, people connecting with my experiences and being grateful someone had talked about it openly **without fear or judgments of any kind.**

Seeing people love themselves a little bit more or implement a new skill into their life was awesome to watch. It was as though my raw accounts of how topics like isolation, anxiety and depression made us feel, deeply resonated with everyone.

This is a typical example of an early response I was amazed to read:

> *Thank you so much for your support in my battle,*
> *I really appreciate it! I am so much better than I used to be,*
> *I can get out of bed every morning now.*

I kept posting and generating a bit of awareness amongst my circle of friends about mental health challenges. I didn't realize at the time that I was creating an important platform for so many people to talk about depression, anxiety or any emotional struggle in a safe, welcoming, understanding environment. During my first few months back home,

BE THE CHANGE

word about my Mindfull Aus Facebook page had been slowing spreading through my little network of friends and contacts.

When I joined the footy club, the coach Travis took an interest in all of his players off field and on. He learned about what I was doing and he wanted to know more. This special footy coach would go on to become one of the biggest influences in my life.

Generally I was the guy running at the front of the training pack, loving the camaraderie and banter. I remember though a few times at training when I first started and I wasn't feeling great, I had some pretty open conversations with the coach. Me in tears and him just listening, holding the space for me and letting me be who I really had to be in that moment, even though I was at training. This was the first time at a sporting club where I had ever experienced open dialogue with a senior coach or in a sporting environment. Not usually the welcoming place men would turn to, to let the walls down, but this coach was different. It felt so good to be able to experience these conversations without judgment, or fear of being thought less of.

After those conversations I'd shared about my own struggles Travis approached me one night, "Matt you're one of the only people I know who is outspoken about mental health challenges. We've got four blokes who are struggling at the club, who are actively suicidal, dealing with their diagnosis and frequently self-harming. We don't know what to do. Can you help us?" To this day I believe this to be Travis' very clever way of giving me purpose during a time that he knew I was stressed and lost. Trav showed me he genuinely cared about the topic and his players in a very unique way.

Travis was that sort of guy. He read the play; treating everyone according to their strengths and weaknesses and did his utmost to make people reach their full potential. I immediately replied, "Yes." Not because I had more qualifications than the person who asked me if I would help. More so because by then I was developing a skill set that I had needed to see, hear and feel when I was at my lowest. I had become pretty good at recognizing worrying behaviors and signs not only in myself but those around me as well. I also knew by then that these environments were the perfect stomping ground for people who could ignore or suppress their emotions by chasing around a red leather ball.

I had been living with depression and clinical anxiety for many years by then and I was racking up knowledge of all the things that *didn't* help. I was still in the early days of learning about what strategies did work but I definitely felt I could bring this growing knowledge to the footy club to make sure nobody else felt alone, the way I did.

Importantly to me even at that early stage, was that the knowledge being offered must be delivered with the right approach from the people that best fit the situation. I felt I did fit the bill in these sporting environments.

Thanks to the courage and compassion of this great coach, a role was unofficially created in the club as somewhat of a well-being coordinator to offer some support to the players off the field. I started delivering casual presentations to the netballers, the junior sides and the parents. I delivered content through storytelling, sharing my experiences and giving people a range of holistic skills that they could take away and implement. It was very simplistic, but even then people were extremely grateful that a male had opened that dialogue, something few and far between in these sporting environments.

The coach didn't have to tell me who the ones struggling were, I could tell the signs by then. Shaun was one of the guys that I could see during training was battling some demons within himself. He was a talented football player but also his toughest critic. He would reproach and blame himself when he thought he had performed poorly. He could be hot headed and impulsive on the field and then sullen and brooding when he came off.

To me now, his behavior is common of most people who don't understand the ins and outs of what they experience. That's what becomes of so many when we grow up in a world with little to no engagement or truthful education about the most important topic there is—our mind and behavioral health.

Not long after I joined the club I reached out to Shaun one night by sending him a message that said,

> Hated seeing you down today mate, you don't deserve to be riddled with injuries. I also can see how much footy means to you and acts as a getaway from the troubles off the field. If there's anything I can do as a senior footballer at the club, I would love to be there and be able to help bro. I know what it's like to be stressed out and down in the dumps, if you ever want to chat, a beer, a laugh, an argument, advice or an honest opinion—I'm your man mate. Love ya bud.

Shaun responded by saying how amazing it was that someone from the football club had reached out to him, that he felt better about being there and knowing someone else was going through similar things.

> Cheers Matty, seriously means a lot and yeah, you're right, I suffer from a lot of stuff and depression is part of it, but footy takes my mind away and I feel free. You sending me this message means so much to just know that I have the support from the older group at the club and I will definitely take that offer up, as I need it.

That was the start of a great friendship. I have held on to so many of Shaun's messages from that time. He would always come to me when he needed support. He was honest and vulnerable with what he was going through and I was able to listen. I didn't have all the answers but I held the space for him so he knew I heard his pain.

Shaun also gave me the determination to look at my own journey. He might have come at me very broken but **his determination to change himself was inspiring** to me and I really needed that at the time. I was trying to help people when I still needed help myself. He'd tell me what was going on in his head and ask me questions about what he could do about it, what options did I know of. He was a tough male covered in tattoos who wanted to talk out how he was feeling and kept looking for options. In many ways, he was ahead of his time going against the stereotype of the tough guy back then. He taught me to confront a lot of my own discomfort more than I ever had up to then. Shaun taught me more than he will ever know.

We enjoyed a great footy season in 2014, winning the premiership under Trav's guidance. Trav finished off his time at the club with another triumph in 2015. This was also the year I watched the entire season from the sidelines out injured, broken, and in pain from the aftermath of doing the 220-kilometer fundraiser to raise money for mental health at the start of the year. Like myself, Shaun also got injured that year and was cut off from the one thing that kept him feeling free, that enabled him to escape. It was during this time that Shaun and myself hit rock bottom again, both having suicide attempts and self-harming.

For the next year and a half we bounced ideas off each other and agreed we would fight our battles together tooth and nail. I shared stuff with Shaun about myself that I'd never shared with anyone. He did the same.

We were able to play football together for another season in 2016, our club winning its third consecutive trophy (none of which was due to my football ability by the way). The season finished up in September of 2016 and I felt satisfied with what I had achieved as a player there, so I decided to go and play football with my brother at another club hoping to enjoy success with my sibling.

As a consequence, I lost my regular weekly chats in person with Shaun. We still kept in contact but it wasn't the same. When we talked he sounded pretty good and that was the problem with just texts and no visual interactions. Then I would hear from friends that he wasn't doing so well so I'd call or message him and once again, provide reassurance and push him in what I felt like was the right direction, he would always bounce back sounding inspired and moved to action.

Even though I had made some inroads in opening up and trying to understand the challenges around mental health, **I couldn't see the truth of Shaun's situation.** In hindsight I was still jaded by my own struggles and so I did not suspect the reason behind his contentment in our last interactions. Shaun had decided the only way to end the pain was to put an end to his life and his outward contentment was ultimately a symptom of him trying to manage his pain and hopelessness through suicide.

It seems obvious to me now, so many years later and with the countless hours I've since devoted to suicide prevention training, discussions, understanding symptoms and strategies that address those feelings and importantly the cause of those feelings. But I didn't know enough back then. I always think, was there something I should have said, or something I should have done? It's guilt that doesn't necessarily belong to me, but nonetheless it exists and I live with it every day. I felt responsible for Shaun.

IF NOT ME, THEN WHO?

I sat fifteen rows back, four seats across at Shaun's funeral that day with a packed funeral home of what felt like 1000 other people who were shocked, heart-broken, confused and some angry at his actions. It wasn't the first time I had seen the devastation left behind by suicide. However this time, there was something more to it. Much more.

Watching the trauma etched across the face of Shaun's mum at the funeral, I felt like it was *my* mum I was looking at as she attended my funeral. I could see the aftermath and wreckage of suicide and could imagine the desolation that *my* family and friends would be left to try and deal with. When I looked at the faces of Shaun's family and friends, all I could picture were the faces of all my loved ones. Even though I had been in these situations before several times, suddenly it became oh-so-real to me.

I hadn't been able to see clearly before. When you're in enormous pain, there is a fog that blocks you from being able to see these repercussions. I thought I was a burden on everyone so people wouldn't be weighed down by me anymore. Suicide is not a selfish option to the person in pain, it is a way to stop the pain and release everyone else from the burden of you. You could argue what is selfish is our negative and uneducated opinions of those who bear emotional pain: selfish not to try and understand.

Now I suddenly had the unique perspective of someone who at one point had thought suicide was the answer, to someone who now saw the monumental need to help people in pain understand that it is not the way, it only leads to more pain.

My epiphany occurred that day, watching so many beautiful people attempt to understand suicide and say goodbye to the most loyal, loving, beautiful, cheeky mate a person could ask for.

I vowed things had to change from that moment. I vowed to be the best I could be in this field, knowing just how many people were impacted by suicide in the communities in which I frequented. I felt an almighty sense of responsibility.

It was Shaun's willingness to get help and support that inspired me. Even though he struggled immensely, he had wanted to know what was available to him; he had an uncanny knack on biting down on his teeth, tenaciously trying to find some other way to get through. It was that part of Shaun that very much drove me to do better and be better, in a way that nothing else had. He had been looking for more options and hadn't found any.

I knew I would have to do it. Whether I liked it or not, I had a foot in both camps and had a chance to speak plainly and openly from experience, speak in a tough uncomfortable new way that would make people sit up and pay attention finally.

I made a new pact with myself that every day when my eyes open, my feet hit the ground and I'm breathing in that fresh air, to know I'm one of the lucky ones, still around and still able to do something about it. A big part of that pact was accepting maybe it was more than depression and anxiety that I was actually experiencing, and had been experiencing for a long time. It was a pivotal time in my life that I reflected thoroughly on.

In order for me to do this and do it wholeheartedly, I needed to be authentic, I needed honest self-reflection and that would mean I would need to begin to tell the truth about how I was in my mind. I had hidden the bulk of my thoughts and feelings from doctors, clinicians and my family in the fear of being mocked, judged or misunderstood.

You see, when I was diagnosed with depression, I was shamed publically and behind closed doors with the typical ignorant remarks that went hand in hand with a diagnosis all those years back. The stigma surrounding mental illness was one full of shame and embarrassment; I could only imagine how hard it would be to tell people that I had a new diagnosis.

 CHANGE YOUR WORLD – TIP #16

Everyone goes to bed with the same damn problems; there isn't anything sexy about pretending they don't exist.

I felt as if I had to keep up this facade, that I was somewhat invincible and strong for all those that had found wellness in my advocacy, for all the amazing people who looked to me for support, but what they really needed to see was me leading by example, acknowledging the struggle, accepting the good, the bad and the ugly of living with mind challenges but who practiced the Art of Wellness, because that is exactly what it is; staying well is an Art form.

EVOLVE OR REMAIN

I was presented with a choice, evolve or remain. If I chose to remain unchanged, stuck in the same unhealthy space, the same bad routine, the same dark storm and situations, no one would benefit from my voice and those that once supported me would be forced away. The lack of stability, negativity and numbness wasn't attractive or healthy for anyone to be around. Until you accept your position, until you love yourself enough to say "no more," until you choose change and find something within that wants to evolve, your mind will control you; and so I knew I wasn't as effective as I wanted or needed to be.

From my learnings and research that I saturated my life with, I could often recognize manic-depressive episodes within myself. I was still on and off antidepressants at this stage treating my depression. However I now questioned whether I was overlooking the mania of what I was actually going through. I thought back to my high episode during the charity event and so many other moments over the years. For the first time I asked myself: *Was I actually living with bipolar disorder? And how long might I have had this for?*

After speaking with my mentors, Joe Williams, Kevin and Margaret Hines and other advocates, seeking clarity and the right path to take, I was encouraged to seek further support and guidance around my own wellness. It was one of the most eye-opening experiences still to this date, one that has fuelled a lot of my passion for going somewhat against the grain of what society says to do.

As I embarked on this professional advice, I found myself some 4–6 months later still without an assessment, being handballed from psychologist to psychiatrist to psychiatrist to expert. No, none of them actually saw me or got to know me. It was one of the most demoralizing exercises ever. I bounced between professionals like a pin ball as they blatantly and outlandishly said in no uncertain terms every time, "I don't think you're the right fit for me" or, "I don't think I can help you, you might be better suited to someone I know," or "I know a person that would be great for you." Weeks would go past as I would wait for their referral. But nothing would eventuate. Endless promises and me drifting further away from well-being.

I remember ringing Dad in tears as I drove home after getting off the phone from yet another professional who was anything but professional. "Any fucking wonder people are killing themselves Dad, it's impossible to get any fucking help and I'm lucky I know how to navigate through the system, I know what I am looking for. Imagine all those people who don't have that experience like me! They are giving up, they are dying 'coz of this shit!"

These experiences would build the fundamentals of my organization to this day. The knowledge of how many people are going out on a limb to seek help as society says to do, only to be turned away, ignored or snubbed. It is why I pride myself on answering every message and every email from all over the world. Yes, it's incredibly exhausting, **but their reach out to me, could be a last bid attempt to stay alive!**

It felt as if every time I sat in a chair and got honest with what I was experiencing, the professional behind their desk would shit themselves in fear and handball me on to someone else. Sometimes when they asked me, "Do you experience suicidal ideation?" and I would reply, "Yes" they would immediately reach for the phone to call the ambulance to have me taken away.

It was no wonder people weren't honest. I was literally having conversations with people so "misguided" about ideation that they automatically believed I was an immediate risk. They didn't even ask or question if I was unsafe or at risk, they lacked the basic understanding that suicidal ideation can be a makeup of someone who is actually not a risk. Still to this day I experience ideation just as many other high functional people do, but I know my thoughts are no longer my actions.

After finally being referred to a professional described to me as "the most reputable expert" in the field, I booked in. After several discussions, my reports being read, my blood being taken, brain being scanned and sessions about what I was experiencing, **I was given the diagnosis of**

bipolar disorder type 2. This was not completely news to me, however it was a move that I needed to take to be honest and authentic with my journey. But also, to solidify the acceptance so I could become more aware about who I was and how to manage what I was experiencing.

BIPOLAR PROUD

Upon getting the diagnosis I was informed that I would require medication to help me regulate between swinging from suicidal lows to manic highs. The medication was lithium. Lithium is a mood stabilizer that is said to help prevent the manic side of the condition. Like all medications it seems, the side effects were extensive and dangerous. I was locked in for periodic blood tests during this treatment to better understand the impacts of lithium on my kidneys and thyroid function.

Through the weight gain of filling my system with lithium carbonate, a salt widely used in processing of metal oxides, I had gone from boxing at 69kgs to ballooning to an unhealthy and overweight 95kgs in the space of months. Speaking in front of audiences, in front of cameras made me extremely conscious of what I looked like and for many years I didn't regain my confidence in getting my shirt off in any environment, even when alone.

My eyes took on a red appearance as if I had not slept for weeks, my kidneys were constantly sore, my mind raced harder than ever, my concentration as a result suffered, my body ached and my agitation and ability to sit still or be patient took an almighty blow. All of which were visible to everyone. Some of these side effects still exist in some form today, I manage them for the most part but it's not ideal.

However, the diagnosis of bipolar ... well, put it this way. If you were to come crashing on my door right now with a cure for it, I am not interested. Before you think I'm crazy and throw insults I've received before like: "Why on earth would anyone want to live with an illness? You are crazy!" Hear me out.

For too long I feared sitting in re-assessment and being labeled bipolar, I thought having depression and anxiety was enough. I regretted ever mentioning to anyone the severity of what I was going through.

Now, the only thing I regret is that I didn't do it earlier.

I am not my illness, I am not crazy, I am not the "Melbourne weather" or dangerous. Yes, I am different and I wouldn't have it any other way. I no longer hold a fear of those people that take a step back, that recoil when I tell them the truth of what I live with; they are not my people.

There are over 2.8% of Americans[1] and 1.3% of Australians[2] living with this condition. Most of which believe it to be fucking hell, because that's what society says it is. "You have a brain disorder," hardly fucking motivating is it?

I want to do it differently, if people want to talk about bipolar disorder then I want as many people as humanly possible to talk about it in a way that also gives hope to those 46 million people across the globe—people like me—living with it. I was inspired to do this by three people. Kevin Hines, Paul Dalio and Andrew Nierenberg the director of Psychiatry at Harvard.

"THOSE PEOPLE WITH BIPOLAR DISORDER ARE JUST THAT, THEY ARE PEOPLE WITH BIPOLAR DISORDER AND THEY WANT THE SAME THINGS AS THE REST OF US, A GOOD LIFE. IT JUST TAKES THEM THAT MUCH MORE EFFORT TO GET THERE ... IT'S A TOUGH JOB FOR THESE PEOPLE. THEY'VE BEEN DEALT A HAND THAT THEY HAVEN'T ASKED FOR. SO, FOR THOSE OF US WHO ARE FREE OF SUCH THINGS, I THINK THAT THE BEST WE CAN DO IS TO TRY TO BE AS HELPFUL AS POSSIBLE, REALLY TRY TO WITHHOLD JUDGMENT AND THEN TRY TO SEE IF WE CAN HELP PEOPLE DOWN A PATH SO THEY CAN LIVE A GOOD LIFE ... PEOPLE WHO ACHIEVE ANY LEVEL OF GREATNESS WHILE LIVING WITH BIPOLAR DISORDER ARE JUST EXTRAORDINARY PEOPLE."[3]

ANDREW NIERENBERG

I wanted to help shift a dialogue that has been created around the condition. That helps people understand it and love it the way I do. The truth is, bipolar disorder doesn't have a cure so the longer I kick back off it, hate it and all that it does to me, the longer I spend not living in acceptance and to my fullest potential. There are enormous amounts of positives associated with the condition.

Bipolar is something to be nurtured and not to be squashed or destroyed. When we learn to nurture our being in a natural way we can feel emotions and really live, not just breathe and get by. To have the choice or ability of lowering medication so you no longer have to be challenged to find your emotions again, so we can enjoy experiences, feel alive, not band-aid emotions, and live in a life we truly deserve, not a life of mediocrity.

Don't get me wrong … at times, living with bipolar can be an incredible challenge, requiring a lot of energy and all of the courage you possess, maintaining the feelings of stability in the "normality" range as I have previously mentioned is much harder than a "normal brain" (whatever that is), however I'm able to experience those emotions much more intensely than most. I don't believe that to be a bad thing anymore. If you're living with bipolar and consistently functional, it's something to be proud of, not ashamed of.

Sometimes I'm good for a while; I'll talk more, interact a lot, laugh constantly, sleep and eat normally. Then something happens, like a switch turns off upstairs and I'll be left with just a feeling of nothing: completely numb, zapped of energy, drained of motivation and a total disregard for my own well-being.

Even worse is the million voices up top trying to understand what went wrong and why that switch turned off. When you don't know the problem, it is impossible to find solutions. It can be exhausting, eating away at your vitality, sometimes for months at a time. Feelings and thoughts become so extreme that I must work tirelessly to regulate my emotion and pain back to that middle zone of normality.

The beauty is every time I do that, I get stronger, I can learn and evolve, making those experiences so beneficial to the next scenario. My friend Paul Dalio describes it perfectly:

> "STILL, I KNOW I'LL ALWAYS BE WALKING A TIGHTROPE, BUT
> YOU GET BETTER AT IT OVER TIME, AND LIKE THE GUY WHO
> CROSSED THE TWIN TOWERS, YOU LEARN NOT TO FALL.
> AND THE HIGHER THE STAKES AND TIGHTER THE WIRE,
> THE STRONGER AND MORE DISCIPLINED YOU'RE FORCED TO
> BECOME IN ORDER TO SURVIVE. IT'S ONLY WHEN THINGS ARE
> SO DARK YOU CAN'T SEE HOPE ONE INCH IN FRONT OF YOUR
> EYELIDS AND IT'S SO COLD, YOUR SOUL IS SO NUMB, YOU DON'T
> EVEN KNOW IF IT STILL EXISTS, WHEN JUST AS YOUR DIM GLOW IS
> THIS CLOSE TO BEING BLOWN OUT BY YOUR OWN LIPS A SUDDEN
> SPARK OF GRIT AND WILL TO LIVE BREAKS INTO A FLAME
> OF DESPERATION, RAGING, TO BLAZE ITS WAY INTO THE
> LIGHT OF DAY AGAIN.
>
> SO BY THE TIME YOU FINALLY RISE, THE LIGHT IN ALL THOSE
> SUNBATHING SOULS COMBINED, COULDN'T HOLD A CANDLE TO
> THE FIRE IN JUST ONE OF YOUR EYES. AND WHEN YOU COMBINE
> THAT WITH THE BIPOLAR FIRE, NO MATTER WHAT ANYONE LABELS
> YOU, THAT'S SOMETHING THEY CAN'T DENY."[4]

PAUL DALIO,
FILMMAKER AND FRIEND

I wouldn't part ways with bipolar, I wouldn't change it for the world. **Bipolar disorder has been one of my greatest teachers. It's taught me levels of compassion and gratitude I wouldn't have known.** It's birthed creativity in me that never existed and has forced me to look at those less-than-shiny parts of my life and learn to love them.

Bipolar disorder is often associated with a tremendous amount of creativity and ambition in people's lives, that's why when reaching the consistent levels of wellness I do, I've been able to identify now with my "illness" truly as a gift. I see the world and hold a value on things so differently to other people and only will it become like that for others if they too—no matter the disorder or condition—work tirelessly to regulate it in favor of their lifestyle and happiness.

Today, many years since sitting in that psychiatry office, being handed down my diagnosis of bipolar disorder, I am more stable, functional, healthy and happier than I have ever been. I still endure all the same thoughts, feelings and chaos from day to day that I once struggled with; the only difference is now I know how to manage it. I'm obsessed with finding new ways forward and obsessed with finding meaning with my emotions and sharing those experiences with the rest of the world.

Yeah, I am diagnosed bipolar, I am bipolar proud.

Do you have bipolar? You should be proud too.

 CHANGE YOUR WORLD – TIP #17

Relax, we're all a bit fucking bonkers,
it's not a competition.

Through the acceptance of my diagnosis and clawing my way back into a place of consistency with my day to day routines and wellness, I made a new pact, for Shaun. I thought it was fitting.

I would dedicate the rest of my life to the cause and be proud to continue to tell his story and everybody else's stories in the way they needed to be told, to ultimately change the situation that I found myself in, the day of Shaun's funeral.

I would do everything I could to stop more people taking their own life. By September 2016, MindfullAus was a fully registered not-for-profit organization.

My advocacy today sees me talking to footy clubs about mental health and how clubs play an integral role in supporting people's feeling of connection and belonging. Footy clubs tread a fine line between bonding and banter. It is a banter culture no doubt, particularly in Australia where talent and ego regularly get knocked down a peg at the expense of a laugh.

Too much constant banter can smother people's voices, they feel they can't be serious for a moment; they can't be vulnerable or authentic because people are going to reply with banter. These guys—and girls too—then practice suppressing their feelings at footy and replace them with their own fake but well-aimed banter and bravado that cuts someone else down to size.

In Aussie culture I find there is a pattern to ribbing someone for not showing up to footy training and slandering them with the seemingly harmless remark, "John didn't show up for training, the lazy prick," then they give "John" hell, with ribs and jibes when he does finally show up.

That's all bullshit. Footy clubs are safe havens for people to come and feel that team belonging so if someone's not showing up regularly, it's time we start asking ourselves why as a first resort, rather than shaming them. **These signs could easily be identified as red flags instead of opportunities for shame and embarrassment.**

SAME QUESTION, SAME ANSWER

The reality is confronting, but I need it to land to all of you reading this. I would hate for you to make the same errors I did and sit at your teammate's funeral in six month's time and tell me you didn't see the signs. We don't know why that person didn't rock up to training and we won't know unless we ask, unless we show we care. This is only one example out of so many scenarios.

Don't create a story about your colleagues, teammates and friends that's not true but has the power to seep into his/her own beliefs about themselves when they hear it.

These banter environments need balance. Ask who your mate hooked up with on the weekend, sure, but also ask how he's doing, where's he at? Need a chat sometime? Or go for a run together, whatever you feel comfortable with in just holding space for your mate, and he can do the same for you.

Ask your friends, "Tell me what it feels like to be you?"

This is a powerful conversation to have and a direct route to helping people feel just how much you care. My mentor Heather Yelland, shared this question with me that I truly believe is a much more poignant way of helping the person on the receiving end understand that you genuinely care what life looks like to them right now. Not just questions that are delivered at a surface level like, "How are you? What's new? Howya feeling?"

While these questions still have a place, I believe if we're going to make breakthroughs into helping people talk about their own vulnerabilities then we have to meet them in the middle with more meaningful questions. Questions that can't be sugar coated, tiptoed around or provide the person the chance to say, **"I'm fine," the most commonly told lie of people right around the world.**[5]

Questions that, out of love, make people feel uncomfortable. It is in that discomfort that they truly reflect on who they are and how they are. Often this question has the receiver sitting in silence either because they don't know the answer if they've never asked themselves that question, or sitting in silence because they feel some fear around sharing their response. But these silences are often signs.

Asking someone what it's like to be you, is a really confronting question that I often use in my workshops and encourage others to use in their environments. It helps build a bridge of connection that can be asked or implemented by anyone at anytime no matter if they are a stranger, friend or family member. It also acts as a reflective question for those who are asked it.

All sporting clubs have to stop turning their backs to the problem. Clubs come looking for answers when it's too late. I get phone calls when it's too late. They ask, **"Can you come in and address our footy club because there was a suicide last week?"**

This breaks my fucking heart.

I get it that people feel scared to act, feel overwhelmed and under qualified to reach out to people. Many parents even ask me, "Here's my son's phone number; he's not doing too good; can you call him?"

Now of course I can call him but he doesn't know me, he doesn't care if I love him or not. It has to come from *you*. You don't need a qualification, you need a heart and to simply know how to hold the space for them to feel you're listening and know you care. That's what reconnects that wire in them that is broken.

In 2016 I was "stood down" and told to "rest" from the footy team after breaking down at training one night, highly suicidal and struggling. I had trusted the environment I was in and had bared all of what I was feeling that night.

After the instruction was given to me, I admit I lost my shit and yelled my head off at those calling the shots that handed down such a callous, clueless decision. I know they were only trying to do the right thing, but if you're ever in the same situation as they were, this is the message to remember: Don't immediately do what you believe to be right when you aren't the one living, or have ever lived in that situation. Spend more time and focus trying to understand what that person needs: understand the person that is hurting. This is the art of listening.

The club effectively removed me, even though only briefly, from my sense of belonging and connection. They took away the only thing that was keeping me balanced and made me even more isolated. It felt like winning was more important to them than how I felt, it was more important than my life.

After we won the premiership that year, a member of the club hugged me in congratulations. "Look how far we've come! I remember the way you spoke to the coaches that night, I wanted to kill you for those things you said!"

I replied, "Don't worry, I wanted to kill myself too," to which they had no response, as if what I had said finally clicked.

Instead of listening intently and holding the space for a person in pain, the club made that decision to ostracize me from the place and the people I needed the most. I managed to hang on that time but how many other people don't? **And then we fool ourselves as we sit at their funeral and wonder why.** We are often gifted the opportunity to listen and we blatantly ignore what that person needs in that moment, making uneducated decisions that can have disastrous implications. Decisions that we make based on our own opinions without considering the person themselves.

This is the urgent message for your team environments: look after the team physically, look after the team mentally. The brain is the general, the body is the troops, and I have never in my life seen an army win a war without the general. Sporting success is derived from the solid foundation of ensuring player well-being as the ultimate priority.

CHANGE YOUR WORLD – TIP #18

The one thing we have, the solvent glue in the world is our love for each other. In a world of broken systems and flawed support, the one thing we should always feel comfort and safety in is the love of the people around us.

WHEN PURPOSE & PASSION ALIGN

Plots were unraveling thick and fast through the following years. Running parallel to the impact of meeting and losing Shaun and my bipolar diagnosis was the creation of Mindfull Aus. As they say from small beginnings big things grow.

The snowball began a short while after the charity event when one of the participants I had become friends with asked me to come and chat to a group of his work colleagues about our experience. *Great*, I thought, *I'm happy to talk about the fundraiser to generate more interest and support.*

However when I found myself in the meeting room, my buddy introduced me to the group in an unexpected way, "Matt's lost quite a few of his mates and he is going to share some of his own mental health challenges and efforts to overcome them and how important it is to break down the mental health barriers."

What! Standing there in the boardroom with expectant faces looking curiously at me was a strange serendipitous moment. I had thought I was just going to promote the fundraiser itself, but there was my friend prompting me to talk about the loss of my mates and my own struggles and encouraging me to explore them in front of others. I wasn't sure I could do that.

I took a huge breath and somehow began to talk.

Had my friend not put me in the spotlight like that unexpectedly I would never have thought I could open up to people publicly about mental health. Without that first spontaneous talk that opened up a world of change and possibility for me, I wonder sometimes whether I would still be living a life full of those old painful edges. Tino, I love you mate.

The people that listened to my story for the first time really encouraged me in how important it was to share and I realized the impact of the knowledge I possessed. From that humble little talk I received another request through Facebook to come and talk at their footy club and so on and so on. **It all took on a life of its own;** I certainly didn't have to go looking for speaking gigs. On the one hand I was excited to think I could help on a bigger scale by literally using my voice and sharing my experiences, because losing numerous mates to suicide is something nobody should have to endure.

On the other hand, my injury from the fundraiser meant I was also spiraling into disconnectedness from not being able to play footy in the 2015 season. I felt I had done all this great work and then had nothing to look forward to; no footy, no mates, no exercise, no friends to see numerous times a week.

I was out of action for months without being able to exercise to the extent I knew I should for my mental wellness. Time away from my normal life challenged all aspects of my life for well over a year. The injury created too much time for thinking and I suffered some serious relapses, that's how Shaun and I supported each other when we both needed it.

So although I wasn't sure I was up to the task of calling myself an advocate or anything, I realized without footy I would have to find another path. This was right around the time I was sitting at people's funerals thinking: *Fuck this*—**something has to change!**

I was more fired up and passionate than ever about mental health attitudes and so the combination of circumstances and timing actually created the time and energy to explore making a difference in a way I would never have been able to had I not been injured—the providence of my life you could say. While it also filled a desperate need for my own sake, giving me value and purpose.

I was scheduling speaking engagements for lots of people, organizations, sporting clubs, schools and everything in between, wanting me to share stories, resources and information. I was known as the guy who did the ridiculous 220kms for mental health and I found the notoriety for a good cause made the injury and repercussions of the event easier to bear. It wasn't that I wanted to be the one to speak publicly about this, I was terrified of public speaking and I practiced what I wanted to say for weeks. It was more that **it was in everyone's too hard basket** and no one else wanted to do it.

 CHANGE YOUR WORLD – TIP #19

Say yes more often and put yourself in the situations
where something magical might just happen as a result.

In my second speaking gig, I had spent weeks preparing what I would say, I organized slide photos for a proper presentation (no boring words to read, just images) but it felt more artificial and awkward than the first spontaneous talk, I was speaking from the head too much. I realized that when I just let the truth of the story flow, I was communicating from the heart and not the head and people really connected with the emotion of the story, not necessarily the details or circumstances.

As the small speaking engagements continued, a big personal challenge was managing my mental health after a talk was over. I replayed my words and rebuked myself: *You stuffed that up—you missed that point—that person was tuned out.* I actually still have those feelings today but not in such overwhelming ways. I wasn't as educated in my message back then and I look back and cringe at my early attempts to share the message, even from six months ago. That's how much I continue to grow in this field of understanding wellness and how to break down the misconceptions around it. I believe continual reflection is a must.

I'm of the huge belief that holding a microphone and telling your story is an absolute privilege. I often say **the right words in the right order at the right time could potentially change someone's life or likewise, harm it.** Creating this awareness in everyone is what drives me.

When I talk to an audience I have to try and connect to 100% of them. I'm always worried about not connecting with that 100th person who could potentially struggle if I don't hit their heart button. To try and hit 100% of the audience, I had to raise the game I brought to them so they would come along with me and then leave the room with wiser eyes to look at people in a new way. This meant arming myself with every available resource, citation, and statistic. It also involved finding more engaging ways to impact the audience using all three styles: visual, auditory and kinesthetic.

"IF YOU AIM FOR THE STARS YOU MIGHT LAND ON THE MOON."

Today I am all about the value in lived experience speakers and lived expertise, meaning skill and knowledge. That's why I feel like I let people down for so long. I felt extreme guilt for a long time about what I was doing—like a fraud—why would anyone listen to the things I had to stay? Afterwards I'd go back over my talk and ask myself: What had I really left these people with? Motivation only lasts 20 minutes. I needed to show them lasting inspiration and tools and skills that they could take away. I needed even more knowledge.

A WORLD OF SUPPORT

In order to show people a beacon of hope and importantly what comes after, I started studying and obsessing and reading everything I could about the physiology, philosophy and psychology around mind and behavioral health. I saturated my life with it. I was Googling, scrolling through social media, reading from the world's most well-known voices in well-being like Deepak Chopra, Sadhguru, Brené Brown, Johann Hari, Joe Dispenza, Martin Seligman, Dr Bruce Lipton and many more people that were real change agents. I studied mindset, subconscious learnings and started understanding that **what we think of as real often isn't**.

My parents were somewhat concerned, "Do you think this is a good idea Matt? Do you need to be around it 24/7?" My answer to them was that it was the only thing that made me feel alive.

Added to that feeling, I was actually being bombarded with requests for help; I felt compelled to do it. I felt purposeful, for the first time since the fundraiser. I almost felt like I didn't have a choice, I felt pulled. **I don't love what I do but I do love seeing people learn to love themselves.** That's what kept me coming back so I strapped in and rode that rollercoaster of emotions and anxiety leading up to a speaking engagement or a workshop, to then experience the euphoria of having connected to people in a meaningful way afterwards.

I still had feelings of suicide, the fraud, the guilt, the responsibility, the weight of the opportunities. I could sense that this was both saving my life but at the same time it was killing me, the weight of it. Unless I came up with a skill set, it didn't matter what I surrounded myself with externally, if I didn't change myself internally, nothing would change. I kept searching for things to help me.

One of the first local advocates I found in my research was Joe Williams, the successful NRL player and professional boxer who became a suicide prevention advocate after his own struggles. I had read about him even before the charity event in 2015 and I felt his story was in synergy with mine in many ways. I sent him a little note of admiration for what he was doing and told him about the fundraiser I was embarking on. I was amazed when he wrote back to show he had reposted the event's information including a picture of me, morphed into Superman; I felt like an excited kid.

Joe and I struck up a friendship and one night when he was in Melbourne, he invited me to come along with him to a boxing match. It was a great night hanging out. Joe was open about his experience living with bipolar and he helped me understand the truths of it so much better, really opening my eyes even though I was not diagnosed myself at this point. Joe would go on to become one of my greatest friends, supports and mentors and someone I continually admire and follow, not only in the wellness space, but that of First Nation advocacy.

In another seemingly predestined move, it was Joe that would go on to introduce me to Kevin Hines' story, which had an enormous influence on my life. Kevin had become an advocate for suicide prevention after surviving his own attempt jumping off the Golden Gate Bridge in San Francisco. I read all I could about him and he became a mentor. Relating to his story gave me the biggest spark of hope I had ever felt which enabled me to find my strength within; Kevin showed that no matter what your adversities, it is absolutely possible to thrive.

Witnessing firsthand the extremes of what Kevin lives with daily and how much more exhausting and challenging his diagnosis and side effects are to mine, but how he succeeds through it, enabled me to put my life into perspective. He gave me great hope and inspiration that perhaps I could live in a more meaningful and fulfilling way too. Kevin has a great quote, "We survived the pain, in spite of the pain, despite the pain, so we can thrive again today."

As my obsession grew, I decided to reach out to Kevin telling him how inspired I was by his journey. I threw it out there and wrote if ever there was an opportunity to meet him it would be a dream come true. I wasn't expecting a reply but I got one and to my luck, Kevin was coming to Australia from Atlanta, USA and mentioned dates and what his location would be. I wasn't missing this so I cleared out the diary and booked my flight to Sydney. This guy was a beacon of hope for my journey.

Unbelievably, I had the pleasure of meeting Kevin in February 2016 when he was shooting *Suicide: The Ripple Effect*. His documentary is about surviving and thriving with mental illness but more importantly the ripple effects, both positive and negative, which come with the loss of loved ones to suicide. He wanted to share the impact of lived experience of storytellers from all over the world in his film and he asked me to be a part of it when they came to Sydney to shoot. I was both exhilarated with excitement and sick with nerves.

While I felt awed at first, Kevin is such a real genuine person that I soon felt comfortable in his presence and soaked up his unique perspective. Time with Kevin showed me another side to the complexities of mental health struggles, as he experiences auditory and visual hallucinations that require unique support and management every day, but every bit worth it. What he brings to so many millions across the world is unmatched in the field of advocacy. I'd never met anyone so passionate about helping others feel seen, heard and valued.

We filmed in Sydney, going to iconic places like the Harbour Bridge, The Opera House as well as Coogee Beach, and Riley Street gym of Russell Crowe fame. Kevin had assembled different lived-experience advocates from all over Australia to be part of his journey. People that were all bereaved or challenged by suicide, trauma or mental health struggles; professionals and experts that brought tremendous value to the field in different ways.

Some of them have become my greatest friends, places for support, resources, guidance and wisdom: David Covington, the founder of Zero Suicide, a global movement; Dr. John Draper the Director of The National Suicide Prevention Lifeline of America; Sam Webb and Casey Lyons the founders of Livin; Stef Caminiti the founder of The Inner

Ninja Foundation; Pat Lawson who started an awareness group called 3Words – I Need Help; Ben Higgs the founder of The Rise Foundation; Joe Williams the founder of The Enemy Within and many other incredible advocates and professionals stretching right across the globe.

Meeting that crew was a crucial part of my journey, that group of people went on to become the CNQR Collective that also featured other advocates from several other countries formed by Kevin Hines and his wife Margaret with the support of Director Lauren Breen to represent a world team. CNQR stood for Courage, Normalize, Question & Recovery; the essence of surviving and thriving in spite of the pain. The CNQR Collective vision is to ultimately eliminate suicide through transforming how brain health and wellness is viewed in the community by creating opportunities and safe spaces for conversations to flourish and for the current landscape of mental health and suicide to be positively disrupted.

 CHANGE YOUR WORLD – TIP #20

Wake up determined. Doze off with satisfaction.
It's the determination that makes you unstoppable, but it's
the satisfaction that makes you appreciate the effort it took.

NO FALL PROTECTION

After the most fantastic few days of filming I returned home to my plumbing job. The experience wouldn't leave me though and I was inspired to keep trying to do more of the same. I was ecstatic to hear from Kevin again in March 2017. He had contacted the CNQR Collective team again asking us to fly out to America to come and work with him and speak across colleges and universities and communities on a speaking tour and attend the National Behavioral Health Conference in Seattle. I didn't have enough money for the trip. When I explained it all to Dad, he was direct, "You're going. Just get on the plane, I'll sort it out." For that, I am forever grateful.

We bounced around America making the biggest impact: Cal State, New Jersey, Chicago, L.A, Kevin was a key name in this field and we spoke to some large audiences filled with hundreds, sometimes thousands of students and community members. Kevin asked me to open for him at all the colleges and to talk on stage before he came out. This was an enormous opportunity that I wasn't sure I was up for at first. But each time I left the stage with sound advice and confidence from both Margaret and Kevin that I was making a difference as I gained more insight into the field.

It helped that Americans have huge admiration for those who speak so openly about the topic, often rising to their feet for a standing ovation and to share stories and trade hugs following a talk. They seemed to appreciate and value this work more than I had seen anywhere else in the world.

In the middle of the tour we went to the major conference in the world for mental health, where all the most incredible organizations and leading advocates would be. This really provided me with the education and the wisdom to continue on more resourcefully with my speaking path.

The problem was, I was away from home and I didn't have any self-wellness plan in place, I had never done anything like this before. I didn't have any home support, wasn't playing sports, everything I'd fallen back on wasn't there, **so I was falling apart.** As much as I was excited to do this work, hotel rooms are pretty cold, lonely places to go back to at night.

Kevin's wife Marg is another beautiful, uniquely perceptive person who could sense I was struggling. She had learned to recognize similar patterns in Kevin and she had some sharp talking words to snap me out of my darkness. I can remember one time where I got the kick under the table at an important meeting with Marg and a collaborative organization.

Marg was always very observant. She could notice when I wasn't fully present and my energy and concentration had disappeared. At the next interval Margie pulled me aside, "Matty, are you thinking about suicide?" In a way, Marg normalized it and confronted it. She knew it was something I had come close to before and she didn't assume I was "over" it or submissive that I wouldn't think about it again. She knew it was in my history.

When I quietly confessed, "Yes," to her question, Margie proved unique in her response technique. Often out of fear it is common for people to internalize strong emotion with a hug; they don't know what to say so they shut the person down with a hug thinking it is processing the emotion somehow. But a hug keeps the person in pain with their head down and not expressing their pain in words, it is still a form of hiding their feelings.

Margie knew to acknowledge it openly and she pattern disrupted my brain in an effective and very humorous way. She simply said, "Well, ya ain't dying on my watch boy." We both laughed. It was her way of snapping me out of the thought process immediately and letting me know she saw me, cared about me and was there for me. She would always follow these moments up with more important, meaningful conversations.

One of the important speakers at this enormous conference was Dr. Harry Kopplewicz, the founding President and Medical Director of the Child Mind Institute. He has been repeatedly recognized in America's Top Doctors, Best Doctors in America and New York Magazine's "Best Doctors in New York," and was named one of WebMD's 2014 Health Heroes for his advocacy on behalf of children with psychiatric or learning disorders.

He started a conversation with me one night when I wasn't coping well. I didn't know who he was or what sort of reputation he had. All I knew was that I wasn't in the mood for another discussion; I was over it. I was rude and brash and didn't want to be there. Everything he said to show how things were working, I had a rebuttal for. I pointed out the negative, how things weren't really working!

Later on Marg said to me, "Ooh Matty, somebody is a big fan of yours. You've made a lasting impression on one of the biggest names in the field."

I barely mustered the energy to care, "Yeah, who's that?"

"Dr. Kopplewicz, that guy over there," she said as she pointed back to Harry. "He works at the Child Mind Institute in New York. He said the CNQR Collective had one of the most impressive, straight-talking people."

Okay—not what I was expecting. For the first clear time, I thought maybe I could do this and I did know what I was bloody talking about, even the times my head was somewhere else. Being with people like Harry, Kevin and other professionals in the field, that constantly had time for my opinions and my thoughts, gave me hope that there was not only room but a need for lived experience advocacy. I may have come home empty and exhausted from the US but I was also feeling validated in the direction my life was taking.

Even though this had been a 38-day tour in the US, I was not yet in full time advocacy. I was incredibly lucky at the time to have a boss that supported me in chasing my alternative dreams. Back in 2016 I had been going for a few interviews for permanent plumbing jobs and I had wanted to be totally upfront with my potential boss.

When the guy asked in the interview, "Is there anything we should know?"

I replied, "Yeah, I live with bipolar disorder." Dad was shocked when I told him what I was saying in the interviews and no doubt it forestalled a few job offers, but I wanted to be real and upfront with people, I had spent long enough hiding. In this particular interview I was surprised to be asked a pertinent, practical question after I told him about it. He asked, "Without being rude, how will it affect your work?"

I told him I manage it but admitted it may rear its face at some point. I just didn't want to hide it anymore. Afterwards I felt pretty proud that I'd taken those steps to share this so authentically. And his response made it all worthwhile. He said he could relate to mental health struggles and didn't make a big thing of it. He was an amazing boss. On one fixture job that should have taken me five minutes, my mind was firing all over the place and my hands were shaking, it was taking me hours because I couldn't work things out in that moment.

I rang my boss and said, "I'm having a stinker. I'm sorry, I think you need to send someone else." And he simply sent someone else out without making a big deal. It was my first experience having a boss like that and I could enjoy going to work for the first time in my life. He actually encouraged me to do my talks and accommodated things from a work perspective when I needed time off to pursue advocacy.

As I came back from America from yet another tour with Kevin in that mid 2017 period, I knew it was time to finish up plumbing. That boss even wished me luck and said if it doesn't work out to come back and see him. If only there were more bosses like him in the world.

 CHANGE YOUR WORLD – TIP #21

Leadership is about having a value system that screams
that your people are more important than any money
you make; where your good will is undoubtedly
stronger than your best product.

LEFT FOOT, RIGHT FOOT

Life was about to get interesting when in July 2017, I finally decided to quit my job to take on full time advocacy for my fledgling charity Mindfull Aus. I started it with a phone and no money, no computer. But I knew it was what I was meant to do. Dad put up some start up money and I was away, trying to keep up with the demands of emails as people and groups were looking for speakers and workshops at a growing pace. Even though I had no financial security I could see people valued what I did and how I did it.

My dad and I learned how to set up a charity with the help of a local organization, roping in some selfless people to become members of the Board to set up logistics and outcomes. Next we needed to fundraise. We received some great support for holding a 24-hour run on a treadmill. I managed to sell all six sponsorship windows of time for $250 each, this felt monumental at the time. I was actually doing it! And thought the

$1500 raised would last the organization a lifetime! How little I knew. The event was exhilarating and intense; all treadmills had to continue and both my best mate and my dad were there every step of the way: literally. I remember Dad let me sleep for a while so he could keep things ticking over.

Despite not being in bed for 24-hours, the fact it was my birthday must have influenced my decision to go on to play football straight after the fundraiser had finished. Perhaps not surprisingly I got knocked out (again) in the last five minutes of the game. I was sent home from the hospital without too much fuss, just instructed to rest but not to fall asleep—what a cruel irony—I was exhausted!

A few days later I was still nauseous with a bad headache so I returned to the hospital where a brain scan showed the extent of the swelling. It was good to have an explanation for how I was feeling yet I was still allowed to play football again the next weekend. How much doctors have learned since then! My list of head knocks over the years is considerable— the repercussions of them are much harder to define.

Within the first three years of the charity, I was already engaging in a hundred plus talks a year. Schools, sporting clubs, community groups, work places and correctional facilities: the groundswell was unexpected and yet not surprising. As I learned early on, I work best without notes and presented organically, as I found the emotion of the truth to connect the most effectively. Through each event we developed programs, work documents, help lines and resources so the audience could go home with tangible information for real changes in attitudes and actions.

That first year of Mindfull Aus was easy in a way. It began in my local community and people were so receptive to what I was doing, they appreciated the risk of what I was doing, the surprise factor of something new and relevant. Even those who had once laughed or made ignorant remarks were being turned around. Donations and bits and pieces came through, enough to keep going, with Dad's help as well. He paid for us to get some exposure, and also paid my wage when Mindfull Aus couldn't.

The second year was challenging, but I never waivered, I didn't have a fear of anything, not even going bankrupt; I'd find a way to do it anyway. I was still trying to find my fear because I'd lost it long ago. After experiencing my own suicide attempts, I had all but lost my ability to fear anything physical. The only fear I've ever had is fear of failure, letting my parents down, not seeing something through, not doing something that makes a profound difference, a fear of judgment and shame, a fear of not being good enough.

The biggest challenge appeared in the third year when things were taking a financial toll on my dad and I admit I was close to quitting. In a cornerstone moment of Mindfull Aus, a large donation came through at the most opportune moment imaginable. An anonymous person had seen the work we'd been doing and the world repaid us ten fold. That timing effectively saved Mindfull Aus and probably saved my life too. I didn't quit. The gratitude and energy I felt from receiving that donation made me get even more serious.

Without that donation, I wouldn't have been able to build the resources that are imperative to the countless workshops and talks I and the rest of our incredible team here at Mindfull Aus give each month, each year. We have continued to grow and build a Blueprint to Wellness, something tangible to support the growing number of people reaching out for help.

It's exciting to share this information with you that will not just give you hope, but an action plan for learning about mind and behavioral health for you and everyone you know. Before I talk about the Blueprint, let's take a look at some of the underlying principles about brain health first.

CREDIT OR DEBIT: THE MENTAL HEALTH CONTINUUM

In my pursuit of real change for myself, the mental health continuum was one of the most valuable and practical discoveries I made. The mental health continuum is a term of measurement from a research paper two decades ago,[6] and considering its simple and universal approach I think it's been vastly underutilized for too many years.

EXCELLING

THRIVING

SURVIVING

STRUGGLING

IN CRISIS

I use it in my workshops to provide a simple yet strong foundation to work from in understanding how our minds, moods and feelings are affected by external circumstances each day. It's like a little barometer to check in with ourselves where our emotions, thoughts, feelings and behaviors cannot be suppressed, they are measured honestly and acknowledged so we can do something about them if needed. As I said at the start, there are no negative emotions; they all serve a beautiful purpose in our lives, for inner-strength, growth and gratitude. Yet we don't want to dwell for too long in the emotions that drain our strength and vitality for life. Using this tool is the reflection people often miss.

From measuring how we are feeling on the continuum, we can ask questions of ourselves to learn what circumstances might have created these feelings. We can't control everything that happens to us, but learning which conditions we can control, can help us make more conscious choices in our actions and environments which then moves our minds, emotions and bodies towards the healthy end of the continuum.

I have been extremely fortunate to have met so many inspiring people in this field along the way; mental health advocates, world-renowned researchers and professionals as well as individuals and families that have lost and battled and questioned "why" endlessly.

As I first began touring as a mental health speaker, an incredible irony was emerging. By day, I spoke endlessly about the need for looking after yourself, yet after hours my own mental health was privately unraveling due to my lack of an applied skill set. I was floundering in a foreign country having brought with me all my old patterns and habits.

Slowly though, I began to see the potential of learning everything I could from the collective wisdom of all of the amazing people around me. I began studying their methods and strategies and ideologies; what they were doing well for themselves; watching how they were implementing rituals and practices into their daily lives that lifted their minds and spirits. With this new knowledge I could see the richness of the resources and options already around us, learning that there is always something tangible a person can implement in their own life, something they can do, or touch, or see or feel that can rewire that connection they are missing, relight that spark.

SO HOW DOES THE CONTINUUM WORK?

Our general well-being is made up of three core areas: emotional, social and psychological. The continuum helps to measure the status of our well-being overall. We are bombarded with potential stress and stimuli all day. Our actions, conversations, environments, companions, physical health and so many other internal and external factors determine where our mind health lies upon the mental health continuum. We all sit somewhere along it.

As equally important as life's big challenges, are the smaller daily struggles. For example divorce, death, or financial crisis are significant stress factors that can severely bruise our emotional and mental stability. But who hasn't replayed in their head a simple misunderstanding with a friend or colleague at the end of the day? Replayed a mistake from their day or just can't seem to shake that sour, unresolved feeling from something that happened that day? Or from yesterday? Or even longer ago?

Sometimes we bounce back fairly quickly, other times we can't shake the anxiety and this is where we need to actively process our feelings to find a healthy balance again. It is an interdependent cycle because our daily mental health can also dictate the way in which we react and whether we are able to shift our position along the continuum!

If I've confused you, think of the continuum like a credit and debit system just like a credit card. Now I am no financial guru in fact quite the opposite, but the premise behind the credit card theory is simple yet it comes with a high level of caution: spend too much and you'll find yourself in debt.

Instead of money, I want you to apply the same warning to HOW YOU SPEND YOUR TIME. If you don't spend your time wisely, you can decline into emotional debit. The good thing is though we get a chance every day to shift the debt.

This means:

✓ Practicing self-care every day and implementing tools and strategies specific to your strengths and values, puts you in mental health **credit**.

✗ Binge drinking, hanging out with toxic people, bottling emotions, eating shit food and whinging every day about your circumstances, **debits** your mental health credit and you'll feel like shit every day and fall into a decline like I did for eight years.

Some people reach the struggling or crisis point of the continuum. The "Crisis Point" is any situation in which a person's behavior puts them at risk of hurting themselves or others and/or prevents them from being able to care for themselves or function.

This is also known as the "problem point" and not necessarily a bad thing. In fact, in my experience this point indicates that **you're finally ready to be real with the place you're truly at**. This will help in your recovery, healing or management of your situation or circumstances. You are no longer suppressing, the pressure has become too great and you can no longer ignore the signs; this acknowledgement is a good thing.

Acknowledging there is a problem is sometimes half the solution. Then you are finally open to knowing how it needs to be addressed. Notice how it isn't called the "suppress it" point or the "I'm fine" point; these mindsets will keep you in the debit zone or red zone. Recovery begins from acceptance of the truth.

Acceptance is the solid platform in which we rebuild; the ability to recognize struggle, challenges or pain. It's important to say to ourselves:

> *Right now I am facing challenges, but these challenges will*
> *subside with support, knowledge, discipline and effort,*
> *just like any I've ever been through and I will be me again.*

People who recognize they are within the "problem point" are then usually able to cope much better with the stress knowing that **recovery is a process**, not a magic click of the fingers. They can start to make changes in their thoughts, behavior, and actions.

However, when someone sits at this end of the continuum for long periods of time we begin to see illness present itself and there are certain strategies for those particular challenges. I bathed in this end of the continuum for eight years, believing a narrative that told me this was my new way of life.

Gaining vital knowledge around the theory and use of the mental health continuum, I was finally able to recognize where I was and began to understand the way to shift myself away from the debit end in a positive direction. The truth is we sit on the continuum by ourselves and no matter the incredible support we have, we are responsible for the shift we make.

You can't cheat your way through this system; nobody else can pick up that pen for you. Don't sit there and think: *No one cares about me—Mum and Dad don't care about me—the psychologist doesn't care about me*, because while good support is evidently easier to have and certainly matters, ONLY YOU can pick up the pen and change where you sit on the continuum.

CHANGE YOUR WORLD – TIP #22

Start the journey all alone;
pick up the right people along the way.

It is a hard but necessary lesson to reveal to people their misconceptions blaming everyone else for their situation. I made this mistake for years and can often find myself falling back into it of course, but **change is only possible if YOU do it, no one else can**. A lot of people complain that they don't have good support. Sometimes it's a shock when I point out that it doesn't matter. Good support can't throw good food down your throat; YOU have to do that. No one can be grateful *for* you; YOU have to feel the gratitude in your heart, which comes from redefining the way you have looked at things for years.

The sole responsibility of our well-being is our own, nobody can put thoughts and feelings inside of us. Just as no one can move us up the continuum—we can have all the best support in the world or we can have none—at the end of the day, the only thing that changes is the effort we put in ourselves. If you only put 20% in, you only get the same amount back.

Only YOU have the power to change YOU.

Everyone is triggered by different stresses and so they move through the continuum at different moments and lengths of times. Many people work hard to keep themselves in the credit zone, spending their time on positive activities that are more likely to put them there.

The credit zones are "Thriving" and "Excelling"; they express contentment and shout times of joy. The distinct marker at this end of the continuum is also known as the "healthy point."

People that maintain much of their life at this point are generally emotionally well balanced, stable, and goal-oriented, living in alignment with who they are and they know how to have their emotional needs met. They have lots of self-knowledge gained through experience and often hardship themselves.

It has taken many years of work and effort for me to be able to consistently find myself in the right place, a place I—just as everyone else—thoroughly deserves to be on the mental health continuum. But my message is clear; my journey is exactly that—*my* journey. When one kid who struggles with poor mental health, when he silences his thoughts and feelings, and marginalizes, suppresses and never shares his feelings, you have one kid who struggles without hope. But that does not have to be their journey; it might be the start of their story but never the end.

When one kid who's struggling finds safe and supportive measures to comfort and reassure him, when he finds an environment of people who are aching to see him smile again, when he shares his feelings this creates a beautiful ripple effect that can not only help them but also others. It gives hope to those people who don't believe they can do it. **The risks of staying silent are too great.** If we can encourage people to choose to share it, the ripple effect can be felt all around the world. I had no one telling me this stuff for eight years. I'm just that kid that decided to speak up about it and it took me years to find the content in this book.

"DROP BY DROP THE LAKE BECOMES; THE RIPPLE EFFECT IS FELT."

By showing up daily and implementing positive strategies into your life such as gratitude, mindfulness, meditation, cold exposure, exercise, good nutritional eating and so many more, you build credit in your mental and behavioral health. Remember someone struggling is often watching to see how well-being is achieved in those around them. Your lead and examples are helping people make their choices, healthier ones that might just inspire them enough to be here tomorrow or to implement the positive tools into their life.

Just as I now have a skill set that helps me stay well balanced and living in alignment, so will you. There is no one-size-fits-all approach for wellness, but there is one thing that certainly doesn't fit and that's sitting in silence, hoping things will change. They won't; and that mentality is entitlement, **assuming that life owes you something when it doesn't**. That was me for many years.

If you are reading or listening to this book, you sit in a privileged part of the world, with access to resources and environments to draw strength from. We are the lucky ones and no matter where you lie on the continuum right now, know that you, just like the rest of the world, face struggles daily and you have the strength within, when you tap into the core of who you are to shift in a positive direction into a more flourishing life.

LIVING IN ALIGNMENT

Wherever you are right now and whatever you're doing, reflect in every moment and decision you make to understand if what you're actually doing will eat away at your mental health credit. Are you moving with purpose or sitting motionless on a couch for long periods, watching the clock and praying for the end of the week?

It's all about balance and by no means do I suggest not to eat your favorite foods or enjoy a sociable drink for fear of declining, just recognize that some decisions and choices require some fall protection to be put in place to stay well balanced in your day-to-day wellness. Finding that balance is critical to joy and contentment.

Falling into debit is just too easy when you don't have the skill set I keep banging on about. Far too commonly we see the cycle of suppressed emotion turn into numbing and self medication through alcohol and a big night out, which in turn flows into the following day in bed, binge watching drama-ridden TV, eating take-away food, no fresh air, no exercise or real connection with anyone and quite easily these debiting days roll into our working week, another one I am far too familiar with.

We then begin the new week already dragging our feet, only gathering some "false" positive momentum when the weekend is in sight, where the cycle begins again. Before we know it, we have gone several weeks with emotions and thoughts that have not been discussed, but constantly suppressed and silenced.

This is how we use the mental health continuum to explain to everyone they are not alone in their struggles; that some actions have slipped them down into the debit zone, which explains why they are feeling so hopeless and helpless. It empowers people to know they can come out of it, rather than what society has often painted for us to believe about mental health and illness. It is not a black abyss or dark hole. **It's just a seat at the wrong end of the table and you can get up and alternate seats if you have the determination.**

You could be struggling alone in the midst of a panic attack, you may be about to perform or speak publicly, you could be taking the game winning shot, "sweating" in an interview room or even at your office desk trying to make sense of day-to-day activity; knowledge of the continuum enables you to use tools and strategies to support yourself back up to where health, wellness, productivity, presenteeism (think the opposite of absenteeism) and contentment is found.

It's not based on new-age mumbo jumbo; **it is science and biology.** My passion is giving people straight talk with straight answers and real options to get themselves out of that debilitating red zone, offering something more hopeful than what many of us have been taught and told. It clears the fog in their minds and gives them that spark of warmth and hope from reconnecting with who they are and with the people who love them.

EVERY MINUTE COUNTS: THE "1440 MINUTES" THEORY

Now that you understand how important the effects are of how you spend your time, let's look at the *value* of your time and how that value is actively applied.

The most common protest I hear from people as I tour around speaking and working among large groups and audiences, is that they don't have time to implement any changes. They say that 5am is too early to get up yet they'll also confess that they don't sleep well or they utter the word that I really hate; they say they're too busy. After the word "suffering," "busy" is my least favorite word in the world, yet I hear it so often in this field of work. It's a word commonly used by people that don't know how to prioritize or proactively use their time each day in alignment with who they are and what matters most to them and those around them.

Not many people question how they actually spend their time, and evaluate the true value of their activity. That's why I started to look more deeply and really analyze time management and ways in which I can show people just how many opportunities we have to help ourselves and reach our full potential each day. I started taking notice of the habits of successful people I met along the way. Not success in terms of financial benefit, success in terms of who embodied a healthy and well-balanced way of life. Often they went hand in hand.

Through this process, I broke things down. We each have 1440 minutes of opportunity each day. **Not 24 hours anymore, 1440 minutes instead.** This helped me to shift my mindset from one of entitlement (remember the world doesn't owe us anything) to one of gratitude and abundance. It was no longer looking down the lens of, "I have to" but rather "I get to."

Through my research I discovered that within each standard day, the average adult spends their time in the following ways:

- 7–9 hours of sleep (often broken and interrupted), which equates to 420–540 minutes each day.
- 8.3 hours of work each day which equates to 498 minutes. (Yet a survey from the UK showed only 2 hours and 53 minutes of that time was spent productively; phone calls, drinks, snacks, stops, toilet breaks, socializing, social media, phone time, reading non associated material or distracting workers made up the remainder of the day.)
- 3.43 hours on mobile phones each day which equates to 223 minutes.

Wow huh! That's 56 days a year lost to being on our phone. Think about how much we could achieve that would be more beneficial to our goals, our dreams and our lifestyle if we culled those hours on our phones.

The sum of those simple things add up to 1261 minutes, so even if you were a phone bandit for an astonishing 3.43 hours a day, you still posses 179 minutes in a day for yourself. If you're playing along at home right now, I don't think there is much argument to support the "I don't have time" theory.

By now though, I can hear the excuses rolling in, "But Matt you try having 6 kids!" Or, "Oh yeah, easy for you to say Matt, have you seen the amount of homework school sends out now?"

I get it, I do. I once gave all my energy and assumptions to all the reasons as to why I couldn't do something, and they are certainly endless if you let them be. I could not entertain any reason as to how or why I could find the time (or inclination sometimes) and so I kept slipping and sliding down into the red zone. It purely came down to what was more important to me, and my life satisfaction rose to the top.

Yes, I was working, paying taxes and getting things done on the outside yet not many knew it was a one-way ticket I was riding on. All my rock bottoms were a hard way to learn that I **simply had to devote time** to my mental health and well-being or I'd have no "time" left at all. Putting yourself in the credit zone on the continuum is your priority above virtually anything else you do in a day (barring saving people from burning buildings of course).

I know it's a challenge but that's the beauty in discovering the answer is within you, you can meet the challenge if you recognize your innate worth. I say that because you deserve what's on the other side of all your reasons why you can't—you deserve to live a fulfilled life with energy and drive and time to do things you want to do.

You are the priority in the situation, because only when you are at your best can you give your best to those you love. So as selfish as the cliché "self-care" may seem sometimes, you are honestly giving those around you the justice they deserve, to be **your most light, most present, most joyful self, engaged in every situation.**

PRIORITIZING FOR NUMBER 1

In all my research and meetings around the world, this pattern of people telling me all the excuses as to why they can't take care of themselves was becoming overwhelming. I still hear so many today, "I'm too tired by the end of the day," "Meditation just isn't for me," all the excuses that get in the way of looking after themselves. This assertion was the main driver behind breaking the day down into its smallest yet most productive components: 1440 minutes to use any way *we choose.*

To each group I speak to I pose a straightforward yet telling question: What do you put more value on, your wealth or your health? The vast majority always come forth confidently and answer, "health!" And yet the evidence, the statistics, the signs all point to the increase in mental health diagnosis, stress and anxiety, none of which aligns with the answer they all emphatically believe. People may say they prioritize their health but turning this belief into action is the path we must take.

So now I prompt *you*: What do you value more; your health or your wealth? If you also answered "health," then further ask yourself: Do I spend more time working and worrying about money or more time focusing on my health? There lies your real answer.

I'm not talking about necessarily working less, fulfilling work adds wonderful purpose to all our lives. The beauty is, self-care doesn't need 40 hours of attention a week like our full time employment does. Self-care can be achieved and implemented in increments as little as 5–10 minutes at a time.

In the last decade or so in Australia, there is a seemingly harmless and humorous expression when someone tells you quietly that they had a pajama day or a doona day. This means a day spent in semi hibernation trying to take a break from the relative stress in their daily lives and hoping to find a quick, easy way to recharge themselves for the next day. This is often disguised as a sick day off work or school.

Australians are some of the best in the world at "chucking a sickie" (taking sick leave from work or school) and studies show only 52% of workers were genuinely sick when they took their sick leave.[7]

A portion of this can be explained by taking days off to look after sick children or family issues, but for many people they are overwhelmed and exhausted with their own thoughts before the day has even begun that they want to switch off from their own life. There are so many reasons behind what creates this cycle of low energy and hollowness. You don't have to sit in your diagnosis of depression and feel like there's nothing you can do about it besides take a pill.

This is letting life happen *to you*.

So many people are unaware of the effects of not eating healthy, being too sedentary, not getting enough sleep, and being under chronic stress and how they all contribute to our mental health each day. On top of that these lifestyle factors have a huge influence on our immune system. When your immune system is depleted, bacteria, viruses, or toxins can overwhelm the body. The result? You get sick!

It's hard to find the positive end of the continuum when you are constantly stuck in this cycle at the lower end, simply swinging between sickness and sadness. We spend so much time in bed trying to recover from the debiting ways we've been spending our time that our body is operating on a slippery slope just trying to get back to a semblance of "normal" let alone reach excelling and thriving on the continuum. Our immunity is down because we're waiting for someone to come and fix us. Society tells us to seek out professionals all the time, and they do have an important place in mental health discussion and support.

But I'm here to highlight how putting wellness back into our own hands, means looking after ourselves from within by aligning and living within our values. *We* have the ability to manage our own state of being each day to reach joy and contentment. By the word joy, I don't mean happiness, I define these words quite differently. Joy comes when you make peace with who you are, why you are and how you are, whereas happiness tends to be externally triggered and is based on other people, things, places, thoughts and events.

SELF-CARE: YOUR RESPONSIBILITY

Self-care is a direct result of *your* ability to put the time and attention into you, it is not reliant on your support network or friends. It starts with small, seemingly insignificant changes in your day, growing bigger as you start to feel different and before too long the results are absolutely profound.

I often use this chart to help explain the enticement and process of getting in alignment with who we are, and the importance of self-care. Take a good look and see the connections between the actions you take each day and how they build up to joy in different aspects of your internal and external self.

BY CHANGING NOTHING, NOTHING CHANGES

PRACTICE ➡	PRODUCTIVITY ➡	FREEDOM =	JOY
MINDFULNESS	TIME	OUTLETS	JOY
COMPASSION	ENERGY	CONTROLS	JOY
GRATITUDE	VALUE	FRIENDS	JOY
PROACTIVE	SELF-WORTH	SLEEP	JOY

As per the first line, if we practice mindfulness and living in the moment, our concentration improves, we gain focus and clarity for the task we are doing and if we are only focused on the one task we are doing, we are going to do it well and more efficiently. This moves us across to effectively creating more time in our life to do things we love, the outlets for how we want to spend our time. And so finally this time spent in positive outlets helps us find more joy, which in an ideal world we would have more time to do the things we love, and living in joy would be a more common state of being.

Does the idea of waking up and rolling over to cuddle your phone seem more romantic than rolling the other way to greet your partner with good morning? This is a sign of a reactive approach to life: seeking external avenues for happiness. Checking our phones to see what everybody else is up to, rather than being proactive and setting intentions and responsibilities for the day ahead. It's a simple but important choice each morning. By focusing more on ourselves rather than the external world, we create our own self worth and value for who we are, we believe in ourselves and listen to our instincts more. This all plays a big role in falling asleep soundly and quickly each night, without the weight of the external world pressing on us, and so leads us to joy.

One of my most effective practices on the way to producing joy is having a cold shower. Now this might not be everyone's cup of tea but once you understand the biology of how our body reacts to stepping *out* of a cold shower compared to a warm shower, you begin to see the potential for managing our own state. Even just a few moments at the end of my shower with the cold tap only, releases positive hormones in my brain as my body thanks me for stepping away from the short discomfort and gives me a mental boost to start the day.

Through the journey of trial and error, you will learn what practices work best for you: exercise, social connection, journaling, motivational podcasts, bibliotherapy or eating certain foods. The key to all these practices is understanding the habit loop, which we will visit shortly.

 # CHANGE YOUR WORLD – TIP #23

Just in case you ever doubted it, nobody has it all.
Nobody lacks it all. We are all just a beautiful balance
of yes and no, wrong and right, strengths and
weaknesses, mistakes and corrections.

Remember I'm human just like the rest of us. I've been there, I slip up and ignore what is important for me from time to time but having this understanding around why it is important helps me each time to pull up and put myself back onto my own particular road to wellness. No one's road will look the same.

I want to reiterate here, the importance of *allowing yourself* the time (the minutes even!) to do what is necessary for you; you are the number one in this situation, everything else begins once good health and contentment are achieved.

IT'S ALWAYS THE RIGHT TIME TO DO RIGHT

Many people squander their resources looking for a quick fix, a band-aid and a solution for their pain, problems and challenges, never quite understanding that they are the pharmacist they are looking for. When you tap into the strength of who you are and the resilience that exists within, you will realize that you always had what it takes. It might have been buried under modern confusion and stress or certain trauma that needs to be worked through, but it's there in every one of us.

I can't tell you your life's going to be better tomorrow, because it's a process and just as quickly as it might feel possible to change your life around, it can quickly turn back to shit if the disciplines and processes of your wellness plan aren't followed consistently, combined with life's spanners thrown frequently into the mix. Discipline plays a huge role in how best to manage your 1440 minutes of the day. The discipline to form good habits and change bad ones.

There's a lot of commonly documented noise that 21 days is all it takes to create a habit. The truth is that it could possibly take you anywhere between 18–254 days to build that new behavior,[8] it's different for everyone. From there it takes on average 66 days before that behavior becomes automatic. How this "automatic" element develops is key to understanding how real change begins.

Our daily lives include hundreds of routine habits such as brushing our teeth, putting on a seat belt, or turning off the morning alarm clock with our eyes still closed. Habits that our brains have automated to the point that we hardly need to think about the actions involved. We have done them repetitively until they are virtually an unconscious yet natural part of our day.

Do we like doing them? Probably not.

Do we feel better after we have done them? Absolutely!

Who doesn't love that "job-done" feeling? Often an important reason behind the discipline of doing these little tasks comes from knowing what it will feel like if we *don't* do them. There are repercussions that follow, even if it's just that annoyed feeling when you arrive home to the dishes still in the kitchen sink or eating something you love yet knowing too much of it makes you feel worse than before you ate it. We draw discipline from the knowledge of the adverse side of doing or not doing something, whichever applies.

Neuroscientists have traced our habit-making behaviors to a part of the brain called the basal ganglia; this also plays an important part in the development of emotions, memories and pattern recognition.

Having discipline and self-determination is one of, if not the, biggest drivers of positive change. Not every day will you feel like doing it and not every day will it be enjoyable. But we know that by doing these things for small 5–10 minute increments daily, we are going to achieve a far better version of ourselves.

If that doesn't get you excited, think about what you could do if you had more free time. That's the reward. When we create habits and lifestyle changes and are living at our capacity, operating with clarity and focus and not weighed down by inevitable life situations and challenges, we find ourselves in *freedom*, with more time to do the things we love and value.

The adage says, "You can't teach an old dog new tricks" but neuroscientists have recently discovered that creating new behaviors can be done by rewiring the brain. That's why there is endless hope for anyone feeling doubt; you can absolutely rewire connections and create new behaviors and habits that will support (and excel) your mental health. We can rewire those signals leftover from adolescence that don't serve us well.

It's easy to overlook how we form our habits but it's really important to take a step back and observe their development. Habit formation has three main components: the context cue; behavioral repetition; and the reward. A habit may initially be triggered by a goal, but over time that goal becomes less necessary and the habit becomes more automatic.

STEP 1 – THE CONTEXT CUE

This step is the understanding of the "why" behind our behavior, behind each habit. This is the reason we are "triggered" into the situation that kicks us into (automatic) action.

When trying to create change, we need to connect the new behavior we are aiming for to as many areas of the brain as possible. Tapping into all five of the human senses often helps to solidify our experiences. Things like smell, images and feelings help create the "stickiness" that helps form neural pathways. We all have experiences that are imprinted in us.

Visualization can be a very powerful sense that can help build new neural pathways toward behavior change. Like the saying goes, "You'll see it when you believe it."

Example: Ring Ring! Your alarm jerks you awake. In response, your arm slaps the alarm, hitting the snooze button, and you go back to sleep.

Think about what's happening step by step:

✗ [Context cue] Horrible sound of morning work alarm going off.
   a. We assign the cue with a workplace we don't like and the idea of having to do eight hours of work; plus—it's cold outside, argh no thanks ...
   b. [Behavioral Repetition] We hit the snooze button and slump back on to the pillow for 5 minutes more "rest."

Or we can rewire the context:

✓ [Context cue] Sound of morning work alarm going off.
   a. We assign the cue with the gratitude we feel for having a job where we can earn money to do things we enjoy. Imagine the dejection of having no job to go to.
   b. [Behavioral Repetition] Disable the alarm within 5-second countdown and immediately move the body to a positive physiological state.

STEP 2 - BEHAVIORAL REPETITION

Neural pathways are a bundle of nerve fibers (comprised of neurons connected by dendrites) that send signals from one part of the brain to another, like pathways or tracks in your brain. The number of dendrites increases when a certain activity or behavior is performed frequently. So the more you do something, the stronger and deeper the neural pathways or tracks become.

The cells in our brain communicate with each other via a process often called "neuronal firing." This is the process in which the road or train track is built. Just as we learn to ride a bike, we fall off at first (and it hurts a bit but the goal is paramount) and so we have to get back on and try again until we find our feet, the rhythm and the technique. Then we ride faster and faster until we see little hoodlums riding around shouting, "Look, no hands!" with eyes closed. This is a prime example of neural pathways strengthening over time between brain cells.

Psychologist Deann Ware, Ph.D, says that when brain cells communicate frequently, the connection between them strengthens and, "The messages that travel the same pathway in the brain over and over begin to transmit faster and faster."[9] Over time, these behaviors (such as writing, speaking and driving a car) become automatic because the pathways have formed from repetition. This means we can almost learn to do anything automatically, if the motivation is there, if we practice it enough.

STEP 3 - THE REWARD

According to Barbara Frederickson of the University of North Carolina, people are much more likely to make changes when new behaviors are associated with positive emotions.[10] We like positive reinforcement, which enables us to be creative and open to trying new things. To use exercise as an example, this may mean working on technique and fitness in order to run a little further each time or improving our running time for a win or a new personal best time. These rewards help release the positive emotions that help us come back and do it all again and to have confidence in doing it.

Example: "But meditation isn't for me. I just can't sit still."

This assumption is often because people have the misconception that meditation means sitting still for hours trying not to think about anything. They may have tried it for a short time and felt like a failure because their mind constantly wandered and explored other things than what they were trying to do. This experience brings them no reward so they don't repeat it. Therefore there is no increase in their neural pathway and the art of meditation is lost on them.

However, rewarding meditation is not just for the likes of gurus and swamis, I admit the way they talk about transcendence and enlightenment takes it to a whole other level. I'm talking about the stillness of meditation to register thoughts and feelings one by one, to slow down the cascade of noise and voices in your head.

Approach meditation with curiosity and optimism and acknowledge your small steps. If you did sit in stillness for one minute the first day and then a bit longer the next day, that alone would be a reward. The problem often is we are looking for big rewards and we want them immediately. We don't get a gym membership one day and cancel it the next because we feel jacked after one workout; it takes work over a period of time, the same way it does when dealing with our behaviors towards our mental and emotional well-being.

With this being said, think about a time you started something and most likely you weren't very good at it. Not being good at something isn't a fixed point, we become good at things by implementing them consistently, not judging our ultimate ability based on the one singular time we attempted it.

**And so I say well done to you reading this book
as a kid with a fighter's mentality, look at you now!
At one point you may have failed to even read the title!**

CHANGE YOUR WORLD – TIP #24

Don't rush the process, do the work. Earn the person and
the titles that other people so freely gift themselves.

THE HABIT FORMULA

As you read through the Blueprint to Wellness, remember this habit
formula can help you map out how to implement the new tool step by step,
increasing your chances of adopting it into your life. One example might
look like this:

- Figure out what it is you want to do (e.g. wake up at 5am to exercise).
  Say it aloud to yourself throughout the day or pin it up on the fridge.

- Plan where the action will happen (at the local gym or training center).

- Use your senses to visualize and plan for the activity to be successful
  (perhaps imagine where you'll park, picture yourself doing the
  workout and what training goals you want to accomplish, how
  many reps? Trying a new exercise? Set a new time for your alarm,
  maybe hit the sack five minutes earlier than usual and lay out your
  gym clothes for a quick "get-up-and-out-the-door" feeling in the
  morning).

- Enjoy the action (your body thanks you for the exercise and tick off
  Day 1!)

- Recognize rewards in the new action (the feeling of completing a
  workout or working up to body composition tests).

- Repeat the habit loop until the new conditioning sinks in.

You can break any new activity down into these habit formula steps.
Understanding the habit loop will give you a huge advantage as you read

through the Blueprint to Wellness and begin to include new practices, concepts and habits into your day.

WHAT'S MINE IS YOURS

My toughest experiences culminated in these lessons I have shared around the mental health continuum, the "1440 minute theory," self-care and behavior reflection. These tools and strategies I developed over a long period of time became the cornerstones of building my path to wellness. Along this journey, there were two clear markers showing me how far I had come.

If you recall, despite me training relentlessly for those 200,000 steps in the charity fundraiser of 2015, my physical training ended up counting for zero and I broke down, mentally and physically. At the time, I swore I would never do anything of that magnitude again. I either lied or couldn't help myself because a few years later, I found myself preparing for a similar event: a 320-kilometer run from Noosa to Byron Bay once again in support of mental health. This event marked a huge turning point in my life and a great representation and learning around the power of my mind.

I had never forgotten my confusion and struggle during the run of 2015 from having no understanding how to be strong and disciplined in mind, behavior or spirit. So this time, I was determined it would be different. Instead of training relentlessly and eating perfectly, I changed tactics. I didn't train physically or exercise or religiously watch my diet; **I shifted my intensity to training my mind.** If I was going to do 320 kilometers again and be tested by doubt and pain, I would prepare my toughest defense yet and knew there would be both big challenges and learnings out of it.

In the lead-up to this effort, I had begun experiencing unusually sharp pains, which I believed were coming from my heart. At one point I ended up in the Emergency Department of the hospital believing I was having a heart attack. Doctors eventually diagnosed atelectasis, which are basically little holes in the lungs. It was described to me as a partially collapsed lung.

By this time I was regularly speaking around the country and overseas, and so I spent a lot of time in the air. The high altitude of flying meant that my lungs would expand because of the holes putting enormous pressure on my heart and so causing those intense pains, so similar to a heart attack. Ironically I now have to take more medication when I fly to prevent this.

Another battle prior to hitting the starting line was the emotion of worrying about a friend who was on life support in hospital. Many people had assured to me, "Matt, you can postpone it," or "Matt, you don't have to do it, everyone would understand." But the mind I had built leading up to this event was incredibly strong, resilient and focused.

To cut a long story short, I found out how much stronger I was mentally by Day Two of the event when I was the only guy left of the three men who took part. I refused stints in the car and pulling out completely. Both my companions on the trip were finding out what I had learned back in 2015; that this sort of adventure was excruciating work for the mind and not for the feint hearted. I finished the event, crossing the finish line in Byron Bay without fail.

Outside of my usual local weekly sporting commitment, I hadn't trained for it physically. I trained the most important thing, my mind; and the proof was in the result. I didn't just train when I felt like it. No— I trained my mind all the time. Every single day I put hours into tapping into the uniqueness of who I was and the strength of who I had always been. I didn't create a new me, I just found out who I really was. My thoughts, my emotions and learning how to regulate all of them.

By merging this knowledge of the mental health continuum with the tools and strategies I have learned along the way, my Blueprint to Wellness was born.

I use it every single day for my own well-being and no doubt I will for the rest of my life. It's not finished and never will be. I obsessively look to adapt, learn and trial new ways of being, that enable me to discover more about who I am and what I need. It has become part of my make-up, part of my muscle memory. This toolset has allowed me to pull myself from the street; it saved my life. Unfortunately, it wasn't there to save my friends.

I wish my mates could have known what I know now.

I'm far from perfect, make more errors and mistakes than most and some days do not follow my Blueprint to a tee but I now have the awareness and acceptance to know what I'm missing and how to realign my well-being again, not only consistently but efficiently. I know that I have another opportunity tomorrow to gain mental credit and rebalance.

But nowadays I don't let the misses roll into two or three days because I know where I'll end up. I still experience the same feelings and emotions as from when I tried to end my life. **The difference is I know what I need to do to combat them** and I have unlimited access to these outlets every day. It might even be as simple as a five-minute reset. It's a confidence to know I am strong enough no matter the situation; it's also a confidence to know I can do it alone when no one else is around. That confidence is what I wish for others.

Originally I developed the Blueprint for myself but now that I'm well enough I want everyone to have it too. It's not groundbreaking or revolutionary and I did not invent these tools, I have learned them from others. Many of them are about reconnecting with the inherent knowledge that we can no longer hear against the clamor and noise of modern life. It is a skill set that is not readily referred to or spoken about enough. For the most part it is dismissed, as we innocently, ignorantly handball those struggling into the hands of broken systems and leave them there, some never finding their way back.

Imagine the difference real self-care could have! Society encourages us to only rely on a set of professionals. They play a very important, vital role but what about the middle of the night panic attack when you're on your own and physical help could be hours away? What about the time you have that relationship breakdown and the idea of a tomorrow without that person seems unattainable?

Rather than trying to numb life and suppress it, we need a skill set to know how to climb out of it right in that moment when we are on our own. **It is the ultimate empowerment to be able to draw upon your own inner resources.** There are many incredible organizations I have become familiar with through my travels and work across the world that offer valuable services in our society but the reality is they are often under resourced and under staffed.

These tools and strategies in my Blueprint to Wellness became the foundations on which I clawed my way back from the person I didn't want to be, a life filled with negativity and exhaustion, to the life I have now. A meaningful one, a highly functional life of continual growth and excitement where I believe in myself again, where I feel alive, where I have the understanding that I can **overcome setbacks and challenges** and I am worthy of love again. I share them with you from only one place within me, a place of hope and love.

 # CHANGE YOUR WORLD – TIP #25

And out of their struggle, strutted the most
beautiful of souls, armored up and equipped
with scars, stories and character.

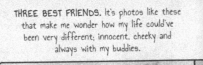

THREE BEST FRIENDS. It's photos like these that make me wonder how my life could've been very different; innocent, cheeky and always with my buddies.

NEVER A DULL MOMENT. Another ten pin bowling birthday, same cheek and laughter with Jakey.

DEBUTANT BALL. My Deb Ball in Year 11 right before it all finished up for me. Some of the more memorable and enjoyable times of school.

JUNGLE BOY. I was shitting my pants patting these lion cubs in the wild of Africa. I learned more here in two months than I did in 12 years of school.

SLOW

WORKING HARD OR HARDLY WORKING. In my first plumbing job in Queensland, at this stage I still had a smile on my face.

BEST FRIEND. Things are never quite as scary as they might have been when you have a best friend like this. The one who checked in, when I wanted to check out.

NO MORE BULLSHIT. Work doesn't have to be a daily struggle. I got a reprieve when I spent 12 months working with one of my best mates. Most days looked something like this.

HOLLIE
We just loved you . We just knew you were worth so much more then what you seen. And we would never give up

UNCONDITIONAL. When I asked Hollie why she saved my life, this is what she said back. This is what I want to do for others.

HOME IS WHERE THE HEART IS. This is the luxurious garage set up I had when Aurora and Hollie took me in, 2013. The biggest room in their family home, the room that supported my erratic thoughts, tears and emotional pain.

HEAD KNOCKS.
It's been great to see the awareness for concussions and the correlation with mental health of late. I have endured many knockouts like this one here and wonder what role it has played on my health.

The good times with Shaun …

EYES ON THE PRIZE.
I have huge admiration and respect for Trav, my coach in 2014. When he spoke, I listened. I wasn't looking too healthy at the time but Trav represented the start of big change in my life.

Shaun & I shared a birthday, it looks a little different for me now, but I love spending time with his mum, Bec.

AND THE LAST TIME.
This is a hard photo to look at but the last time I ever saw Shaun, our end of year football celebrations. He was crying because of how far he had come. I miss him every day.

KEEP YOUR GUARD UP!
My first-ever sparring partner; don't let the size fool you, Shaun had lightning hands. A great friend and mentor.

PICTURE PERFECT. Day 1 of the fundraiser. The backdrop sums up how finding like-minded people made me feel in 2014.

YOU GOT THIS!
Over 100kms done, stress fractures in my foot but a heart to see it through.

BIG HEART.
Laying in Emergency after being rushed to hospital with excruciating heart pain. I thought I was going to die that day. We would later find atelectasis in my lungs.

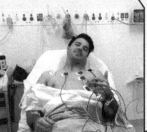

EVERY STEP OF THE WAY. I'd be lost without my mum & dad, sharing this journey with them into advocacy has been a highlight of my life.

THE ENEMY WITHIN. One of my lifelong friends in the field of advocacy and one of the first people to support me. Joe Williams is a former NRL player and champion boxer, but his work away from professional sport has been his most important. Joe is a champion of the cause.

ZEROSUICIDES. It's been an honour to work alongside and learn from the biggest change agents in suicide prevention; here I am with David Covington on set filming *Suicide: The Ripple Effect*.

LIGHTS, CAMERA, ACTION. With my mentor and good friend Kevin Hines behind the scenes filming the International Award Winning Documentary, *Suicide: The Ripple Effect*.

NEW YORK, NEW YORK. Out for dinner in New York with the CNQR Collective, while catching up with the Director of National Suicide Prevention Lifeline Dr. John Draper and The You Rock Foundation's Joseph Penola.

A NEW WORLD. My first ever-speaking gig abroad in America: a long way from someone who avoided class presentations at school.

UP IN LIGHTS. Proudly wearing Shaun's memorial T-shirt on stage at the Kirby Centre, Pennsylvania USA with Livin ambassador Dan Price & Founder – Sam Webb.

I HAVE A DREAM. A CNQR photo shoot "Brain Health is Sexy" initiative outside the steps of the Lincoln Memorial, Washington DC.

MY INSPIRATION. These two guys have shown me a new level of acceptance for what I live with. Two of my greatest inspirations; Kevin Hines and Paul Dalio enjoying a laugh as we finish speaking at Kansas University in 2018 in the midst of a 38-day tour.

THE GIFT THAT LASTS FOREVER. Most people are lucky if they have one good family. I'm blessed to have two. This is the Alexander Family. I'll never have the words to articulate how grateful I am.

EYES OF DETERMINATION. I've fallen in love with seeing how far the body will go. The cold is my friend, a doorway to my soul.

NEW WAVE OF AWESOME. My greatest achievement will be creating this primary school program. The thought of kids saved my life, the program could save many more.

OVER THE RAINBOW. Finished over 300kms from Noosa to Byron Bay by foot. Raising $20k for mental health; this smile represented the "Thank fuck it's over." moment.

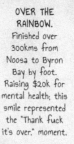

CONNECTING TO MOTHER NATURE. I am blessed to be able to facilitate workshops right around the world, using our natural and inner resources to heal and strengthen our relationships with self.

MODEL BEHAVIOR; these kids light my world up, seeing them learn and implement the skills and articulations around mental health is truly my life's greatest achievement.

ONE OF THE LUCKY ONES. Not all kids get the love and support that I have received; this is my family, my three best friends.

SAME, SAME. Heather and I in Queensland 2020. We didn't plan to wear the same outfit, but we often share similar thoughts and perspectives.

HOLD ON, PAIN ENDS. Keynote speaking at a packed memorial event. These are the hardest gigs known to a mental health speaker.

PART 3

BLUEPRINT TO WELLNESS

"By doing nothing, nothing changes."

WELLNESS IS IN YOUR OWN HANDS

This is the education and validation I focus on so much in my advocacy. Too often we rely on external sources to sustain us. I want to help people better understand just how strong they are when they tap into the strength they were born with. The exact strengths that I never knew existed to me.

Creating my Blueprint didn't happen spontaneously nor did the inspiration for it. In 2017 I was speaking on a 38-day tour of America with my great friend and mental health advocate Kevin Hines. On one of these particular days, we had the privilege of speaking at my favorite college,

Kansas University. It's where a lot of my favorite NBA and NFL players have been drafted.

Often, as the packed-out auditoriums slowly evaporated and people headed back to their lives following our keynote talks, a line of people would often stay behind to ask questions, get a photo or sometimes even an autograph. It's often where I meet the most incredible people, who have also had to walk through the gullies to find the mountaintops. A lot of them also offer sound advice and learnings that I take on board.

On this particular day I was fortunate enough to meet John who was a staff member at The Bert Nash Medical Centre, an impressive facility in advancing the health of the county community through comprehensive behavioral health services. John greeted me on stage, shook my hand and shared that our journeys had many similarities. During our discussion John pulled from his bag a book. He had not planned on giving this book away until he heard me speak.

He said, "Matt, I want you to have this book as I know it will help you the way it helped me." I thanked him but asked if he was sure, as I could just buy one, "I don't want to take yours." John then replied, "I know I am putting this book into the right hands."

Upon returning to Australia this book found its way onto my bookshelf and to be honest I had no initial urge or intention to read it. Fortunately though, it kept grabbing my eye every time I sat down and the guilt of John's parting words ran through my mind until I pulled the book from the shelf and started to make my way through it.

The book is called *The Strengths Model: A Recovery-Oriented Approach to Mental Health Services*[1] and presents a compelling alternative to traditional medical approaches. The strength model demonstrates an evidence-based approach to helping people that may be identifying with a psychiatric challenge or disorder to build a life more meaningful, bridging the gap between recovery and living a life disabled by the effects of mental illness.

This gift from John that day provided me with the inspiration, drive and energy for something better. Inside the cover it reads; *From one believer in recovery to another, thank you Matt.* John, I will never forget that moment.

Strengths-based approaches focus on individuals' strengths (including personal strengths and social and community networks) and not on their deficits. Strengths-based practice is holistic and multidisciplinary and works with the individual to promote their well-being and I fell in love with the idea that mental health recovery could look more like this. It is the basis of the programs in which I deliver right around the world. Equipping ourselves with things that enhance our way of being, the way we want to, by doing things we enjoy, the things we are good at and not this one set menu society continues to shove toward us. It puts wellness back in the individual's hands. Which I find is always much safer for myself, than relying upon others unfortunately.

Yes, it helps to have good people around but they can't lift our pen to paper, they can't express our emotion, they can't release endorphins for us. Only when we embrace a self-supported approach to our wellness will we actually consolidate the efficacy of the medication we take, or the therapy we seek; they go hand-in-hand. Without holistic self-care, we are putting limitations on our ability to shift up the positive end of our own mental health continuum.

The tools, habits and values within the Blueprint offer you choice to manage your own self-care as it suits your preferences and personality. This means **you might relate to just one or two of the tools or you might embrace them all.** Any and all of them can help you to lead a more productive, enjoyable and fulfilling life. They are small-scale distraction techniques, and strategies that help us put "repetitions" or good habits into the most important muscle, our emotional one.

They are easily attainable tools that belong to us already; we actually possess them in unlimited amounts. When we use a strength-based perspective to build our own Blueprint to Wellness, we then begin to believe that we have the strength to recover from, overcome or guide ourselves through adversity or challenges.

This is my go-to approach for everyone because it can be done by anyone, at any time, as many times as humanly possible. These small self-motivated actions actually create and strengthen our ability to navigate through life;

it is like awakening the resilience that we were each born with. Yet also provides people with the gratification of knowing they did it themselves.

AN UNBREAKABLE DAY

Let's set the scene of the Blueprint by setting up an Unbreakable Day; win the morning/win the day. While things might happen in the day that you don't like, if you've already put 90 minutes into your mental health continuum that morning, the chances are you have provided your neurology with the serotonin, dopamine, oxytocin, and endorphins that promote positive feelings like pleasure, happiness, and even love which all go toward counteracting virtually anything negative.

It all begins with those important **first 90 minutes after you wake.** Think honestly about how you spend your time from your first conscious moment each morning; do you continuously roll over to delay getting out of bed for as long as you can? Then finally reach for your phone just to scroll through social media notifications or twitter or tinder—whatever tickles your fancy?

Unfortunately, these actions mean we are starting our day looking for external validation, looking for external happiness. How we spend those critical wake-up minutes determines our sliding scale for the day. Without conscious thought, we are setting up our day without any direction, intent or discipline; we are influenced by others and take no responsibility for our own well-being. We are letting life happen to us and our movements are simply reactions to it. We are setting up our day for nothing in particular and our well-being is slipping down the continuum even before we have stepped out of bed.

CHANGE YOUR WORLD – TIP #26

Nobody gets up each day with the intent to make your day
hard. Don't rise with the opinion that it's going to be.
Wake up with determination!

If you haven't already, I encourage you to take a listen to a stirring speech called *Make Your Bed* written by a retired US Naval Admiral. I'll admit the title may not light your fire initially but its basis is a game changer. In 2014, the graduating class of the University of Texas got more than they imagined when Admiral McRaven delivered their commencement address, a speech that would become something of a YouTube phenomenon. Admiral McRaven spoke of his time training as a navy SEAL and with clarity and conviction, he imparted his advice to the graduates before they headed off into the wide world. This is just a snippet:

"If you make your bed every morning you will have accomplished the first task of the day. It will give you a small sense of pride and will encourage you to do another task and yet another. And, if you happen to have a miserable day, you will come home to a bed that you made, and this will give you encouragement that tomorrow will be better."[2]

McRaven's message is both simple and yet profound. Whatever your tedious task might be, don't underestimate its role in setting up your day. It is important to start the day with those small tasks that snowball into other tasks and these accomplishments set the benchmark for a good day. Let's break down exactly what makes a proactive approach to start an Unbreakable Day.

TAKING INITIATIVE

"THE POWER OR OPPORTUNITY TO ACT OR TAKE
CHARGE BEFORE OTHERS DO."

An Unbreakable Day begins with laying the foundations of well-being within those first 90 minutes. The right moves will give you the focus, stamina, and positive outlook you need to plow through the day. Taking initiative means implementing little things that might be so small you overlook their significance. It might just be flooding your room with natural light upon waking up, or having left curtain space to allow the dawn's light to slowly fill your bedroom so you wake up naturally with the sun.

Another initiative could be setting out your gym clothes the night before so you feel focused and committed to the task as soon as you wake. Or as simple as leaving a glass of water by your bed so you can replenish yourself with an effective shot of cognitive energy straight to your brain as soon as you wake up. Your body is unconsciously looking for that straight away.

The initiatives are up to you and can be as simple or as efficient as you need so you don't roll over and hit the snooze button or lay there wishing for that extra five minutes sleep. Gradually this Blueprint to Wellness that you're developing will make you feel more grateful, content and ready to start the day when your eyes pop open and your feet hit that floor!

RESPONSIBILITY

"THE STATE OR FACT OF HAVING A DUTY TO DEAL WITH SOMETHING
OR OF HAVING CONTROL OVER THE OUTCOME."[3]

This can be a tough one to face. Taking responsibility for your well-being in the morning is the ability to re-evaluate the position you are in, accepting the repercussions from your decisions you made the day before, asking yourself, are you capable of better? Or are you truly helpless to your state of being?

Some ways to take responsibility for your well-being include:

- Take an active, rather than passive approach to solving problems. Don't expect others to provide solutions or simply wait; hoping the problem will go away on its own. This is called "shit stacking." Self-explanatory really, don't let your pile become overwhelming, pay good attention to the things in life that are causing you to feel any way but the way you deserve to. Don't "shit stack."

- Manage your environment. Surround yourself with people and activities that support a healthy mindset and body. Your internal radar will get better at recognizing people and situations that don't support your needs and values. It's okay to walk away, you're not missing anything, you're adding to your mental health credit by focusing on you. Nothing is more empowering than walking away because you have made a conscious decision that will positively impact your own well-being.

- Engage in physically healthy daily habits, like balanced eating and getting enough sleep.

- Notice when you are stuck in negative thoughts or when your body is tired, tense or run down. Once you begin to notice these times you can ask questions about how you came to feel like that. You can determine how to manage those emotions (trace them back to the environment you might have been in) instead of suppressing them. This positive habit to observe and question your state of being overflows into other areas of your life.

- When the negative is overwhelming, take the time you require to re-group, process, reflect and prioritize. However don't sit and bathe in the "shit" for too long, otherwise it becomes hard to get off.

There are many ways to take responsibility for your well-being. Although there are circumstances and events that you are powerless to change, you can change how you respond to them and how you take care of yourself during difficult times.

DISCIPLINE (OR FLOW)

Firstly, let's start by changing the feel of that word. The word "discipline" has all sorts of connotations. You can instantly feel restrained by the word, thinking that discipline requires deprivation of things we love, but this isn't the case. It can become your ally, helping you to live your best life. Discipline is showing up each day, each moment.

> *"A DISCIPLINED MIND LEADS TO HAPPINESS, WHILE AN UNDISCIPLINED MIND LEADS TO SUFFERING."*
> **DALAI LAMA**

If the word discipline scares you, shift towards a term like "flow." This can help you simplify and understand when you are "in" it. Where our attention goes, our energy flows. This creates a sense of calm and ease, understanding that the onus is now on us. If you are not in flow, feeling roadblocks or blocks in creativity or enthusiasm, you could be putting your time, energy and resources into things that do not serve you, or align with who you are.

Your job is to actively create more moments of flow in your days or, more longevity in your flow. The notion of flow enables you to create the space to relax and pursue what really matters in your life. Rather than it feeling like a chore, as the word discipline can often do.

We all know that feeling of self-recrimination when we've given in to laziness or allowed ourselves to be distracted by our phone, social media notifications or YouTube videos. You can feel quite down on yourself when you know you've avoided things that needed to be done or squandered time that could have been used more productively. You can make excuses that you needed the break but you know deep down this is often not the case. Be aware that **avoidance and procrastination can become chronic and even lead to more serious mental health issues.**

Life is a game that requires you to roll up your sleeves each morning. It was never designed to be easy, nor will it be. **It requires 100% effort and 0% talent.** Yet many sit on the sidelines, never taking chances in the game of life. Whether they battle their own internal resistance and doubts or perhaps lack purpose or motivation, they don't make things happen and wait passively for life to happen for them.

And then there are those who are aware that tomorrow isn't guaranteed, they don't wait, they go for it and it's these people who make magic happen. They work towards their goals and are driven by purpose and pursue it wholeheartedly, often not knowing the next step but learning and trusting the end game along the way. The more they persevere, the more mistakes they make and the more they learn and the more unbreakable they become on their journey.

The secret is that anyone can do this. All you have to do is decide to be disciplined, too jump into the flow of life. Remember that doing those things that you don't often feel like doing, are altering life's trajectory to a more meaningful existence, shifting you up the continuum to the thriving zone.

INTENTIONS

Mindset is an intention. You can't fake an intention. You need to be in a healthy, positive frame of mind to set an intention. An intention is something you need to firstly set, and then the action must follow. Intentions create our energy and how we go about achieving things.

Often of a morning, I repeat one very important sentence I learned in my head: *how I show up in the game is how I show up in life.* I roll this statement into many different aspects of life and have found it to be really beneficial in times where I find myself slipping, avoiding, rejecting or not doing as I should.

NOBODY CAN SAVE ME

The brain, while biologically and chemically complex, is actually quite simple when we understand how to communicate effectively with the conscious and the unconscious parts of our brain. Setting an intention is simply instructing the unconscious brain with a statement, goal or question. It's a form of goal setting: an oven is heated before the dish goes in; a seatbelt is secured before turning on the engine; you stretch your body before exercising. Setting intention establishes what you want with the belief and energy to drive it and so it becomes more than just a passing thought.

It's laying a foundation of strength and conviction to energize yourself to complete the activity in order to meet your intention. The unconscious brain then works towards satisfying the intention for its (or your) gratification.

Here is a simple example. My intention for the day could be that I want to show gratitude to everyone who passes me objects, open doors or smile at me. I have set up my day with a strong and positive intention. You can say it aloud or write it down in the early days so the words float around in your subconscious better.

From this intention set early in the morning, I am then consciously aware of it while my *unconscious* mind seeks opportunities to satisfy the intention. The more your subconscious looks, the more opportunities to show gratitude it will find. Showing this gratitude more openly, often surprises those receiving it and they reward me with a bright, surprised smile in return. These moments of connection are refilling (or rewiring) my need to be seen, heard, loved etc.

Setting intentions to begin the day can have a powerful influence on the hours ahead and may serve to remind you if you are going off-course and can reward you when you are on track. Other intentions for the day could be letting go of any negative conversations, listening more, talking less, reading more body cues in conversations, calling someone you haven't connected with in a while, the list is endless.

ALL THE SMALL THINGS

Just as Admiral McRaven touched on in his speech, understanding that all the little things matter is possibly the most important element to starting your day with a proactive approach. Your life is the sum of the small actions you do every day, and every choice you make is significant. While you may not physically see the difference that a morning stretch, first glass of cold water or jumping out of bed on time is having, all of these actions are the "one percenters" and will eventually add up to 100% of our day.

Like a mosaic picture, each small piece is necessary in contributing to the overall beauty of the art. If even one piece were missing, it would be incomplete. The same principle is true for all the small things in life that we often overlook. Achieving these small things build us up to bigger change, one small action at a time. They contribute to how you feel, how you perceive something, how you receive something, or how you respond.

This is how your well-being really comes down to the details of your choices throughout the day. While you might not see it physically like the results of a new training regime at the gym, trust that you will begin to build that emotional "six pack," small task by small task, and will find clarity and focus once again.

GRATITUDE: THE NATURAL ANTIDEPRESSANT

"IT IS NOT HAPPINESS THAT BRINGS US GRATITUDE.
IT IS GRATITUDE THAT BRINGS US HAPPINESS."

The two most debilitating and exhausting emotions in the human face are fear and anger, I experienced them a lot for a long time, I'm sure you have at some stage too. Fortunately for us when we consistently practice gratitude— not just saying we are grateful, actually practicing it—we overcome those two emotions.

There have been so many studies around the benefits of gratitude over the years. Through following the work of leading researchers like Robert

Emmons and undertaking various positive psychology courses of Martin Seligman, we know that gratitude is more than just saying, "thank you" or being appreciative of something.

Numerous studies are demonstrating how consistently practicing gratitude can increase one's joy and contentment and leads to a more positive outlook on life. More so, it might not necessarily be what gratitude can do for you, but more of what practicing gratitude *doesn't* create for you, such as consistent toxic thoughts and feelings of envy, resentment, regret and depression, which can destroy our emotional state.

Imagine a five-minute practice a day that could turn the following things in your life around:

- Sleep that you could look forward to.
- Stay on top of and aware of emotion.
- Shift out of your mood and feel more alive, grounded or present.
- Rediscover hope and be driven by optimism.
- Rid yourself of overwhelm that can often lead to stress and burnout.
- Increase resilience in times of hardship.

Gratitude practice is broken down into three parts: **recognizing** what you're grateful for; **acknowledging** it; and **appreciating** it. I do this in multiple ways, but here are just two examples.

Firstly each morning I practice gratitude for the big things, things that most likely won't change from day to day but are a constant reminder of just how fortunate I am. These might be my job, my parents, my apartment, having fuel in the car, food in the pantry, my dog—you know, the big things.

Secondly is an option to deepen the practice by asking yourself "why" you are grateful for something below the surface. I use this strategy about five times or so following whatever I said I am grateful for. This ensures I am giving enough time for true gratitude to positively influence my behavior and mood towards different aspects of life on any given day.

I call it the practice of "Five Whys" and it looks something like this:

What am I grateful for?

I am grateful for work.

Why?

Because it keeps me feeling purposeful.

Why?

Because I have a core limiting belief that I am a burden so I want to help others not feel the same; work gives me purpose.

Why?

Because I know if other beautiful people have these skills they too can realize their potential and live a healthy, happy and fulfilling life.

Why?

Then we can save lives and prevent suicides.

Why?

Because when dealing with mental health, I believe suicide is 100% preventable when associated with mental ill-health.

This example is a regular one I use, it gives me great clarity to my day and is my "why" behind everything I do.

 CHANGE YOUR WORLD – TIP #27

When your "why" is compelling enough,
nothing is impossible.

In the morning I also write down one thing I will let go of from the day before. For example:

- A recent rejection.
- An argument.
- Someone else's behavior or reaction to an event or situation.
- A bad score on a test.
- Not having been productive.

Letting go of what you can from the day before, sets that clear intention for the day ahead, focuses on what's in front of you and not the past. At the end of the day we have the opportunity to practice gratitude for the small things as well:

- Create a list as long as you wish with all the things that you are grateful for in the day that happened to you.
- Compliments that I would like to give myself today.
- People I am grateful for today.

Here are some tips for more effective gratitude practice.

- Be authentic: Don't fake it or pretend you're grateful when you're not. This leads to burying feelings that need to come to the surface.
- Little is more important than big. If you are struggling to find things to be grateful for, start small. Think of all the little things that have eventuated in the hour, day or the week. Remember how important the details are in our day.
- Validate: Deepen the practice by understanding why exactly you feel gratitude for something. Show your gratitude where possible.
- Express: Share your gratitude where possible, the more people around you that understand the practice of gratitude and exert positivity, the greater the environment you live in.

Scientists have suggested that by activating the reward center of the brain, gratitude exchange alters the way we see the world and ourselves.[4] How powerful is that! This means tomorrow morning when you wake, flip the equation from, "I have to go to work" to, "I get to go to work." A simple but effective intervention that helps us understand just how lucky we are each morning.

It might come with my own bias, but we Australians live in the best country in the world. If you have this book in your hand right now or are listening to it on audio, firstly is your blessing of good hearing or eyesight, which many do not have. You have also been fortunate enough to cultivate the money required to purchase it or have been blessed to receive it as a gift. From those opportunities alone, you are considered to be privileged and I think we should do our utmost to never forget that. We should constantly check in and remind ourselves that there are millions of people who would wish to be where we are in a heartbeat.

"GRATITUDE IS OUR MAGNET FOR MAGIC AND MIRACLES."

MINDFULNESS

Mindfulness is a simple but effective way of slowing down the manic rush that society can demand of us if we let it; it helps us find clarity, gratitude and awareness.

Mindfulness is the quality of being present and fully engaged with whatever we are doing each moment: not thinking behind or ahead. Living mindfully has three simple but powerful parts to it; becoming more aware or learning to observe your thoughts and feelings; being non-judgmental in the moment of mindfulness; and becoming more proactive as you practice mindfulness in more and more moments each day no matter what situation is unfolding, your awareness reduces your reactiveness to it.

Mindfulness is bringing ourselves 100% into the present moment. It's about being aware of our thoughts, feelings and emotions without feeling a need to remove them, ignore them or suppress them. It that moment, feelings just *are* what they are without any manipulation; they will likely change in the future but not at that moment. Mindfulness is the practice of being free, suspending all judgment.

When we practice mindfulness, our thoughts tune into what we're sensing through all our five channels in that one moment rather than flicking on a slideshow of what happened yesterday or imagining what will happen tomorrow. Feel the texture of the task you are doing, watch your fingers do the task, feel the wind or temperature of where you are, be aware of the elements that make up that moment. Mindfulness reduces our feelings of overwhelm, confusion and complacency and replaces them with the **pure simplicity of being**.

Researchers at the University of California San Francisco, and California State University have looked closely at the impact of the brain's function while we're engaging in more than one task at a time, otherwise known as the fallacy that is "multitasking."

Multitasking and trying to live in the current world of doing, doing, doing wreaks havoc on several areas of our brain. Firstly in the prefrontal cortex: the area that processes the information given to us and decides how to respond. Secondly multitasking causes chaos for the hippocampus: the area that is responsible for storing information otherwise known as our memory.

Multitasking also affects the auditory and visual areas of our brains, and we're more likely to interpret incorrectly or make mistakes. By focusing our attention on just one thing at a time, all the parts of the brain work harmoniously. When we glance at something else during an activity we are inviting our brain to take in additional information.

Mindfulness doesn't eliminate stress or other difficulties; instead, by becoming aware of our thoughts and emotions that arise because of challenging situations or moments, we have more choice in how to handle them thereafter—and a better chance of reacting calmly and empathetically when faced with stress or challenges.

Of course, practicing mindfulness does not mean we never get angry— but it does allow us to be more thoughtful in how we want to respond, whether that's responding calmly or "cracking the shits."

One practical way to equate mindfulness to a task is to practice listening, really listening, a sense that can be underestimated for its value to living well mentally. Listen to the moment you are in and listen to others that need an ear. Listening is filtering the distractions (or removing them) and finding a comfortable place to open up so you can listen with eye contact, allowing you to read body language and knowing how and when to best intervene or respond.

Mindfulness can also be practiced by just *being*. By focusing on the one thing you are doing and not everything around you. Again, probably the most important tool when it comes to helping people feel comfort or open up, is being present to them; that's how we show up for others.

Practicing mindfulness can be done in any moment and may look like this.

1. Pay attention—slow life down.
2. Live in the moment—give attention to detail.
3. Observe your thoughts—notice that you are noticing.
4. Focus on your breathing—refocus and bring the mind back to the moment.
5. Observe your surroundings—fine-tune your senses, creating gratitude.
6. Notice sensations—the body keeps the score.
7. Awareness of attitude, state and behavior—accepting what is.
8. Intentional being—productive and meaningful actions.

Mindfulness has been a critical and important daily practice of mine in helping to reduce overwhelm, stress and anxiety. It is very easy to get caught up in the fast pace of the world we live in and the demands of those around us. By having a conservative approach to the way in which you disperse your minutes or time in a day you become even more present to the moment you are in. Progressively having this knowledge is more likely to produce a moment that is of high value with purpose and meaning for your life.

CHANGE YOUR WORLD – TIP #28

Thoughts; the shadows of our feelings.
Being able to feel, not having to think.
Being able to see it, without having to attempt it.
Being uncertain, but being clear.
Not always fun to look at, but always worth it.
The one tool we have at our fingertips
where we get time back in return.
A purifier of the mind.

NUTRITION

"A HEALTHY OUTSIDE, STARTS FROM WHAT WE PUT INSIDE."

One of my biggest challenges is nutrition. I admit I don't set the best example but I know how important it is. A balanced mood and feelings of well-being can be protected by ensuring that our diet provides adequate amounts of complex carbohydrates, essential fats, amino acids, vitamins, minerals and water. Healthy food provides stronger, faster brain functioning.

Every time I allow myself to shift away from good clean eating and balance with my diet, it is like a tumble weed that picks up pace and negatively effects the rest of my functions. I stop exercising, my thought process and clarity is clouded and shady, my productivity diminishes and my ability to control the voices, paranoia and erratic thoughts of anger begin to run rampant through my mind. Nutrition is something I'm very much still working hard toward and learning more about each and every day. We are what we eat and so it was any wonder for ten years of my life I had poor mental health and well-being.

This is something I am continuing to work on, the hardest area of my wellness plan and something that I continually lack the self-discipline for.

Even so, I have come a long way from the chocolate milk and chicken nuggets on the regular, when I used to go by the phrase of "If nobody sees me eating it, the calories don't count."

As you can tell I don't claim to be a nutritionist, far from it. I would simply say go on the journey to get to know your body and what it needs, how much and how often in order to function at your best. But don't ignore nutrition thinking that you can make it up in other areas. Be aware of what you are putting into your system, what exactly is in it and what effects it can have on you.

FOR THOSE THAT HAVE A DIET LIKE MINE

CHANGE YOUR WORLD – TIP #29

70% of your serotonin is produced in your gut.
Healing starts in the kitchen.

EXERCISE

This is kind of a no-brainer. In fact I contemplated not even writing about it at all, but it is a crucial part of the Blueprint to Wellness. For anyone out there reading and doubting right now, who in an ideal world would prefer not to exercise (like me), just take a minute to appreciate that 30 minutes of rigorous exercise can produce enough endorphins for up to 12 hours of good positive brain health. "Rigorous" meaning exercising at an intensity that is enough to lift our heart rate, have us breathing deeply and causing us to sweat. 20–30 minutes of physical activity stimulates the release of dopamine, norepinephrine, and serotonin. These brain chemicals play an important part in regulating your mood and triggering those positive feelings.

And for those that are sitting reading this next to a box of deep-fried chook and a bottle of soft drink or who are struggling to make sense of the day-to-day or to shift themselves from the bed they collapse in—trust me I get you—I've been in those exact places. **I would be the fattest, laziest and most depressed bastard if I only worked out when I wanted to!** I don't really enjoy it, but I know it works and more importantly I know I am my best self when exercise is one of the cores of my wellness plan.

As previously mentioned, it was only in 2015 when training for the 220-kilometer charity event that I really found a sense of peace from exercising. It was in running that I learned more about my thoughts than anywhere else; it was in running that I released a day's stress; it was in running where I found clarity and focus. In every step and foot that hit the pavement did I understand myself more and more.

The beauty of exercise is it doesn't have to be done alone, or it can be, whichever way suits you. Remembering that everything in life is much easier done when we share it with someone else. Go for a walk, start a meaningful discussion, get your thoughts off your chest, breathe in that fresh air and listen to a podcast; right there you have ticked off five elements of good well-being in **exercise**, **talk therapy**, **connection**, **nature**, **mindfulness** & **education**, all shifting you well and truly toward the right end of your continuum.

BREATHWORK

For so many years whenever I heard someone say, "Just breathe," as if it was a magical superpower that solved all of the world's problems, I wanted to slap them!

Then somewhat sheepishly, I found out that it wasn't far from the truth. Focused breathwork can actually help us to navigate through the uncertain and unknowable moments in life. It's a way to feel less stressed, release tension, help us sleep better, enrich creativity, improve our focus, aid positivity, boost immunity and most importantly regulate our emotion, temperature and pain.

Yep, believe it or not, the art to breathwork can unlock a hell of a lot of benefits.

And for those friends of mine out there, cuddled up to their sleep apnea machines at night or to the girls out there that are sick of throwing combination punches at their partner nightly because they sound like a Mack truck as they snore profusely, breathwork might just be the tool that helps create more meaningful solutions come sleep time.

In the time it takes for you to read to the end of this breathwork section you will have experienced close to 260 breaths. In an hour you will clock up between 720–1200 breaths. Every single one of these breaths is critical to your overall health and well-being. So as you continue to read this piece, consciously make the effort (or attempt at least) to breath through your nose and not your mouth.

Here's why:

Three things we cannot live without in life are food, liquids and oxygen. Unfortunately for many people, we pour all our time into fad diets and making sure our intake of water is spot on and yet not many of us put any consideration into the art of breathing properly and are actually doing it inefficiently. I often talk to people about the benefits of breathwork only to hear them reply skeptically, "But breathing is breathing," and they simply take it for granted.

But it certainly is not that simple. Breathing through the mouth, including the hours when you're asleep, can lead to many problems. Mouth breathing in kids can be related to bad teeth, speech impediments and poor growth and posture. In adults, chronic mouth breathing can cause bad breath and gum disease.

When I was younger I vividly remember waking up bleary-eyed after a big night with my friends and feeling disgusted by the taste left in my mouth. I would later learn that this was due not purely from the alcohol itself, but the body relaxing from the effects of the alcohol and then sleeping with a slack open mouth, similar to the way snoring occurs. When the tongue muscles relax or the airway muscles are floppy and not taut, they create that horrible art of snoring and likewise, cause that disgusting taste and feeling in your mouth after a big night.

Even more worrying than that, mouth breathing can worsen symptoms of other illnesses that are directly related to mental health. Mouth breathing caused by nasal obstruction is likely to cause sleep disorders, which severely impacts our ability to recharge and find energy for the following day or respond to situations and challenges. Sleep disorders also increase symptoms similar to those of ADHD while for others they create symptoms like "brain fog," fatigue, insomnia and irritability.

But when we choose to consciously breathe through our nose instead of our mouth, we make a positive decision that can help prevent those adverse effects on our brain functions, reactions and moods.

When I tried meditation and yoga practices for the first time, the instructor would say, "Focus on your breath, in through your nose—out through your nose." I could never really breathe through my nose so it required huge concentration and struggle for me to do it. It didn't feel particularly comfortable and I couldn't initially keep it up so I actually reverted once again to mouth breathing.

My continual research however, kept guiding me to explore something called pranayama. Pranayama is the practice of directing the breath. It teaches you to breathe consciously with awareness and intention. I kept trying to make an effort to change my unconscious breathing habit from mouth to nasal breathing, and over time it worked and I could feel the difference in terms of self-healing and therapy. Understanding pranayama was transformational and intrinsic to understanding the beautiful systems within our bodies that support our optimal function.

The first process to the art of breathing relies on the oxygen specifically passing through the nasal passages. The nose acts as a filter lined with all of those nose hairs you like to think you don't have. But those fine nose hairs are critically important to the transfer of breath; they humidify or cool the air as required before it enters our lungs. Those nose hairs protect us against roughly 20 billion foreign particles every single day: bacteria, viruses and other particles stick to the wet surface of nose hair and are prevented from entering into our lungs and causing infection.

The air then enters our lungs where oxygen is transferred into our bloodstream and circulated throughout the rest of our system and body. As a parting gift the air that leaves our body takes with it carbon dioxide from our cells, which is the toxicity we need to remove. There is no filter through mouth breathing; this critical process is bypassed.

In an early video module that I studied, I distinctly remember the instructor summing up the difference between mouth and nasal breathing, "Breathing through your mouth is as practical as trying to eat food with your nose. It's so important to focus on our breath more, and make sure we are doing it consciously and correctly."

The words have stuck with me ever since and are a constant reminder to consciously check in with my breathing. I felt like I was a late bloomer to this knowledge around the importance of breathwork and I had a lot to catch up on.

Along with some simple techniques that can be utilized and tapped into daily, I found the benefits stem from one of these three core elements to breathwork: Body, Mind and Spirit.

BODY

The physical benefits of breathwork are both incredible and efficient. By taking deep breaths correctly and in alignment with your chest, belly, back and mind you can activate what is called the parasympathetic nervous system. It's the part of our system that helps to control and slow the heart rate and reserve our energy. As a result this lowers our blood pressure, which is the quickest way to create a sense of calm.

Often in today's society we are finding people overwhelmed, stressed and operating from our amygdala, which controls the flight or fight response and is responsible for the release of adrenaline or cortisol that causes our nervous system to be heightened and overwhelmed, which in turn causes anxiety. This prevents us from thinking straight or making sharp and calculated decisions. The role of breathwork is to reverse this and create an environment where we are relaxed and operating consciously.

MIND

In a study conducted with 21 US Army veterans in 2014, all of which served in the Iraq or Afghanistan war, a controlled trial split the 21 vets in half.[5] Half of which were put through breathwork practices, half weren't. One year on from the controlled trial, research showed that the half that were given the skills and tools to practice breathwork based meditation dramatically decreased in anxiety symptoms and respiration rate, lowering their PTSD Scores. However the controlled group did not decrease in symptoms.

The art of breathwork encourages people to find a much more meaningful and deeper state of mind. Within this state of mind is often the place where buried trauma, emotional blockages and negativity are deeply engrained. Through breathwork practices you can find release from these areas of your life and find focus and clarity again in your mental state.

SPIRIT

Breathwork is very much a spiritual journey where consistent practices can lead to connecting with your innate self, your own spirit. A chance to meet ourselves and create or identify with an increased sense of who we truly are and a way to navigate through our own healing process and whatever that might look like. When we provide spaces to connect to our innate well-being and spirit we find balance in life, which is imperative to align with the things that best serve who we are.

I practice my breathwork in several different ways including the Wim Hof method, which is a relatively new technique, based on the ancient pranayama methods. I combine the Wim Hof method with my cold exposure practices.

Disclaimer, before we jump into the practices and you get excited about them, please note that practicing breathwork can be dangerous for those with pre-existing heart conditions or those women who are pregnant. Please seek further professional advice before diving in to this beautiful art form.

Here are two of the more useful and practical ways to achieve immediate and incredible results:

ALTERNATE NOSTRIL BREATHING OR *NADI SHODHANA*

An ancient yogic breathwork technique that is both practical and easy to help you calm yourself down, relieve sudden stress or anxiety and find that innate peace. Alternate nostril breathing focuses on aligning the two hemispheres of our brain, the left our Ida which is used to calm and purify the mind and our right hemisphere, the Pingala which is used to increase our energy and flow.

To practice Alternate Nostril Breathing simply:

1. Sit in a comfortable position and bring your hands together letting your ring fingers and little pinkies touch each other.
2. Your index fingers and middle fingers remain folded down meeting at the knuckles.
3. Close the right nostril with your right thumb and inhale slowly through the left nostril.
4. Now alternate. Close your left nostril with your left thumb and exhale slowly through the right nostril.
5. Keeping your left thumb over the left nostril, inhale slowly through the right nostril.
6. Close the right nostril with your right thumb and exhale slowly through the left nostril.
7. You have completed one cycle, repeat 6–12 times then return to your normal breath.

BELLOWS BREATH OR *BHASTRIKA*

An extremely energizing practice that is often referred to as Breath of Fire is a good exercise for the morning that can replace your cup of coffee. Producing exactly what you need if you are feeling sluggish without the need for an expensive cup of coffee or the shakes of caffeine.

Bellows breathing is also a practice to consider if you're trying to lose weight, as simply a few rounds daily can help speed up your metabolism.

This practice is more tailored towards the start of a day, but certainly not before bed, as it focuses on increasing energy on those days you feel a little out of sorts.

To practice Bellows Breath it is as easy as:

1. Sitting up tall and relaxing your shoulders. Start by taking a few deep, breaths in and out from your nose. With each inhale the aim is to expand your stomach to its maximum expansion with every breath.

2. Begin Bellows Breathing by exhaling forcefully through your nose. Follow by inhaling forcefully at the rate of one second per cycle. You might begin to notice an increase in your temperature.

3. Make sure the breath is coming from your diaphragm; keep your head, neck, shoulders, and chest in alignment and try to maintain stillness of the body while the stomach moves in and out.

4. For your first cycle, move through a round of 10 breaths, then take a break and breathe naturally, observing the sensations in your mind and body. Notice what you notice, feel what you feel; an important part of any breathwork experience. After a 15–30 second break, begin the next round with 20 breaths. Finally, after pausing for another 30 seconds, complete a third round of 30 Bellows Breaths.

You may feel some sensations during this breathwork practice, including possibly light-headedness; this is completely normal and will diminish as you deepen the practice. Breathwork is a practice not made to cause discomfort, if some light-headedness does occur, wait until the discomfort passes, or use the discomfort to focus back on the breath.

Breathwork is one of, if not the, most overlooked and most effective tool to stress management, available to us at any and all times offering a huge array of benefits. It is your friend, the friend that is there to comfort you and support you.

Whenever you need a burst of energy, breathe.

Whenever you need to process heavy emotions, breathe.

Whenever you need to calm down, breathe.

Breathe in and cultivate freedom, breathe out with LOVE.

COLD EXPOSURE

Let me introduce to you my absolute favorite aspect of my Blueprint to Wellness: cold exposure or cold training. Does the thought of it make you roll your eyes at me? Everyone does when I introduce this concept to my audience. And if you were flirting with the idea that I'm crazy, well this won't help my case straight away. But it is truly my belief that the people who are crazy are those who would rather live in a lifetime of stress instead of trading it out for just two minutes of relative discomfort a day.

Our intrinsic physiology is truly incredible and the principle of cold training can be explained through an analogy I heard a long time ago. As someone who has visited the jungles of Africa, I can attest to the following theory as well. When we see animals in the wild, for example a lion hunting a zebra; we can't see the physiological responses going on inside their bodies. The difference between them is that the predator wants to be there; the prey however, does not.

In the realm of cold training, it's the same; physically you don't want to be there but its mental stimulation has something enormous to offer. The cold will always be cold and it's your choice if you want to experience what it has to offer or not. The same principle applies in the realm of life: how we show up in the game is how we show up in life. Cold training is a mindset and a strong mindset helps us achieve more, be more and do more. I know I would like to do that trade every day if it means I live a life of fulfillment.

By exposing ourselves to the cold we experience a 25% increase in blood flow. It's not about being tough or being a big scary lion or getting your kit off and being the brave one in an ice bath; it's about bringing more blood flow to the brain stem. From there we can achieve a greater balance between serotonin and dopamine (our happiness chemicals) and endorphins that we need to release in order to feel fulfilled and content.

Benefits of cold exposure affect both physical and mental aspects of your body. Some of the most prolific benefits aren't ones you'll see, but rather feel.

For a long time my life theory and mantra has been that if I can build a healthier relationship with everything in life that causes me stress, pain or discomfort then life again becomes simple. The option isn't to spend my life running from it, whining about it or wasting effort being annoyed by it. Cold exposure has shown me how you can turn a physical stressful situation and use it to your mental and physical advantage; there is a gift in each moment of stress. We become not a victim of it but an observer of its benefits.

When we dwell in a stressed or overwhelmed state, our over-stimulated mind from these thoughts leads to chronic inflammation. Inflammation is capable of producing depression, anxiety and fatigue. It's a tough cycle to break out of. Cold water or exposure can help on a few fronts. Firstly it lowers the temperature of our muscle tissue constricting the blood vessels and over small periods of exposure this helps to reduce the swelling and can even numb nerve endings, bringing immediate relief in panic attacks and anxiety-ridden situations.

Splashing cold water on my face, or dunking my head in a pure cold shower has, on countless occasions now, helped bring me back into my body, and provided instant relief from heightened situations. A cold shower can temporarily take your mind off the things you might be worried or fearful of. It helps you tap back into the moment, to our breath and to the capacity we possess to change our state. Being aware of how the cold water feels on your body can act as a mindfulness practice, keeping you in the moment as you feel your blood pump vigorously around your body. It reminds you that you are okay, right in that moment you are alive and breathing and anchored.

Always do your research before practicing cold-water exposure safely for the first time. Cold water or ice baths are best practiced for just minutes at a time. If you have any underlying conditions, chat to your doctor about how it could work for you.

If ice baths are not *yet* for you, or a cold shower is still a few steps away, you can still achieve many benefits from splashing your face upon waking up or by drinking several cups of cold water.

For those who are ready to take the plunge, the good news is that you can still have your hot or lukewarm shower. In the final moments of the shower, turn the hot tap off giving yourself the final 15–30 seconds of the shower cold, use those seconds to breathe deeply in and all the way out, before you know it you will have exited the shower with a release of dopamine so you think: *Thank fuck I'm out of there!* which is positive.

Your body will experience heightened sensations, your concentration for the morning is improved, your willpower to test yourself in other areas of life becomes increasingly high and your immune system has your back.

It's a simple but effective avenue to start the day in a real and positive way if you choose to do so.

The alternative is to exit a warm shower, feeling wet and cold and thinking: *Shit I want to get back in the shower,* which releases cortisol the stress hormone. This is letting the cold control you as oppose to you controlling the cold.

I'm not saying there aren't benefits of hot showers too, however when trying to improve our current situation, right now many of us are wired to only ever step foot in a hot shower, I am asking you to question this conditioning and rewire those habits so you know you have the power to change your state.

The great Wim Hof, also known as the Iceman, is a Dutch extreme athlete noted for his ability to withstand freezing temperatures. His extraordinary feats of human endurance have made countless Guinness World Records and also advanced scientific understanding about the potential to influence our own nervous and immune systems. His personal story is truly incredible; after losing his wife to suicide he was desperate to show his four children that a happy life was absolutely still possible for them and he began exploring the power of the mind over the body to inspiring and groundbreaking depths. His abilities are even teaching the scientists to rethink a thing or two.

When I met Wim Hof in Sydney at one of his workshops in 2019, just as I was about to take the plunge into his freezing cold ice bath, he put one hand on my right shoulder as he revealed his secret, "How you show up in the game, is how you show up in life; breathe Motherfucker."

A tip for those who are going to get brave with their life, remember that same sentence as you take the plunge into the fleeting stress that is the cold. Do you tip toe into the depth of the cold the same way you do in tough situations in life, or do you make a splash and rock a big smile, the same way you attack a challenge in life?

It was in that moment with Wim, that my mindset shifted and I sat in the ice and watched as all the other participants had their eyes closed, shivering, sitting in the ice, struggling to control their breath and some were just counting down the time to get out.

I sat there peacefully, smiling and recognizing that the only difference between those that hated it and those who didn't was the ability to make a conscious decision in that moment. It was those who embraced the cold that did it much easier.

We can run from challenges or we can run with them. We can make excuses why we can't do something or we can make excuses as to why we should do something. Life is much easier when we turn to the latter. To practice cold exposure try the following:

- Splash your face immediately when you wake up.
- Dunk your head and/or chest only in the cold shower.
- Put your hands in a bucket of ice water.
- Start a shower cold for 15 seconds before returning to your normal shower, and then finish with cold again.
- Have only a cold shower.
- Full body immersion in cold water.
- Train in ice extremities.

It's best to pair this with the previous segment; Breathwork. They go hand in hand. If you find like me that your overall health and well-being is increasingly improved and you now attack the day with a greater sense of clarity and focus, you will never have a hot shower again. The added bonuses are the great savings on water, electricity and there are no side effects at all!

FOR THOSE WHO
HATE THE COLD

CHANGE YOUR WORLD – TIP #30

If we always choose comfort, we never get to witness and understand the capacity of both our mind and body.

POSITIVE AFFIRMATIONS

What you tell yourself every day will either lift you up, or tear you down. Release negativity by replacing it with positivity. When you can't think positive, listen to something positive and that might come in the form of YouTube clips, motivational videos, positive affirmation videos, cards, words or maybe it's a routine list you pin somewhere for yourself to see so that you create that habit first thing of a morning.

For me when I was at my lowest I would begin each day in the worst possible ways, waking up every day with the attitude that: *Work sucks—the weather's crap—I just want to stay in bed.* This immediately fed my system and wired it with the belief that those were all true, forming negative neurological pathways that affect behavior and actions for that day ahead instead of taking onus, acceptance and control of my life.

What we can or can't do, what we often consider impossible or unachievable is rarely a reflection of our true capabilities, but more a reflection of our old-wired beliefs, whether accurate or not. Now of a morning, I phrase my sentences with the two most important words combined, "I am ..." followed by a sentence that feeds those reassurances that I need or silences that voice in my head that tries to tell me otherwise.

The beauty of positive affirmations is that we can trick our brain into believing something that isn't necessarily true. The same way the brain often tricks us into believing we aren't good enough or that life carries no meaning, or my limiting belief for over ten years that I was a burden on the world.

We must remember that our thoughts are just brain cells firing off fleeting ideas, they're just thoughts *we* create in our head. Our brains can get a little mixed up on the difference between reality and imagination, and is quick to trick us into believing a negative narrative about ourselves. As we begin to believe these thoughts about ourselves, many of them cement themselves as "facts." This is where the danger lies, however this little deception can be surprisingly useful if we learn how to tap into it for our benefit.

I want you to create a mental image of yourself achieving something you consider challenging. Maybe it's acing a nerve-wracking interview or conquering your fear of heights by bungee jumping. Replaying these successful images in your mind activates many of the same brain areas in the same way as if we *actually* experienced these situations. Similarly, by consistently arming ourselves with the repetition of re-affirming statements we can cheekily trick our brains into believing something as fact. So when you truly believe you can do something, your actions often follow.

For example, let's seek to replace a negative or anxious thought like this one:

I am unlovable; I will never find anyone that will want me. The more I talk about my thoughts and feelings the more I scare people away. I am a burden on those around me and maybe I am better off being alone.

Replace this with a positive reinforcement:

By being open and honest I am presenting my best self to the world. Through this I will find the people that create a sense of belonging, who love me for me. By loving me, for who I am I allow myself to be loved the way I truly deserve.

So, why don't we practice cementing the stories we should believe, rather than the ones that don't serve us any good at all?

Affirmations generally work as a tool for shifting our mindset and achieving our goals, but I admit they're not a magic wand for instant success or healing. Repeating an affirmation can help boost your motivation and confidence, but you still have to take some action yourself. Affirmations act as a positive step towards change, but are not the change itself. To get the most benefit from affirmations, you'll want to start a regular practice and make it consistent:

- Start with 5 minutes at least twice a day. I call it "brush and prime," easily achieved on the two instances you brush your teeth each day (please tell me you do that).

- Repeat each affirmation about 10 times. Listen to yourself saying it, focusing on the words as they leave your mouth. As you say them, believe them to be true.

- Ask a trusted loved one to play. Ask a family member to give you their affirmations of you, to help reinforce your belief in them.

- Make your routine consistent. Try not to skip any days. This practice can be done as you brush your teeth and gaze into the mirror, it can be done lying down in bed as the alarm goes off. It is simple and time effective.

- Be patient. Just like any of the tools shared, it may take some time before you notice any changes. Don't quit; trust the process. I have made these changes myself and remember my initial doubts but I knew what it meant if I didn't try them!

A recent study from the Queens University in Canada suggests the average person has more than 6,000 individual thoughts every day.[6] However 91% of those thoughts are identical to the day before. Only 9% of what we think about alters the direction and outcomes of our following day. It's about getting really curious about that small percentage of variables and how they can change the path of life moving forward.

Your obsessions really do become your possessions which means whatever you're thinking about expands in your life. It's a powerful notion because it works for good and not so good thoughts. **If you are sick of feeling the way you do, you need to try something different.**

Instead of tirelessly repeating all your old negative thoughts—you know where they will take you—try a different road. These simple small practices for your mind teach you to become self-aware of your thoughts and their triggers. This awareness starts to drastically change the outlook of your life with more favorable, clear thoughts and decisions.

Instead of; I am shit; I am a failure; I am worthless; I am stressed; I am hopeless etc. It's time to rewire the brain with the knowledge that we can be what we want to be. We control who we are, by the thoughts we think and importantly the actions we take.

Positive affirmations didn't heal my trauma; positive affirmations helped me to carve out a different possibility for myself to work through it. It was not always about removing the negative thoughts; it was rewiring them to be of more benefit to the next chapter of my story, my "I am" story:

- I AM no longer a burden on the world.
- I AM a better person for experiencing what I have, no matter how painful it was.
- I AM fortunate that I have always had the loving support of my family.
- I AM blessed with opportunities to share these experiences.
- I AM not perfect, but perfectly stitched together with flaws and scars.

 # CHANGE YOUR WORLD – TIP #31

Tomorrow is only a new start if you don't have
you hands still full of yesterday's bullshit.

EMOTIONAL AWARENESS

"EVERY EMOTION IS A MESSAGE. NEGATIVE EMOTIONS
ARE A SIGNAL THAT CHANGE IS REQUIRED."

We all have those friends or colleagues that we envy, who can seamlessly manage and deal with all of their challenges and their emotions in a completely different way to how we would. They don't get angry in stressful situations, they don't feel overwhelm in the pressure cooker of life. Instead, they have the ability to look at a problem and calmly find a solution; they are sharp with clarity and focus. They're excellent decision makers, and they know when to trust their intuition. They have what appears to us as a keen eye for decision-making.

Regardless of those strengths, these people are usually willing and not afraid to look at themselves in the mirror, with honesty and authenticity. They take criticism well and make educated decisions to take what part of it they desire to grow and what they wish to ignore and leave behind. People like this have a high repertoire of emotional intelligence.

They understand themselves very well, but also they have this uncanny knack to identify the emotional needs of others around them. It is not something you have or don't have. The good news is that emotional intelligence and awareness can be learned and developed. Just like any of the other skills previously mentioned it is something that needs to be consistently practiced and understood.

Throughout my life, I would go through challenging times and throw my hands in the air, pointing the finger at everyone else about why I was in the predicament or situation I was in and avoided all responsibility that it could potentially be solved or managed internally.

The reason that emotional awareness is here in the Blueprint section is because it has become increasingly common for people to isolate themselves, to run away from or suppress their emotions and thoughts and they blame many of their problems on the lack of support around them.

Emotional awareness gives us the acceptance and knowledge to know that we are capable, that we can overcome and navigate through difficulty, that we can see something positive up ahead. It is our ability to put our hands back on our own steering wheel.

When we understand this theory, we make positive progress for ourselves, we are not reliant on any one thing or person to push us or provide for us. Every single emotion we feel, whether anger or sadness, joy or disgust or maybe fear or shock, they are all valid and none are negative. They only become negative when we don't deal with them through these forms of expression and take the learning from them.

Rather than suppress or ignore what society has mislabeled "negative" emotions, my point is about embracing them, and using them to inspire growth. They are a way to empower yourself to make meaningful changes in your life and make the most of those emotions you feel to avoid spiraling down into bad behaviors and habits or stewing in your own situation.

It is about taking back control of your own emotions instead of letting your emotions control you. If I was to trip over and cut my arm causing it to bleed, and then I left it like that overnight, I would wake up with a cut on my arm, blood everywhere and possibly within days or weeks it would turn into a scar, depending on the severity of the cut. That cut would continue to be a nuisance and possibly cause infection and further problems if it wasn't dealt with.

The same can be said of our emotionally heightened situations. We have all experienced something that was hard or unkind, perhaps in the form of bullying, or an emotional setting like the loss of a loved one, or perhaps even failing some sort of test or being embarrassed socially in front of friends.

If we take these situations and ignore them, suppress them or pretend they didn't happen and try to move on, it is essentially like a cut on our mind that will continue to metaphorically bleed out, causing us continual pain and struggle. As the cut on our mind becomes more infected by numerous other situations and problems that we experience in the same time period, it will begin to scar. The scarring represents our traumas and memories of a situation. That scar can lead to anxiety or depression.

The theory of "just sleep on it" or "tomorrow's a new day" is a potentially harmful way to operate when dealing with emotionally heightening situations. Unlike the common expression, time does not heal everything. If left unattended or ignored in the hopes that the challenges and painful areas of our life will disappear, unfortunately they won't and will continue to show up in other areas of our life.

It is with emotional awareness of these events and settings that we can productively and proactively work through them to create a healthier way of life for ourselves.

Here are some tips for practicing emotional awareness:

- Observe your feelings; *live with presence in every moment: consciously conscious.*

- Pay attention to your behavior or actions; *are you living in alignment with your values?*

- Question to understand your own bias and opinions; *know the truth, all of it!*

- Take responsibility for your feelings; *nobody can put a thought into you.*

- Celebrate the positives; *reflect on the good work and small wins.*

- Don't avoid the tough stuff; *understanding the negative is the key to balance and reacting positively and finding growth.*

Why should we care about developing our emotional intelligence skills? Being able to understand your emotions is a key fundamental to understanding what will lead you to flourish and become higher functioning in the process of loving who you are and the life you live.

Take back the wheel of your life and drive forward to a much more meaningful space to thrive in.

"YOUR INTELLECT MAY BE CONFUSED,
BUT YOUR EMOTIONS WILL NEVER LIE TO YOU."

ROGER EBERT

COMPASSION

Through my journey to mental health and suicide prevention advocacy, one element that I can always rely on to help lift me up, no matter how badly I'm feeling is by helping others. With an abundance of the five essentials (love, kindness, empathy, support and care) we can begin to alter the stories that people write in their mind about how their journey is meant to play out.

The most valuable of all tools we each possess is not a head full of knowledge but a heart full of love. The reflex head nod that shows we're trying to understand, the eyes that show you value someone and the ears willing to listen with no intent to reply, followed by the hand ready to help someone up. We all have a unique gift in this world and make a difference to other's lives the moment we all start spreading it.

Imagine how horrible this world would be if we weren't inspired by the random acts of kindness we witness, our good morning messages, the smiles of passing strangers or the wave and hello from next-door neighbors both reaching for the morning paper.

Imagine a world without those past figures that have inspired generational movements and messages for humanity: Mother Teresa, Martin Luther King Jr., Maya Angelou, Nelson Mandela, Mahatma Gandhi, and so many others that have epitomized compassion, not only for themselves but for those millions they will never meet.

Imagine a world without the countless individuals who risked their own lives to save others on the frontline, those compassionate people who work on the hardest and sharpest edges of love and life in communities, or those everyday heroes like Aurora, Hollie or Mum or Dad for me, who are there in every moment, on every call who act for the betterment of others, more frequently than they do themselves.

Having compassion is an incredible element in our Blueprint to Wellness because it not only increases positive behaviors in others but also gives back deep, fulfilling benefits for ourselves.

"IF YOU WANT OTHERS TO BE HAPPY, PRACTICE COMPASSION.
IF YOU WANT TO BE HAPPY, PRACTICE COMPASSION. "

DALAI LAMA

The Dalai Lama's words describe the emotional benefits of compassion for those who proffer it to others and also those who receive it. In other words, the rewards of practicing compassion work by reciprocation.

But what exactly is compassion? And how do we in fact feel it and practice it without having to buy the next person in line a coffee or bombard our friends with compliments and phone messages?

Among emotion researchers, compassion is defined as the feeling that arises when you are confronted with another's suffering and feel motivated to relieve that suffering. Compassion is not identical to empathy, although the concepts are related. Empathy refers to our ability to identify with a person's perspective and feel the emotions of another; compassion is when those feelings and thoughts include the desire to help.[7]

Compassion is also the ability to not get caught up trying to reason with and attach ourselves to the "story" of what someone experiences, rather it's about attaching ourselves to the pain the story has caused the individual. We don't have to understand what somebody is going through because it's often not possible. But it is our role to recognize and remember just how pain felt to us in our worst situation and imagine it was equal with the pain the person on the other end is feeling.

When we understand people are hurting, we help them. When we make up stories or comparisons about why they are in a situation, we judge, we belittle, we ignore and we offer apathy—the exact opposite of what we are born to do in these situations.

Not only does showing compassion for others make us feel better about ourselves, but self-compassion also serves an important function for well-being. Unfortunately, people often bathe themselves in hatred over mistakes for which they would readily forgive others. Yet, when we look beyond our flaws and treat ourselves with forgiveness and understanding, we increase our psychological health and well-being.

The human condition is wired for several key elements; certainty, uncertainty (or variety), growth, and contribution (or significance).[8] Along with those conditions, there is something particularly important when talking about the effectiveness of compassion and that is ***belonging and connection***. The only thing we want as a human being is to love, be loved, be valued, be understood and seen for who we truly are.

When society begins to grasp the idea that we are all as qualified as one another to offer the exact elements of what it looks like to live a healthy, happy and fulfilling life, that every single morning when we wake, we have choices, then the world will begin to look a lot different.

- Love or hate?
- Empathy or apathy?
- Compassion or cold-heartedness?

It has been the alignment of purpose and passion that has led me to find all of the tools and learnings that I share with you now, that have helped me push past my trauma and my challenges, **by finding and feeling compassion.**

When all was lost and life was seemingly over and I truly believed I would die by my own two hands, that I willingly gave all of what was left of me each day to others; I didn't want other people to feel the same way I felt. It was in those acts of kindness, of sharing of stories and holding space and listening to others, that woke up something inside of me that enabled me to connect and rediscover my own hope.

Loneliness is one of the biggest causes of depression. However loneliness is not the feeling of being alone. Loneliness is the ability to feel no sense of connection to anybody mentally, emotionally or physically, even when surrounded by others.

From here I hope you feel the importance each day to tap into the unlimited amounts of kindness you have to give and spread it like confetti across the community. I believe that it is there that you will find more of yourself, that you will find endless amounts of opportunity for meaning and purpose and connection; the exact feelings we are wired for.

Here are some simple ways to cultivate compassion

- Practice self-compassion with positive self-talk.

- Put yourself in other's shoes frequently.

- Move beyond thinking of only yourself.

- Practice those Random Acts of Kindness; with no reward or gratification, it can even be anonymous.

- Relax judgments; remind yourself: *What if everyone is just doing their best?*

- Listen generously; give more of your ears and less of your mouth.

- Do the dirty work; heal your own shit before it leaks into other parts of life.

- Practice being fully present.

- Incorporate your own Blueprint to Wellness with self-care routines.

- Respectfully share hugs.

- Learn about other people's situations to be better informed.

- Positive expression; find your outlets to release and recharge.

- Encourage and empower others.

- Volunteer or give back.

 # CHANGE YOUR WORLD – TIP #32

Being vulnerable with the protected, being strong with the upset, outgoing with the reserved and wise for the confused. Compassion is going where it's uncomfortable, where it almost begins to hurt. Opening our arms and embracing the uniqueness of those who walk before us and behind us. A world where charity becomes unnecessary.

CHANGE ONE, CHANGE ALL THREE

Fun little fact to remember the next time you're in a foul or shitty mood, the answer is to MOVE! It takes six seconds for emotions to absorb in our system. We can immediately shift our state by moving, changing our posture, taking a deep breath, smiling, laughing, exercising or dancing, all of which will elevate our heart rate. When you've been stationary for a while and then shake up your inert state, it changes your mental, physical and emotional state.

If you change one you can change all three.
If you change your physical, you change both
your mental and emotional.

A practical example of this is when a teacher makes a kid laugh; it affects their whole body and stance. When you try and smile, you trick your brain into believing something that may not be true however your brain is still tricked into releasing good chemicals. This is powerful for those disengaged kids struggling with the endless rhetoric of adults preaching at them.

You can still feel what you're feeling; often it's natural or useful as you wrestle with a challenging feeling. But being aware of this concept to change your state in that moment, really helps battle the lethargy of the 21st century for people who are disinterested, don't want to go to the gym or stay in bed for days; you can change out of it. All of these things can change our state or pattern disrupt our brain:

- A 20-second hug releases oxytocin the love hormone and alleviates stress.

- Dance; 3 seconds of music can improve your mood and attitude.

- Clapping and star jumps have positive effects on blood circulation and blood function.

VALUE ALIGNMENT

"ALIGN YOUR VALUES WITH YOUR BEHAVIOR AND
LIFE BECOMES MORE SATISFYING."

Your values are the things that you believe are important in the way you live and work. The way you carry yourself and what people think of you. These values should determine your priorities everyday. Each day I get into the habit of practicing and modeling to the best of my ability the person I want to be, the person I am. I need to replicate authenticity and act accordingly with my values, when I do so life is not only kind to me, but I find my overall satisfaction and joy is much more elevated than if I was pretending, faking or mimicking the behavior of someone I am not.

This I believe is the reasoning behind a lot of people's downfalls especially with the way in which social media and the world presents itself in this day and age. The continual need to compare our lives, or have a representation on our Instagram or Facebook of this farfetched lifestyle or appearance that doesn't actually exist. It opens people up to hurt, to believing that they are inferior to others.

Practices: Write down five core values that you believe represent the person you are or the person people would say you are, e.g. honest, compassionate or loyal.

If I pride myself on honesty as my value, yet my behavior for the day suggests that I lied to someone, are my values aligning with my behaviors? No, so expect that life satisfaction, relationships etc. will diminish because of this. Am I really compassionate if I left a mate upset and walked past? No.

Follow the process with every decision you make every single day. Self reflect, get honest, improve where you're lacking and grow. You have to represent and behave with authenticity and only then will you see change.

Watch the world part for you when you're giving your best version of yourself to it.

CHANGE YOUR WORLD – TIP #33

Repeat after me: "I know who I am. I am clear about that.
It is not negotiable. I belong here, perhaps I don't fit in,
but I refuse to negotiate my belonging to myself."

STANDARDS

*"IF YOU WANT TO CHANGE EVERY ASPECT OF YOUR LIFE,
RAISE YOUR STANDARDS."*

What changes a person is when their "shoulds" becomes their "musts." Friendship groups, relationships, time for yourself etc. What we allow and accept grows, so make sure you don't lower that bar in your life.

How do you expect to run with the cheetahs when you've been swimming with the turtles? Yeah they're cute, they provide the odd laugh but they're not bringing any growth to your life. Keep the people who truly motivate you, show their love for you and remind you of your value. Self-love, self-acceptance and self respect all start with self because you hold the fort. Don't allow people to take up room in your life, when good people are waiting for their turn. Your boat has a maximum capacity of so many people; don't allow it to sink carrying the wrong people.

OUTLETS

"FALL IN LOVE WITH TAKING CARE OF YOURSELF.
MIND, BODY, SPIRIT."

Small-scale distraction techniques can really help when you're surrounded by dangerous thoughts and waiting for talk therapy. Occupy your mind; don't allow it to occupy you. I always encourage people to find the outlets and hobbies that would make them feel uncomfortable, because as we are distracting our mind, we are also equipping a new skill set.

In 2014 after returning from Queensland, I walked myself into the boxing club, I was scared, I was embarrassed, it was something new to me, although I loved the idea of it. Week in week out I would go home from the boxing gym with bruises and cuts, the odd broken nose but more importantly the biggest smile. It made me feel so uncomfortable, but through that I grew, I found levels to myself I didn't recognize and boxing and combat sports became the tool I used to vent and get rid of excess energy on a punching bag when manic or distressed.

Boxing was also extremely beneficial for living with chronic suicidal ideation. When I was sparring with an opponent, and I looked across the ring absolutely crapping my pants, it was near impossible for me to feel suicidal or have those thoughts when I was faced with someone trying to break my nose. The clarity it brought to my head through discipline and concentration was tremendous and has always been an anchor as an escape outlet for me when struggling.

You might enjoy sports, painting, art, photography, meditation or maybe it's just going for a coffee with a friend, everybody is going to have a different set of outlets and escapes, whatever they may be it's important to have fall protection to that outlet.

If your hobbies include sport and you break your leg, then you're without a hobby. So work on finding other alternatives that are not similar to sport that can act as a backup plan if something ever goes wrong. The black fog of depression would often pull me back in when I was injured or

NOBODY CAN SAVE ME

when football season finished, it became clear to me that I needed other alternatives so that my mind was distracted all year round and not just for the footy season.

SELF-REFLECTION

This strategy or task in the Blueprint fits in towards the end of an evening, usually right before meditation and bed. In the current world we live in, the business of life and the urgent demand to just "get things done" at all costs, has created an environment where we often avoid the dedicated time to turn inward, to look at ourselves, our day and the emotion that created our thoughts and feelings.

But there are many people who believe or who'll confidently tell you that self-reflection is a waste of your time; that we should always be aiming to live in the moment and not to dwell in the past. However, I truly believe that reflection is one of the most critical elements to achieving my wellness. It has acted as a simple but effective process of closely examining my thoughts, feelings, behaviors and motives from a position of objectivity. It has allowed me to take a step outside of myself to evaluate my experience of the day and to then make calculated decisions on my next move, my environment, relationships and many other facets of life.

Every day I am given the opportunity to look back at the previous 24 hours or 1440 minutes, to ensure that all of the situations and decisions were in alignment with who I am and who I wish to be. Years of living without reflection was like I was driving blind, jumping in a car without a navigation system and just guessing which streets to turn down on my way to an unknown destination in the middle of fucking nowhere. If you don't have any clue as to where you are going, you will most likely end up lost.

Reflection is the navigation. It is the process of understanding where my decisions get me, and then considering what direction my current thoughts are pointing me in. It is the ability to see which passengers you want to accompany you on the journey and which passengers are on a different route. It is the ability to pick and choose which toll roads you want to take or if there is a more efficient and cost effective way. It is the plain and simple ability to **live in the conscious mind.** Making purposeful decisions that impact your life in a positive way.

For many years I was living the alternative, believing in a sense of entitlement, that **life owed me something; that good things would happen to me because they "should"** and that when bad things happen somebody else would help me out of it. That life would work itself out. It was an ignorant and narrow-minded way to think and strangely enough, having that attitude on this journey only brought me repetitive trauma, challenges, pain, struggles and rejection that left me throwing my hands in the air, saying, "Poor me," "Life sucks" and, "This isn't fair!"

It's the entitlement trap that I see so many people fall into. Being self-aware by utilizing the tool of reflection is a mechanism for self-control. It's not a tool used for self-criticism, but a tool that is an inevitable part of being human and helps us do it in a comfortable, non-judgmental way.

When you have awareness for what transpired each day, you can begin to regulate your own behavior in accordance with your values, strengths and goals. You begin to notice the discrepancy between your current behavior or emotional state and the direction you're aspiring to better yourself.

You see, I still experience the same negative thoughts, suicidal ideation and fluctuating moods that once led me to try to take my life, the only difference is now through practices of reflection and being self aware of my journey I have the ability to transform the negative thought into the next stepping stone towards wellness or my dreams. When I trip and misplace my foot upon the wrong stone (which is often) through reflection, I am able to retrace the steps and adjust them accordingly in a more favorable direction.

Self-awareness and reflecting isn't a difficult process, but it is confronting. We as a society, just don't tend to look inward enough and when we do, we push back on the thought of feeling somewhat insecure and threatened by what comes up, and so continue to feel lost, struggling to find our footing in this world. And the debilitating and exhausting cycle begins; we find it harder to contemplate doing anything of value for ourselves.

During my time and travels around the world, I noticed several common elements to the people that are very self-aware and are mentally and behaviorally strong, calm and controlled which stem from some pretty effective self-reflection. This is what I noticed and learned from them:

- His/her life is filled with flow, because he/she attends to areas of life that are most beneficial. Playing in strengths and acknowledging and outsourcing weakness.

- He/she doesn't get caught up in anything other than what is here right now and therefore makes great decisions and reacts appropriately in the majority of situations.

- He/she continually strives forward, completely locked in on the difference they were born to make and creates actionable steps to achieving it.

The process of self-reflection can be broken into two parts. "In the moment reflection" helps us to make thoughtful and purposeful decisions, with awareness for how we treat people and behave. Then there is the bigger picture, reflecting on the day that was, to help us remove thoughts and moments that caused us distress, but also providing us opportunity to take forward into tomorrow more of the things that made our day great; a pretty simple process.

Ever since starting Mindfull Aus in 2016 and receiving my diagnosis of bipolar disorder in the same year, I experienced several burnouts throughout the three years that followed. Burnouts that saw me struggle to lift my head up, would slur my speech some days and I became achingly suicidal. In March of 2019 I got to a point where I even attempted to resign from Mindfull Aus, the organization I started as a dream. The burnout and exhaustion I experienced were incredibly difficult to experience each day. Feelings of being worthless and a failure riddled my mind manically every day. The responsibilities of people's wellness and running an organization alone, was becoming crippling. It was difficult on me but more importantly it was also taking its toll on my family.

Mindfull Aus had a pretty wonderful Board of Directors who had encouraged me to keep going and try to see more clearly the difference we were making and they inspired me to commit to the organization with new determination; we adjusted the sails to be more sustainable.

This became part of my motivation behind creating the Blueprint to Wellness. I knew I wanted to spend my life making a difference just like I had promised myself at Shaun's funeral. In order to make a difference I had to maintain my own self-care to operate on the level I needed to but also on the level that I deserved. I was finally (and consistently) incorporating all these tools and strategies in the Blueprint but a lot of this action stemmed from the lessons of reflecting properly and deeply for the first time.

I was building enormous discipline and for nine months I didn't miss a day of reflection. I was driven to finally look for and learn from the continual thought and behavioral patterns that came up for me. I actually grew to enjoy the internal competition that was sub-consciously going on, seeing how many days in a row I could enjoy or find contentment in. I didn't have any previous target for a personal best but starting January 1st, I lasted just over nine months of the year before reflecting on my first "bad" or "exhausting" day. I have not experienced another burn out to this day.

Of course, my Blueprint to Wellness tools continue to play an integral part for why this is. But more so, my ability to understand myself, others and my thoughts using reflection enabled me to break down each day and work out what I needed to do to ensure consistency in feeling good emotion and enjoyment in every day, something that I believe we take for granted. It also held me accountable to practicing what I preach as a mental health advocate, not that I wasn't beforehand but this time I really leveled up. Let me show you what I do for reflection.

SELF REFLECTION PRACTICE: STREAM OF CONSCIOUSNESS

Stream of consciousness writing is freestyle journaling where you write down exactly what you're thinking without censoring or editing it. It is a flow of words onto the page just as they are appearing in your mind. It requires you to find presence and encourages authenticity and honesty. The rules are simple.

Each night, ask yourself a series of questions, however the pen is not to break contact with the paper. Each question is to be answered for two minutes. If you don't know what to write, just write that. Wherever your brain goes, just go with it. This will clarify your thoughts and remember no thought should be ignored. The questions for this practice are as follows:

1. My life is great because …
2. The reason people enjoyed me today is because …
3. Today was good because …
4. One area of my life that I am proud of is …
5. Today I enjoyed …
6. One thing I will let go of for tomorrow is …

The beauty of this stream of writing is that after you have done it, it is entirely up to you whether you choose to revisit it or work through it. There is no right or wrong, but putting words on a page is an effective way of reflection and letting go simultaneously.

An alternative to the stream of consciousness writing is a simple daily reflection.

Each question allows for comments and a score out of 10.

The questions are as follows:

1. Am I using my time wisely?   /10

2. Today my exercise was … ?   /10

3. Today my nutrition was … ?   /10

4. My sleep last night was … ?   /10

5. Today I lived in alignment with my values.   /10

6. How I treated others today ... ?   /10

7. How I treated myself today ... ?   /10

8. Did I have a productive day today?   /10

9. My self-care today was ... ?   /10

10. Today I felt ... ?   /10

Bonus questions

- List all of the things that happened that were positive today.

- Out of that list, what will I incorporate again tomorrow?

- What was negative or challenging about today?

- What can I do to manage those thoughts of negativity and move forward?

To improve our chances of reaching our goals and living a healthy, productive life we must remain aware of our current behaviors. While it is important to understand *where* and *what* happened in the day, it is equally important to understand *how* we can achieve it again if that is our selection. This is how consistency is developed.

Through frequent self-reflection, we can make sure that we're on the right path. Lack of self-reflection can cause us to seem lost or without a purpose. Life flies by and before we know it we haven't evaluated our circumstances, we can let so many important and beautiful aspects of our lives slip away: our health, our relationships, our goals. It's necessary for us to unplug for a few minutes every now and again, when possible, and address a variety of the questions, including those listed above.

"EVERYTHING THAT IRRITATES US ABOUT OTHERS CAN LEAD US TO AN UNDERSTANDING OF OURSELVES."

CARL JUNG

GOALS AND OBJECTIVES

"IF YOU DON'T KNOW WHERE YOU'RE GOING,
YOU'LL END UP SOMEWHERE ELSE."

Life takes on meaning when you are inspired, motivated and driven by goals and dreams. The same way it is equally important to have a similar set of goals for well-being and health. Write them down; go to bed knowing what you want from tomorrow. Wake up and action those achievements. Celebrate the small victories. Even if it's a job list for work for your job, write it down, physically tick them off, it will help produce self gratification and joy knowing you complete your list each day and gives you the empowerment to set much larger and meaningful goals and the steps required to achieve them.

It also helps with accountability. When things in life get tough—and they will—it is helpful to have this set of goals visible to others to help support you. The same goes hand in hand for your own well-being, keep people informed about where you are at and what you are up to. By doing so, you might even inspire the next person.

Here are my set of rules for goal setting for good well-being and health.

- High accountability; the journey is easier when shared with others.
- Be realistic; baby steps, plan the steps wisely.
- Measure up; be able to track your progress and celebrate it.
- Remain Positive; some days are tough, remember the "why."

If you dream big and just miss, you still end up with a fantastic reward. Put the wheels in motion and appreciate all the steps you adhere to, towards the end goal. Dream it, believe it, map it, vision it, achieve it.

MEDITATION

Just as the clouds appear every day and often cover up the sun, our thoughts, senses, sensations and surroundings can cloud our judgment and dampen our joy. Yet each day we don't attempt to lasso the clouds and pull them down, remove them or see past them, we are patient, attentive to what is important and we wait for them to pass, we understand they are there to play a role, they are part of life. Meditation helps us be patient and understanding to the clouds that appear in our lives.

Continually I'm told by people that they struggle with the idea of getting their thoughts to stop and that they'll just get caught in the cycle of: *Oh fuck, just stop thinking!* They don't yet realise that that's the idea of meditation, to recognize just how busy your mind is and continuously practicing it will create more awareness and more space to think calmly. So when you think a thought during meditation, don't panic or reprimand yourself, let the thought flow and be aware of it and what it's trying to show or teach you.

We are going to do a little exercise now.
I'd like you to say the alphabet to yourself as quickly as you can. Go!

Now, I'd like you to count from 1 to 26 to yourself as quickly as you can. Go!

Next, I'd like you to combine these two tasks by saying "A 1" and then "B 2" and "C 3" and so on matching the next letter to the next number each time. Do this as quickly as you can. Go!

You would have noticed that the easiest part of that activity is the moment when you do either task 1 or task 2, when our only purpose is to simply count 26 items individually. But when combining the two tasks it becomes more challenging, creating fog and confusion. Some of you might have started to re-trace your steps; some of you might have just given up.

Welcome to our beautiful minds and the art of meditation.

If you're like me when I started, there might be a few misconceptions that you have to undo about meditation. It's not all about crossing your legs and humming silently while trying not to let a single thought in your head. The easiest way to see how meditation can work for people as part of the Blueprint each day is to firstly understand the main components to our brain's function and their roles in supporting us. They have official names but you might better connect to the way I think of them as our very own superhero, librarian and judge.

Amygdala "protects" (our superhero)

The role of this part of the brain is our superman/woman that tries to protect us at all costs, it is our flight or fight response kicking in. Our superhero often mistakes stress for real threats when it is rushed, confused or struggling to fight off multiple thoughts at once. Ideally, our superhero would be better at dealing with one thought at a time.

When working fluently, superman/woman passes thoughts, memories and information to our hippocampus.

Hippocampus "stores" (our librarian)

Our librarian, much like in real life, loves a quiet environment. This helps our librarian to put attention into ensuring our thoughts, information and memories are stored in the correct place and are easy to find, as we need them.

Our librarian, when not under attack from loads of items to store, is able to find the correct information to pass to the prefrontal cortex.

Prefrontal Cortex "decides" (our judge)

Just like in a courtroom, our judge makes the decisions based on the information it is provided. Our judge likes to make well-balanced choices for our benefit. Just like in real life situations, our judge requires a quiet courtroom and stillness to marry up the best decision and response.

The judge is able to provide the right information to make the correct decision that is favorable for ourselves and others, the decision is based on the information we possess and is passed from our librarian.

It's important to remember that the judge is in control of our actions, however if superman is overwhelmed, the judge is of no use to us as superman takes over. Often when this happens we see brash decisions being made, bullying or nasty behavior take place, we offer apathy instead of sitting with someone in distress or perhaps we have no clarity and focus in the classroom or at work. I think this simplified model speaks to everyone to emphasize the importance of stillness and breathwork, and the need for the modern world to embark on a meditative journey.

All three components of our brain do not function in synergy without some form of peacefulness, however we all know that it requires work and often we are left with a thousand racing thoughts, ideas and emotions happening to us all at once.

The aim of meditation is not to push aside stress or block out thoughts, but to recognize them, just like the clouds that exist, and behind the clouds, clarity and sunshine again.

Suzanne Westbrook, a retired internal medicine doctor at Harvard University, describes meditation as a means of, "Noticing what happens moment to moment, the easy and the difficult, and the painful and the joyful. It's about building a muscle to be present and awake in your life."[9]

Meditation is the habitual loop of training your mind to have laser like focus and a redirection of thoughts. The popularity of meditation is increasing as more and more people discover the awareness, clarity and sharpness it brings them mentally, the improved sleep, decreased blood pressure and its ability to increase our tolerances to pain or to help control pain specifically in those that experience it chronically.

A small study, published in September 2016 in the journal *Frontiers in Human Neuroscience* found that meditation helped people manage negative emotions. For the experiment, one group of participants listened to guided meditation while another control group listened to a language-learning presentation. At the conclusion of the controlled group sessions, the participants were shown photos of distressing scenes, such as a bloody corpse. The researchers recorded the participants' brain activity and found that those who were involved in the guided meditation session had a quicker recovery from their emotional response in their brain after seeing the photos, suggesting meditation helped them manage their negative emotions.[10]

I mentioned the stereotype and misconception that I had around meditating when starting out, but the truth is you can practice meditation anywhere: sitting at your desk at school or work—not a problem. On the toilet while finally getting that moment of time away from everyone else undisturbed—hell yeah! On the train so people leave you alone and avoid contact—if you need to do that—then absolutely.

It is a simple task that can be driven by yourself or guided by someone else and practiced daily without any disruption to your schedule. All you need is an ability to be disciplined in the practice, to not give up because your mind wanders elsewhere and remember that the thoughts exist to you for a reason. It can be a quiet place where you can be left alone to practice for a few minutes a day, where your world essentially stops.

There aren't any rules or right or wrong as to how often we should practice, although just like anything that has featured throughout this Blueprint, the more we do it, not only the better we will become but the more we strengthen and thicken areas of the brain, specifically the prefrontal cortex (our decision maker) that helps us control our attention and emotion. If what I have mentioned thus far still has you believing that "meditation" isn't for you; that is entirely up to you and your clear and honest reasons why not.

However some of the positive effects of consistent practices of meditation are:

- Reduced stress.
- Emotional balance.
- Increased focus.
- Reduced pain.
- Reduced anxiety.
- Increased creativity.
- Reduced depression.
- Increased memory.

The answers, the truth, the next step and all of life's clarity lie within meditation and stillness. As a society I wish for us to collectively return to the days of hearing, "I'm bored." Being so-called **bored is where genius is born**, it is where we stop and just look around at the miniature worlds going on in nature all around us, it is where parents start to pay close attention to the needs and thoughts of their kids without being submissive, it's where we dust off our imagination again and get creative, it is where we fine tune our strengths or passions and it's where we wind back to the times we picked up a phone or visited friends for communication, and not relied on technology to judge how someone might be feeling.

Boredom is our friend, stillness is our friend: not this rat race of a world that is killing us and making us unwell. Slow down your world, we only get one of it!

"QUIET THE MIND, AND THE SOUL WILL SPEAK."

MA JAYA SATI BHAGAVATI

SLEEP

For so many years living with sleep insomnia, falling asleep seemed like an impossible dream when lying awake at 3 a.m. It was beyond frustrating, screaming into the pillow. My body was dead but my mind was racing a million miles an hour, creating stories, narratives, and trying to find solutions to problems that didn't even exist. Sleep challenges were one of the most debilitating and exhausting experiences of my entire journey through poor mental health.

Sleep helps restore the brain by flushing out toxins that build up during waking hours. Lack of sleep can lead to cognitive decline, memory loss, anxiety, depression and paranoia. Yep, that was me; all of these things I experienced for many years.

But achieving good sleep is more under our control than we think. Following healthy sleep habits can make the difference between restlessness and restful slumber. Researchers have identified a variety of practices and habits, known as "sleep hygiene" that can help anyone maximize the hours they spend sleeping, even those whose sleep is affected by insomnia, jet lag, or shift work. I will also add that not only are the last couple of hours before bed time crucial to laying down the mind, but the whole day's lead-up to sleep. The moment we wake up to the moment we turn the light off is pivotal to the overall quality of sleep we get.

Sleep practices:
- Stick to a sleep schedule.
- Practice a relaxing bedtime ritual.
- Avoid naps.
- Exercise daily.
- Turn your bedroom into a sleep-inducing environment.
- Establish a soothing pre-sleep routine.
- Lighten up on evening meals.
- Reflection and goal setting.
- Meditation.

For a long time society has painted a picture that an adult requires 8 or more hours of sleep a night. As with many aspects of human biology, there is no one-size-fits-all approach to sleep. I personally function at my very best after 5–7 hours sleep. Everybody's sleep patterns vary and are generally different. Oversleeping, much like getting too little sleep, can have major impacts on your health too. These can include increased rates of heart disease and stroke and has often been associated with fertility issues, cognitive decline and obesity issues.

I can't stress enough the importance of routine and awareness when it comes to sleep. Nothing in life will catch up with you quicker than disregarding the importance of sleep. **Sleep is an investment in energy we need, to be effective tomorrow.**

BLUEPRINT TO WELLNESS FINAL LEARNINGS

"Scars that hold a lifetime of valuable lessons."

Do the things you don't necessarily want to do because you know the positive impact and growth you will achieve from them. The same correlates towards overall mental wellness and good positive brain health. Me, I don't love running or eating healthy food, I hate it. But as I've already said, I can only imagine how I'd look and feel if I only ate healthy and exercised when I felt like it.

I'm not running and eating healthy to look good, I'm not doing it for any other reason but to prepare. Prepare for the phone call to tell me there has been a death, a phone call to tell me I've lost my job, a phone call that something horrible has gone wrong, preparing for each time I get treated poorly or for any of life's "inevitables" that get thrown our way each and every day. I'm preparing for those crap days and challenges so I can pull myself out of them. I'm built ready for those wars. The effort you put in today will be the reward you get tomorrow.

If you don't brush your teeth, your breath smells. If you don't shower, you stink. If you leave a cut, it gets infected. If you don't change your underwear, well, I'll leave that to your imagination.

So why is it that we don't have the same approach and emphasis on our emotional hygiene? Just as we practice daily routines to look after our physical hygiene we need to observe our emotional hygiene to preserve a healthy mind, behavior and attitude.

So before you brush your teeth tonight, or have a shower, or jump into fresh clothes, take some time to do a workout for the mind. Incorporate a 5- minute evening practice of each of the following:

- Gratitude
- Goal setting
- Self reflection
- Compassion
- Meditation
- Value alignment.

When you wake up for work tomorrow, don't be that friend that sends that silly Instagram or Snapchat message, "I hate work!" "F*$k work!" "Omg! 8 hours left of this stupid job!"

Start the day on the right foot, and wire yourself with positivity:

- 5 minute morning practice of:
  - » Gratitude
  - » Mindfulness
  - » Compassion
  - » Affirmations
- 25–30 minutes of rigorous exercise.

Your mind is the garden, you can tip toe around the weeds and get prickles in your foot or you can pull them suckers out and make way for roses to grow. But if you leave the garden unattended for a day or two, you know what's growing back.

Wake up every day and do the gardening. Do the things others won't, so you can live a life others don't.

You have to have more than one thing that gets you up each morning, that feeds you drive and energy. You have to be bold. Mental health, well-being and prevention is a huge priority and part of my life, it has become my obsession, my passion and purpose. It's also something that has made me a much better person, that has made me proud of the person I am becoming, at one stage becoming this person was an impossible thought and an exhausting task. It's the reason I am surrounded by beautiful people and compassionate environments. Mental health advocacy is the tree, the branches that come from that reach very broad and are what give my life growth and meaning that makes up all of the things that life is about.

For me it's not about being able to change the person I once was. We can all be better people not only to ourselves, but to others, with every waking day. The only reason we should ever look back is to be proud of the person who has come so far. I want to continue to utilize my rediscovery of kindness, compassion, love, support and value to help others. And to share the many physical and emotional scars I have experienced in 30 years to tell my story in a way that could potentially change or positively impact somebody's life.

I'm just ecstatic with life, I go through all the same challenges and thoughts I once did and always will—right to the day I depart of natural causes. Bipolar is not going anywhere, there is no cure, neither will I sit and waste time wishing for one. I just know how to manage those thoughts and behaviors now. For so long I didn't know these emotions existed or that this way of thinking about life was possible, now I do. I hope you can too.

I am not superman; I am no different, stronger or better than anyone else. I'm just someone who was sick of seeing people struggle, who couldn't bare the thought of sitting up the back of another funeral.

The future belongs to those who prepare for it today. From one believer in recovery to another I hope you too find the beauty in your journey, the same way I found mine. You are loved, you are worthwhile, you are unique and at the very least I love that.

CHANGE YOUR WORLD — TIP #34

People, events and situations can take the life right out
of you, I know that. I've felt that. But you don't have any
other plan right now other than to give this thing called life
absolute hell for a while and see what it gives back.
You got this; the choice is now yours.

PART 4

MY PAIN, MY GIFT

A wrong turn, the right place. Welcome to the less attractive parts of my life, but where the most learnings took place. The following set of eight emotional experiences which I call The Emotional 8 have no doubt caused you discomfort, pain and many headaches throughout your life already. They may have really challenged you or made you question who you are. You may second guess them, doubt yourself through them or wish they never appeared.

But what happens if we take what we have always thought about them and flip it on its head? What happens when we look at the situations in front of us, through the shiny lens? What happens when we stay and wrangle in our sadness, our frustration, our anger and confusion? When we take time to play in the ugly or confronting parts of our journey? Where we no longer believe that it is sexy to hide it?

What if absolutely everything that has happened to you, may have actually happened *for* you? What if the reason it happened was to assist you? Acknowledge the shit to remove the possibility of stepping in it again and again. **I sat with my anger long enough; until he finally let slip his name was trauma.** The idea was not to carry him around anymore—not a second longer than I already had—but to put him down and utilize him to climb the next hurdle.

THE EMOTIONAL 8

BE SAD

*Sit with your sadness; those tears come from your heart, not your head.
If you feel sadness, you are alive and leading with your heart; that's a
beautiful thing. What brings us sadness; shows us the perspectives of
joy and happiness. Feel that beating heart? That's purpose.*

BE ANGRY

*It will help you identify what, who and where you need to remove yourself
from; anger is the action signal for positive change. It is okay to feel anger,
however holding on to it is not and will cause aggression. Don't let it
sit long enough to become that. Aggression is like holding on to hot coals
expecting them to get burnt like you did, they won't. Throw them away and
find the learning.*

BE FRUSTRATED

*It's where deliberate actions take place, where our focus is on the
outcomes and not the obstacle. Turn all of your frustrations into
curiosity. Create magic with it. Again, remember why you are
doing it. Nothing is impossible when your why is compelling enough.*

BE BROKEN

*What we heal becomes stronger. Restoration and refurbishment always
look and feel much better. Acceptance for where you are is the solid
foundation on which to rebuild from. Use your pain as your gift and
your emotion as the glue in the rebuild.*

BE LOST

*Life isn't about finding yourself; it's about creating yourself.
What you find has always existed, what you create will depend on
how badly you want it. The only limitations are the excuses as
to why you can't.*

BE ALONE

*There isn't anything more satisfying in life than to find your best friend
and realize you were with them all along. To depend on nobody, that is true
strength. Feeling alone is an action signal that you need to work on
loving you a little more. Only when you love yourself will you find the
love from others you truly deserve.*

BE BEHIND

*Appreciate the life-miles you have already covered, the setbacks, challenges,
pain and triumphs are what makes you, YOU! Fall in love with the life you
are creating, don't fall into tune with the walk of someone else.*

BE AFRAID

*This is the part that shows us that it's worth it. Bravery and courage
come from doing the things that are unknown and not guaranteed.
What doesn't kill you simply makes you stronger.*

THE EMOTIONAL 8

❧ BE SAD ❧

Sit with your sadness; those tears come from your heart, not your head.
If you feel sadness, you are alive and leading with your heart; that's a
beautiful thing. What brings us sadness; shows us the perspectives
of joy and happiness. Feel that beating heart? That's purpose.

I hated plumbing, not the physical work or the practices of it and most certainly not the ability to be around new friends and colleagues on a job site in sunny Queensland. No, unfortunately my time as a plumber was jaded by the run of challenges and situations I faced amongst my apprenticeship. I no longer enjoyed it or felt the inspiration I once did when I was fresh out of school with my Mercedes Vito Van, a false floor and sound system, when every tool had a place and I enjoyed the challenge of the learning.

Nope, not anymore. It was 2013 and although I sometimes enjoyed my place of employment and had finally found a better space and environment in which to work, I was becoming seriously homesick. Clinging to the inch of hope and seeing the light at the end of the tunnel, I knew I had to get home back to the people who had always loved me and supported me; my parents and my brother, I knew I would be better for it. But the lingering promise of finishing this apprenticeship still smacked me in the face every morning, it was like a shit advent calendar, where I opened a little door each day in search of the chocolate, only to be left disappointed, and the days on the calendar didn't seem to have an end.

I had just finished my last stint of trade school in Mackay, Queensland, spending a month away from my home in Gladstone, which always presented more challenges. Being flipped out of routine, staying in hotel beds and hanging around a group of people that only seemed to have the one common interest—we were plumbers who wanted to just get this shit done and get out of there.

I had been signed off; trade school component done. I remember driving out of the Mackay area and immediately ringing Mum and Dad, "I've done it!" I burst out with the utmost joy and excitement, remembering that this was not the first time I had finished trade school but the second, as my transfer from Victoria to Queensland two years earlier meant they couldn't transfer all of my trade school modules and credits.

I had fulfilled my promise to my parents, completed my apprenticeship studies and got that golden piece of paper to say I was a qualified plumber. That certificate resembled hell for me, in every definition of the word. It was also a gentle reminder of the resilience I had shown over many years and the promise that I had kept to my parents.

My parents were just as excited for me; they knew how much this meant. I think it is important to detail that the promise I felt obliged over five years to fulfill was not forced on me, my parents have only ever wanted the best for me and if I wanted to walk away, they would have supported it no matter what. Unfortunately when you live with a mind and behavioral health challenge and a voice that seems uncontrollable the only thing I ever heard in my mind, no matter the support from anyone was: *You're a failure, you're worthless and you're a burden.*

Therefore it was not even a question to walk away for me. No matter how much pain I was experiencing, as I've mentioned before I could be heard saying quite regularly, "This plumbing apprenticeship will be the death of me," and I honestly believed it. This is a real indication and example of the power of the mind when we aren't in control of it, because I would have comfortably taken my life before I let down my promise to my parents and felt like a failure. Strangely enough I never once viewed taking my life as a failure, I believed I was the failure and that the failure would then be gone.

In amongst the excitement of that phone call that day, I had plotted my return to Victoria and just talking about it overwhelmed me with joy. It was that light at the end of the tunnel moment. My parents had mentioned to me over the phone, "You're on the home stretch now mate, you just have to put your head down and complete the last little bit of time on your apprenticeship in the field and you're home."

But I wasn't having it. I had obsessed over the idea of reaching out to my boss after completing trade school and requesting that he sign me off three months early so that I could return to the safety, love and care of my family in Melbourne. I hadn't even considered that the idea would be rejected,

NOBODY CAN SAVE ME

and I couldn't understand why it would be. Surely any good soul would recognize my struggles and desire to go home and grant me that wish.

I turned up that next week, organized a meeting to sit down with my boss and his wife. I thanked them for the opportunity and they also congratulated me on finishing my trade school modules. Then I awkwardly swung around on my rotating chair, uncomfortable, nervous but excited. "I don't think it's any secret of my struggles and I'm incredibly homesick, I would love it if I was able to be signed off to return home to my parents, I'm really battling being up here and I think it's best if I go home. Is that something that you think we could make eventuate? I would be really grateful."

My voice shook as I got the sentences out, there was no awkward thought process or silence in between. My boss looked straight to his wife as if she was the real boss and she looked straight at me. "No, nice try, but we don't sign apprentices off early, we pride ourselves here at having the highest quality apprentice and it's our reputation on the line. By signing you off now before your required time we risk that something could go wrong in that time and that falls back on us for gifting you an early sign off."

I was fucking devastated. I immediately fell back in my chair and tears wept from my face. It wasn't just a "NO!" It felt inhumane, like there was no empathy shown toward the situation.

There were many things I wanted to and could have immediately mentioned in rebuttal. They had signed apprentices off early before, it was a common practice in the field of construction when an apprentice had done all the right things, a way of rewarding them for their honest approach to the last four years. Not only had I done an extra 12 months and doubled up on trade school, I could have sworn right then and promised I would never touch another tool in my life, I just wanted home. I wanted to be safe. I just wanted to see my parents.

I had felt rejected. I had felt like I was not seen, heard or valued.

Maybe it was my excitement that clouded my understanding that it was not a certainty, maybe I just thought people were better than that and when given a situation between saving my life and not having me on their books for three months, I thought they would swing towards the compassionate answer.

I don't hate them for it. It taught me something very important that day as I sunk in the chair and wiped tears away from my face. I was alive. I could feel, I could hurt, and I could be sad. Something that for several years of my life I couldn't feel, shut off and numb to the world and the actions of myself and others: a real-life version of a zombie. Hoping a car would hit me, that someone would bash me, just so I could feel again.

It was in that moment, as a wiped away the tears that I felt my heartbeat.

That heartbeat told me in no uncertain way that I still had reason and purpose.

So often we get caught up believing we cannot go on, just as I did. That this decision was rejection, but it doesn't have to be. It was just the gentle reminder that there are other means and ways forward. That perhaps I needed a few more learnings before I returned home to Melbourne. I had done five years of this shit previously; I could do three months more.

Sadness has helped me understand others, provided me with the empathy for others that I once did not possess. **Sadness is the most important emotion I ever felt.** It shows me every time that I am alive and while that heart beats, the journey will continue.

 CHANGE YOUR WORLD – TIP #35

Don't let the "out there" get involved with the "in here."
Regulate your emotion before it regulates you.
Protect that inner peace.

❧ BE ANGRY ❧

It will help you identify what, who and where you need to remove
yourself from; anger is the action signal for positive change. It is okay
to feel anger, however holding on to it is not and will cause aggression.
Don't let it sit long enough to become that. Aggression is like
holding on to hot coals expecting them to get burnt like you did,
they won't. Throw them away and find the learning.

Being locked up in a watch house isn't fun for anyone, it's just as you imagine it. Handcuffs, stuffed in a four-by-four cell with a thin piece of foam to sit on and a toilet to shit in, a buzzer to talk to the officers on watch and adjacent cells with other people who have done no good. Well, that's what it looks like for the majority of people. However when you have a history of suicidal ideation, attempts on your life or self-harm it may not. Unfortunately my experience was a little different to most.

In 2012, the year at my lowest, I was doing whatever I possibly could to not feel, self-medicating—not because I enjoyed it but to mask or suppress something below it. At the time however, not recognizing, accepting or aware of what I was masking, I could keep up with the best of them; make myself look like I had it all together, but still waters run deep and all that.

I was to find out the truth of the saying, "Pain that has not been transformed, gets transmitted," true to a tee. I found myself out regularly either hustling for a place to fit in to the world or I was out finding a place to feel. I had rustled up a trip for myself and three friends to Rockhampton; about an hour north of Gladstone. It was a night away with the "boys," boys that I trusted and at the time thought the world of. A perfect example of trying to fit in, having to bring something to the table to be accepted, instead of focusing my attention on finding the people who accepted me for who I was. Booking this hotel in Rockhampton was avoided by the other boys so I took it upon myself to do it and provided the hotel with my identification and payment.

Cutting to the chase, the boys and myself returned to the venue in the early hours of the morning, full to the brim of alcohol after a big night out.

However the boys had no intention of going to bed like I had imagined, and this is where I discovered we were not on the same page. We were one hundred percent different in our ideas of knowing where the line is and taking things too far.

For the next several hours, the boys went on a rampage of sorts, plugging the communal hose in and filling up the hallways' ducted heated units, flipping the beds upside down and playing wrestling, smashing windows and TVs and finishing it off by jumping wildly on the beds, breaking every spring and corner stand.

I sat near the little bar fridge in disbelief the entire time this was happening, I just kept repeating, "Guys, I am not part of this." A little bit into the chaos I was joined by the second friend who also said, "Nah, this has gone too far I am not involved in this."

I knew the outcomes weren't going to be favorable, but innocently I thought it wasn't going to be my problem, as I did not participate. I was all about having fun, but the idea of disrespecting people's property or wrecking shit has never been something I've been a fan of. While I am not perfect and certainly wasn't in these earlier years, I was not that person.

I managed to check out while the boys rushed off to the car. The damage was soon discovered and I want to draw your attention to what followed in the police station afterward, I will never forget it. I had received a call from the police asking me to come down to the station. Unlike my friends, who had avoided the calls and cards left at their door I had called the police back immediately. They were kind and assured me that everything was okay and that I had nothing to worry about, that they knew I wasn't the perpetrator but needed to ask some questions and that would be all.

I organized to go in and see them after work. Walking into the police station, I was greeted by an Officer who asked me to follow him to the interview room where he wanted to get my version of events. Knowing I had nothing to hide, I shared my involvement in the evening. I admitted to knowing that I knew they inflicted damages yet didn't at the time think that I would tell police about it. My first mistake! Telling on your mates in a dire situation like that might be the right thing to do, but easier said than done. I had just assumed they would get found out and be dealt with: my second mistake.

After a long interview in which I was transparent and detailed about the events, the police officer proceeded to charge me. The first time I had ever been in trouble like this. I was shocked but I still played ball. The boys had apparently caused over $16,000 damage to the hotel room and because I was the only one to answer the calls and respond to the police, I was the only one charged. Again, my so-called mates sat back and watched from a distance as I copped the full wrath of their fucking pathetic behavior. Due to the severity of the charge, the Officer took me down to the watch house. All of a sudden the so-called, "we just need to ask you a few questions," line had deteriorated rapidly. I was ordered to remain locked up for 12 hours.

This is where it gets even better. I was fucking fuming, not anger where I was uncontrollable or rude or abrupt, it was the quiet anger, reserved yet seething. Incredible resentment and hatred for these boys welled up.

The police officer in the watch house took my photographs, took my fingerprints and then proceeded to punch my name into the system. I had never been in trouble with the law before, so I am still not entirely sure why or how this eventuated, but they stopped me from entering the cell in the clothes that I was in and told me to strip down butt naked and put on a police station jumpsuit. I could see other the people in remand were allowed to keep their civilian clothes on. I was pretty familiar with protocol so I didn't think that removing all of my clothes was warranted unless they had good reason.

Then the police officer said, "Place your hands up on the counter," and when I did so, the police office on my left caught sight of my elastic wristband and said, "And you can take that bit of mental health shit off."

That bit of shit he was referring to, was my Beyond Blue[1] wristband, it was my "must-have" bit of hope that I attached to my wrist every day not only as a reminder to myself, but awareness for others and the mates I had lost. I was already feeling like a defect of humanity, wearing their fucking stupid police jumpsuit, handcuffed for something I didn't do.

Now I was wild, that resentment bubbling below had surfaced. I calmly took off the wristband and turned to the police officer on my left. He quickly motioned to me; "Put your hands back on the counter!" As if he knew I was about to do something I could regret. I dropped the wristband to the ground, and seethed, "That is not a bit of mental health shit. I suggest you pick it up and read it!"

They then ushered me off into my cell. No ordinary cell that any "normal person" would get. Nope, I got the four-by-four padded cell, where they keep people who are a threat to themselves or others. Again, I don't know what they knew about me, I was never a threat to anyone else, but they seemed to think I might have been to myself.

A demoralizing twelve hours later, no toilet, no food and no water I was let out. The door slid back, and the police officer said, "Matt, how are you feeling mate?"

I was clear. "If I wasn't fucking crazy before you put me in there, you've definitely made me feel like it now," and I walked out.

A week later, I bumped into the Officers that I had had the run in with, as they waited for take away at the Thai restaurant. Not in handcuffs this time I felt immediate aggression bubble up. I didn't have a fear for trouble at this stage, nor did I have a fear for physical injury, all I wanted to do was die and there was nothing anyone else could do to me that could be worse than that.

The police recognized me and immediately upon locking eyes, I wanted to do something about it. I let the anger from that night in the cells and the disrespect they showed to the wristband overcome me with an aggression that I wasn't used to.

On cue, both police officers looked down at my wrist, as though to check if I was still wearing it and remembering what it meant to me, as if maybe they felt guilty about it.

"Hey Matt, how are you going mate, you been keeping well?"

Fuck—what! They weren't supposed to be nice. They sounded genuine in asking how I was doing.

I swear from then on, every single week I would run into those police officers in every environment possible; in the supermarket or at the sporting fields, I couldn't escape them. Somehow though, every time I ran into them,

I felt a little less of that aggression and I never acted on how I initially felt that night in the watch house.

Yes, I still wished they didn't call mental health "shit." Yes, I wish they were more understanding of me and my wellness and not have treated me like a defect of humanity that night with a station-issued jumpsuit and a padded cell but it no longer served me to feel aggression towards all of that.

Throughout this situation I learned a pretty important lesson that frequently comes up in life for me and whether it's true or not, I wish to believe it.

Nobody wakes up of a morning and bounds out of bed with the attitude of: *How much can I piss off Matt Runnalls today?* Absolutely nobody. No matter the situations and challenges or run-ins I have with others, I believe that nobody's purpose is to make my life harder. They may make it so from time to time but adjusting my mindset to this has enabled me to let go of aggression. To help me control and express anger positively and productively.

People make mistakes, people say shit they don't mean, people speak without thinking, and people make decisions without recognizing the impact they might have. I can't control that, but I can control how I choose to view it and what I choose to do in response.

I am no longer weighed down by the want to fight, or to lash out or to hurt someone who has hurt me. It never served me, and I never won.

Anger is okay, I'm going to feel it from time to time, but aggression is not.

I will no longer hold onto the hot coal of someone else's decisions or behaviors and have it compromise my joy and happiness.

Never again.

By the way, I paid the hotel back for the damage that was caused by my mates. I wrote a letter of apology for my part in the evening. I now understand that it is more important in every situation to do the right thing, no matter if it impedes on your friendships with those doing the wrong thing. I learned from that in a big way, an expensive way, in a traumatic way. I will never ever spend another minute in a padded cell, contemplating how I can end my life, as a result of hanging out with people who are not my people.

CHANGE YOUR WORLD – TIP #36

I sat with anger long enough; until he finally let slip his
name was trauma. The idea was not to carry him around
anymore, no longer than I already had. But to put him
down and utilize him to climb the next hurdle.
There is no victim, just a victor. Evolve or Remain.

➳ BE FRUSTRATED ➳

*It's where deliberate actions take place, where our focus is on the
outcomes and not the obstacle. Turn all of your frustrations into
curiosity. Create magic with it. Again, remember why you are doing it.
Nothing is impossible when your why is compelling enough.*

Imagine being down to your last dollars, last twelve dollars to be exact. Your head is down, feet are dragging and you're trying to work out why you ever began this stupid mission. Well, that was me.

Starting Mindfull Aus in 2016 meant basically saying goodbye to any financial security for many years, putting everything that I had towards making this not-for-profit charitable organization functional with a maxed-out credit card at ten thousand dollars that I struggled to pay off for years. Some weeks I got paid when the organization had something to spare, many weeks there was nothing. Not to mention I didn't actually draw a wage at all until eighteen months after starting it up.

I was stressing out my parents and hurting them financially asking them for money from time to time, missing out on the things that I would have loved to do while watching others around me accomplish them. It was frustrating, I had set out on a goal to run an organization that would help change and save lives, the same way I knew it was possible.

Logistically, the organization was inundated with opportunity, however financially it wasn't reciprocal. Everyone wanted to be helped, everyone wanted my advice, my time and my expertise and I was too nice to ask for anything in return on most occasions. When people would rebut our prices with their ridiculous and ignorant mental health budgets, I would do it for free so people wouldn't miss out.

I did over 150 free speaking engagements in my first four years as CEO. I only wanted to help, but helping others wasn't helping me or helping to keep the organization alive. As an organization not supported by government funding we relied heavily on community donations, or people who valued our work. Our incoming payment were often few and far between. We didn't spend a lot and my ability to keep costs down was good, but my ability to make them was also in question. The plumber-turned-charity-CEO was a bit shaky for some time.

But one thing stayed true. My father's ability to back me in, when I didn't believe in myself and my ability to bounce up and go again and even when I wanted to go back to bed and never see the light of day. My dad continuously provided for me in the times it was tough, often paying me a wage and creating jobs for me to get me by. Often, he would "donate" to Mindfull Aus and tip another few thousand in, sometimes ten. He is a legend, my idol and the only reason Mindfull Aus still exists. Fact.

It's easy for me to get the rewards for the work Mindfull Aus does, but what others don't get to see is the people like my dad, who keep it thriving, who continuously back me in and support me in doing the work I do, no matter how shaky the ground is under me.

This particular day I was driving back from Geelong, a regional city about an hour out of Melbourne. I had gone out there to do an interview with a local newspaper and radio station for an initiative called Thick & Thin as an ambassador for mental health. It aimed to engage people in the local community to don blue socks for this specific weekend as a show of solidarity and raise awareness and support of mental health; a great opportunity for me to be heard and more lived-experience stories to be shared.

After the conclusion of my interviews with the local media, I sank into the car for the long drive home. I had an enormous amount of anxiety hovering over my head as I put the seatbelt on. I knew damn well the Mindfull Aus bank account had just $12 left. Yes, we might have had some fundraisers due in soon, some invoices for speaking engagements not yet paid, but nonetheless we had just twelve stinking dollars left at that moment in time and I knew the car needed fuel. It was going to be touch and go, maybe I would make it, maybe I would have to ring the old man and ask him for yet another handout.

I hated doing it; it feeds me full of limiting beliefs of worthlessness, failure and being a burden. The same three things if you recall by now, that are the cause of my suicidal ideation on a regular occurrence.

I pulled up to the petrol station and carefully began filling the fuel tank in a little game I know we all play at the petrol bowsers, trying to stop the counter on our favorite number or in my case on exactly the right price. However mine was embarrassing, I had to stop mine at $12. No more, no less. I couldn't afford to go over; I had already used up every loose coin in the glove box to get by the week before.

With stressful precision, boom! $11.99. Close enough. Embarrassed by my deficient purchase I strategically waited for there to be nobody in the queue before I called out my bowser number, "Just number 6 thanks mate."

Of course, the attendant couldn't help himself. He returned fire with, "Just $12 mate, nice and easy one today." Little did he know it wasn't easy and that my palms resembled the Nile, a river of sweat, shame and guilt. So much so that I asked the attendant for a brief minute to transfer some funds. This is a common practice of the anxious, there were no funds to actually transfer but I needed to triple check that I even had the $12 I had presumed.

As I logged onto the bank and scrolled down to the Mindfull Aus account, I couldn't believe my eyes. The balance read **one hundred thousand dollars!** *What the fucking hell is going on here? Is this some sick joke?* I said to myself as I scrolled through looking for clues. Finally it dawned on me, it was an anonymous donation!

"You are kidding me!" My surprise burst out and the attendant wanted to know what was wrong. I replied, "Nothing, just the fuel mate, it's all good." I paid for my fuel and strutted back to my car on cloud nine. I had never ever seen that amount of money, not personally or in business. I had just been a plumber previously who struggled to make it week to week.

I rang my father before even pulling out of the petrol station, "Dad! Have you seen the fucking bank accounts!"

"No, what's happened?" He replied so calmly! *He mustn't know,* I thought.

"We just got a fucking donation of $100,000!"

He gave a short bout of laughter, "Who's that from?"

"I have no idea, it's anonymous." We wracked our brains as to whom it might have been. It was my real-life example of *Charlie & The Chocolate Factory,* I felt like I had won the golden ticket. It wasn't my money, but I rode every bump of Mindfull Aus as if it were.

I now understand who donated that money and I will forever be indebted and grateful to the wonderful and generous person it was. It saved Mindfull Aus and our existence. Again, it's easy for people to say I do important work, but I can only reiterate I am not able to do this work on these sharp but beautiful edges of love and life without the support of our amazing community. I could write a list of achievements of Mindfull Aus and share stories of people who have credited their life to our work, but the book would require a few too many pages, but what I will say is this: those lives may or may not have been here to read this, had it not been for the generosity of that one individual that day.

My mentor Heather Yelland has always said to me, "Matty, when your why is compelling enough, nothing is impossible," and she urged me to push on and continue. My father Andrew has articulated a similar line every time it seems I am being overwhelmed with challenges that the organization faces or as a young CEO with no prior experience, I juggle it all from day to day. And it's true, there is absolutely nothing that will get in the way or has got in the way of us making things eventuate at Mindfull Aus, because we are as passionate as ever when it comes to the cause. We are tied to the initial reason as to why we got involved and we have not waivered or lost an inch of that motivation.

The focus every single day we go to work is not on the obstacles, but on the outcomes and when it seems hard and roadblocks appear—or the countless times individuals have tried to stand in the way of our good work—we remember those we've lost, I personally picture myself back at too many funerals and remember that without pushing forward, the world unfortunately will lose more to the same silent killer that got them, and that breaks my heart.

Be frustrated but get fascinated about it and what it's trying to tell you. Not everyone will value the work we do because they haven't yet (fortunately) felt the punch in the face I have on many occasions, but that's not my prerogative. What is, is doing the best I can with what I have and putting my best self forward every day, tirelessly and working as hard tomorrow with the same passion as I had day one. People see that, and people will support that. Good things don't happen for those who wait, no, good things happen for those who are living in alignment with their values, passion and purpose.

Feeling frustrated? Ask yourself why, then create your magic with it.

 CHANGE YOUR WORLD – TIP #37

Life will never get any easier.
Only your ability to withstand the challenges does.

⤳ BE BROKEN ⤳

Where we heal it is stronger. Restoration and refurbishment always looks and feels much better. Acceptance for where you are is the solid foundation on which to rebuild from. Use your pain as your gift and your emotion as the glue in the rebuild.

As I have alluded to at times already, I am in no way, shape or form perfect. I have made mistakes that have landed me in hot water, I have said things that have made people feel in ways they don't deserve to and I have made decisions that I have not thought about the consequences of prior to putting them into action. This story unknowingly began decades ago.

In 1995 I was in grade prep and about five or six years old without a worry in the world. There was the excitement of starting school, making new friends and swinging from monkey bar to monkey bar, as I innocently wondered how any one's life could be different, but it was. I loved primary school, loved my friends and especially those sport days where we spray painted our hair green, spiked it up as tall possible and tackled the athletics track as if we were the fastest people on the planet, oblivious that our little legs just looked like we were running on the spot.

I don't remember much from primary school unfortunately and I don't recall this specific situation; that's not to dismiss it or say it isn't true, because more than likely it was. Let me fast forward the story, to the end of the year in 2016. I had just launched Mindfull Aus as a not-for-profit and was enjoying the new opportunity and a new life where my passion and purpose was aligned, and I was just 25.

I was living life back on my terms, still with struggles and ongoing challenges, but with a newfound acceptance for them. By no means in the clear but I understood mental health the best I ever had, and I was medicated and receiving consistent therapy and reaching out when required to other professional services. Work though, was the driver behind my wellness. I wanted to do it authentically and I wanted to know everything about mind and behavioral health, so that I could help myself and externally support others with that newfound knowledge.

Living in St Kilda by myself at the time in a studio apartment, an apartment where all sides of my bed nearly met the walls and each night, I ate dinner on my bed because it wasn't big enough for a kitchen table. I lived by the beach and implemented everything I had learned into a wellness plan that I needed to live by in order to be more myself and who I deserved to be.

Mindfull Aus at this stage was nine or so months into its existence and just registered with the Australian Charities and Commission Board; a dream achieved and in play. People were starting to familiarize themselves with the work and services of Mindfull Aus, especially those in the country community in which I grew up. I had their support and people really rallied behind me in getting the wheels turning. There was no hate, no negativity like I had received in plumbing all those years and the only comments made about Mindfull Aus were five-star reviews pasted across our social medias, specifically Facebook. Facebook was our platform to share, at the time I don't even think we had a website but used social media as our tool to educate, share stories and make the community aware of upcoming events.

It was an early morning ritual to stroll down the beach to begin a short meditation, often in my ears as I walked was a podcast of the likes of Joe Dispenza, Brené Brown or Tom Bilyeau; anything to help shift me in a positive direction. The phone buzzed and I whipped it out of my pocket in hope it was some more opportunities or excitement to do with Mindfull Aus, but it wasn't.

It was the opposite. A good friend of mine had sent me a message, "Hey mate, have you seen Facebook? Just wanted to know if you're okay?" I freaked out and hurriedly replied trying to work out what he meant. I immediately started frantically scrolling to see if I could work out what he was on about. Sure enough my notifications had skyrocketed.

There had been a girl, a girl I was not familiar with, who had shared a status about Mindfull Aus being fraudulent, not because of the organization itself, but a personal attack on myself as a person. It was short, it was sharp, and it mentioned that I had traded words with her years ago and that nobody should support the work I do, as I am the total contradiction to mental health and supporting people.

Underneath was a social media war between what appeared to be her friends and on the other side of the fence, people who had wanted to support Mindfull Aus, either from my friendships or because we had supported them. Comments were made about my living arrangements in St Kilda and that I must be profiteering off mental health initiatives in order to live there. Little did they know my house was the size of a shoebox and at the bottom of the building, cars were broken into and used syringes were often lying around.

Not taking anything away from her comment, but her anger was rampant, it didn't matter if she knew the facts of the story she was out to attack me on all fronts. More importantly to me, she was out to attack the charity's reputation before it really had begun!

I had obviously at some point in my life really hurt this person by things I had said. The comments were getting out of control and the fighting back and forth—as it does on social media these days—showed no signs of slowing down. I didn't fire any shots; I was simply shaken and overwhelmed with the situation. I had no idea what I had ever done to her, but the body keeps the score, and I knew I must have upset her, which had never been my intention.

I reached out to her via inbox and asked her what had transpired, if we could talk about it? She fired more shots and didn't want a bar of it. Initially I let it be and turned my phone off. I had sunk into an extraordinary amount of guilt. I didn't deflect what I might have done but sat with it. I could feel the pain of what I had unknowingly done at one point in my life through the pain of her abusive messages.

I fell into a deep state of depression, the feelings of being a burden hit me like a ton of bricks and the thought that I had caused someone that amount of hurt ate away at me. To be publicly shamed for it was the icing on the cake and no amount of support that I received on that Facebook post made me feel any better.

I couldn't get a hold of this girl to talk it through, as she didn't want any of it. That night would be the last suicide attempt I ever made. It wasn't a get-out-of-trouble clause or a way of making me feel better, I couldn't live with the fact I had made someone hurt so much, it didn't matter that it was a stranger. The unknown of what caused it weighed heavily on me and I began writing one more note to leave behind. How could I run a not-for-profit mental health foundation if I was a bully? If I was someone who had hurt someone so much? I couldn't live with that and I felt that this world would be truly better off—that this anonymous girl was right.

In the days following my attempt at my life, I received a message from this girl, she seemed to have calmed down. She mentioned that when I was in prep (five years old), she was in grade four (nine years old) and apparently, I had bullied her on my way home from school one afternoon and made fun of her in front of other kids. Uncovering the truth made me feel somewhat better and my friends tried to help me put the situation to bed by assuring me that I had only been five years old, "You weren't to know Matt, it doesn't matter now."

But the fact that words I said when I was five had lived with this girl for two decades (until she posted about it) showed me just how powerful our words and actions are on others. That no matter how much time passed or the fact that I was only five when I said them, did not matter.

For a long time I have lived as what I describe as broken. Numb, shut off to the world and a shade of the person I once was. I have believed narratives about myself that aren't true based on the opinions of others and on things people have said to me or about me. I have believed similar narratives that I tell myself that prevent me from being who I know I can be.

They caused me continual hurt, they did.

There lies the opportunity. We can believe these narratives about who we are, or we can shift them. I can believe that I am a bad person because of the comments I made and let them outweigh the positives and find myself in suicidal situations again like the evening of that Facebook post; or I can choose to use them as my fuel to be better for the world. To take the learning from the situation and ensure that not only do I do my best to avoid making people feel that way, but also act in a way that encourages and supports people to be the best they can be for their communities too.

I will never be able to change what I have done and the mistakes I have made, but I can make sure that I lead a different life moving forward. I can choose to be broken in parts and let those parts hurt others, or I can refurbish and restore those parts of me and come out shining, a better version of the person I was not just years ago, but even a day ago. That's the goal: to continually move forward in a positive way. To live life in the betterment of others, to serve, to help, to support and to be here for people that believe those narratives about themselves.

All of my past failures, frustrations, broken parts and challenges have paved the solid foundation on which I rebuilt my life, from the very bottom up. It came down to *loving* myself and all the parts of me, or *losing* myself and bathing in the pain: two words with only one letter difference, but two words that store years of pain.

Let go of what hurt you, let go of what others believe. The only thing that matters is that you have a choice right now to change the outcomes of whatever it is you have been through, but only you can make this happen. No one else can.

You are not a bad person. Let it go. Life is up ahead and worth living.

 CHANGE YOUR WORLD – TIP #38

Our words have the ability to lift up and heal people, or
pull down and destroy them. Make a conscious choice;
it is always the right time to do what's right.

 **BE LOST**

Life isn't about finding yourself; it's about creating yourself.
What you find has always existed, what you create
will depend on how badly you want it.
The only limitations are your excuses as to why you can't.

It's bizarre to think that the guy who was either mysteriously absent on the days he had to present in front of the class or who would happily fail rather than to get up and share—who by the way is still challenged and living with social anxiety today—is in fact the same person who speaks publicly in front of thousands of people a year.

Yet I do.

Often, we avoid tough situations because we believe "stories" about ourselves that we can't do it, we overthink the situation until it's not even feasible. There is no merit to this thinking but how often do we see people holding themselves back from things that we all know they can do, but they don't.

How often do we judge ourselves based on our ability or inability to do what others can, most of the time without even giving it a go?

Nearing the end of my journey as a plumber, I was volunteering for other mental health organizations but mostly sitting back watching other people do what they did, feeling lost, like I had no sense of purpose and belonging, I was feeling connected to the cause but without anything worthwhile to give towards it. Believing that nobody on the planet would want to listen to my story, silencing it and hiding it in fear of judgment and shame. Remember that this is going back quite a lot of years where mental health wasn't as readily spoken about like it is now.

I would talk to people who worked in the field and pick their brains, listen to them speak, read their books, put their podcasts in my ears and drown myself in their work. I was frequently being given opportunities to share my passion for the topic but quickly knocking them on the head thinking to myself: *Well, I haven't been through too much, I've only witnessed some people close to me struggle,* or *Yeah I had depression but I don't any more,* as if it was something I had magically removed forever. For a time I even minimalized the loss of so many friends because I hadn't been their best friend for 20+ years or sat front row at their funerals.

I silenced who I really was because I believed someone else always had it worse, which they do but that doesn't lesson my experiences. I silenced myself because I thought: *What value do I bring to any of this? I am just a twenty-something-year-old plumber who's been a bit wayward for a few years and troubled by his thoughts.*

And it's common to diminish your own experience. Actually, I prompt you to ask yourself if you have ever felt the same way. Have you sat still and silent when conversations were happening around you about the exact topic you knew you could contribute to, yet you didn't because you didn't think others would find value in what you shared? I bet you have.

You hear people talk about "finding yourself" all the time and yet from what I see so frequently in the circles of people in which I play, most of us tend to have the term twisted so that it alludes to being this thing we "do" after we get the less important shit of life done and out of the way. We forget just how dangerous it is to live blind folded, in a life **guided by the person we are not, instead of the person we are.**

We forget there is very little progress to be made in this life if we don't have a firm grip on who we are and why we matter. It is not about finding out the essence of who we are, it is about creating a more meaningful version of the person that already exists. Sure, you can cruise through life and be happy with mediocrity, accepting all challenges as if they are "part of life" or you can accept that you have the ability to live a more fulfilling lifestyle, aware of challenges and maneuvering around them, through them and with them with insight, intuition and purpose.

Professionals, specifically psychologists recognize that when a person lacks a sense of personal identity, their problems spill out and into every other aspect of their life.

People who refuse to do the work to understand themselves, who bathe in the idea of "it's a part of life" rather than creating something more meaningful for themselves with the skills they were birthed with, tend to be frequently challenged in all areas of their life from relationships, career and more importantly mind and behavioral health. Those same people who have no strong sense of their own identify tend to go down the same paths I did, the path of anxiety, addiction, feelings of emptiness, isolation from things of value, pushing away great support and feelings of helplessness.

Lacking in self-confidence often ends up in manipulative relationships, settling for something far below par. Decision making becomes harder and you lose confidence in things you were once great at, that you could do with your eyes closed, it gets buried and becomes a feature of your past.

I could no longer wade around in the environments of construction, waking up every day to put on the work boots, only to dream of taking them off again, but I had no exit strategy. Continuously landing on the idea that I had nothing to offer the world. I was plumbing to make ends meet but dying by installments: the true definition of suffering—though this was self-inflicted, my choice or lack thereof.

Until I was totally caught off guard when I was asked to speak about my journey in front of a team of people in a corporate setting. Not long after that I began receiving emails and inboxes through word of mouth asking if I would come to their sporting club or community. To think of all those years of turning down opportunities to speak in front of my peers and failing automatically because of my own shame cycle I chose to sit in as to why I wasn't good enough to do it. And the deliriousness of thinking nobody would get any value out of what I say.

I had wasted enough time.

Organically I became a keynote speaker in 2014, in the following three years I would speak between 50–100 times a year. This would increase to 150 times a year in subsequent years and I would accumulate over 550 speaking engagements in more than ten countries, and 40 plus states around the world. My story and learnings would go on to be shared with millions across podcasts, media, documentaries and short films, interviews or mainstream media. None of which was advertised or solicited on my end, all of it was word of mouth. People who believed in what I did and how I did it, communities of people who were sitting on every word, starting to believe something else was possible for them, the same way it was for me because of the hope visible in stories I heard from speakers and advocates like Kevin Hines many years prior.

What I was doing wasn't revolutionary, it was just articulating the topic from my viewpoint, the same way I needed to hear it from someone else on my journey. The realization that the one thing that has been lost on the world is authenticity and people love it when people are real. My goals have always been the same from speech one to this very moment.

My goal is not to be liked; my goal is to be authentic. That way when I leave the stage and microphone behind, I am not fazed by how many people like me because that wasn't my goal. If they do, that's a bonus, if they don't, **I just hope they walk away loving themselves a little bit more.** Because if they can do that, they will get to a place where they no longer feel lost in the world and get back to being more of who they were born to be and make the difference they were born to make.

If I remain authentic in every situation in my life, I will continue to find what's true to me and for me. In the process, we will give that same permission to everyone else.

And because of that, this socially anxious, nervous wreck of a keynote speaker will continue to front up and do it, because it is now that I recognize that the gig is not actually about how I feel, but how I make others feel. So, for 60 minutes an evening I can comfortably put what I feel aside and focus on others and I bloody love doing that.

In July 2017, I made the big move to full time. **I had no bloody idea what I was doing.** I had no background in business or not-for-profit governance, I didn't own a computer, I had no home internet and absolutely zero understanding of what it was going to take to be good at what I do or make a profound impact on those I spoke in front of. But I put my head down and followed the directions that my heart continuously pulled me towards. I obsessed over the field of mental health, studied daily, course after course and with every minute of the day I was researching papers, noting citations, asking questions of professionals and surrounding myself with those who walked the same path. They showed me it was not only possible, but took me in and didn't alter my articulation or passion, but sanded it back in a way that was the best fit for me.

I had gone from lost and not sure as to when or if I would ever leave plumbing, to giving away all my tools to friends and removing any traces of construction in my closet. Still to this day I no longer own any plumbing tools, steel-capped boots or high-vis clothing.

I had become a full time speaker, delivering content on stages across the world in every environment you could think of, it wasn't the ideal way to get there but I recreated myself from what already existed. The only thing that stopped me previously was not believing I could do it or that I wouldn't provide any value in doing it. I was wrong all along.

The art of creating yourself is the process of shining a light on who you are now. It's the beautiful elements of acceptance, those where we learn to appreciate our strengths and triple down on them, simultaneously looking at the uglier parts of us, locking eyes with our weaknesses and outsourcing them or strengthening them.

Creating yourself is not about achievement or competition with anyone else. It is the part of learning where we begin to back the sound of our own voice instead of finding ways to silence it or requiring someone else, it's recognizing thoughts exist and being zoned in on what they are teaching you.

It is action, it is intention, it is intuition. It is taking control of your every move with authenticity and positive inner dialogue. Overall creating ourselves, from what always existed is the one place in the world that presents true peace.

Being in tune with the life I have now created from what existed to me, has enabled me to live with more spontaneity, more fire and more excitement. When you create a strong sense of purpose and belief about who you are, you are more competent to balance changes, emotion, uncertainty, adversity and hold yourself accountable to things or people in your life that are simply not your people.

It's a hell of a task in creating that person, it's something that is continual and not met with an end date or expiry. It's a daily habit of mastering challenges that life throws at us and turning them into your ally, your friend and your strength to drive forward.

Life isn't easy; it can be painful and ugly. Sometimes the overwhelm of your next move creates this abyss that makes it seem as if you are lost and unworthy. Push through that pain and emptiness, roll up your sleeves and get dirty with things that are coming up and lingering through important parts of life.

You might be "lost" but you do not require saving or finding. You are there, just as you always will be. The very path you find while "lost" is the one you are meant to ride on and remember that when the wheels go flat, you can always get off and walk. Unzip the costume of "I can't" and step into the suit of "I can."

CHANGE YOUR WORLD — TIP #39

Some of us aren't meant to belong, some of us are
designed to turn the world upside fucking down and
shake the hell out of it until we find our own place in it.

✈ BE ALONE ✈

*There isn't anything more satisfying in life than to find your best friend
and realize you were with them all along. To depend on nobody, that is
true strength. Feeling alone is an action signal that you need to work on
loving you a little more. Only when you love yourself will you find the
love from others you truly deserve.*

It will come as no surprise that not many of us are naturals at carving
out space, having time to just be, without completely losing our minds.
Boredom, once upon a time was a word used to describe the time in which
we didn't quite know what to do with. However it was during this uncertain
time, that we birthed ideas and creativity that enabled us to fulfill parts of
ourselves that we didn't know existed.

But in this day and age it's a word hardly heard, we have a phone in our
hands most of the time and we rarely ever find ourselves not overwhelmed
with a long list of things we need to do or places we must be. It is in these
situations that we often forget about Number One: us. Right now, we live in
a state of being that is constantly reactive to the things going on around us,
rather than being proactive to things right in front of us. We are so caught
up in taking photos of the toilet we sit on, the food we eat and people we
are with, we avoid the one thing that is insanely important to the human
condition: connection. And I don't mean to others, I mean to ourselves.

Right now, one of the biggest causes of depression is loneliness. However, loneliness might not be what you assume it to be. Loneliness is when our emotional needs are not being met, both physically and emotionally. Loneliness is not just from physical separation or distance between people. It's a worrying sign when people in this world are increasingly feeling like they are alone, in a saturated world of people.

In the year 2014 I made the bold decision to live on my own. I recall hesitation from my peers and family believing that being on my own would only enable me to sit longer inside my own thoughts, stew over situations and isolate myself from people who cared about me. Naturally I am somewhat of an introvert and comfortable in keeping to myself, problems included. I was not yet finished plumbing at this stage and only freshly back in the state of Victoria. There would have been some concern over how I was settling back in. Until this point, I had always had someone in my life not too far away to keep me in check when things were tough: Aurora, Hollie, my housemate Michael or my brother around the corner.

But nevertheless I began renting a tiny place in St Kilda, barely big enough to swing a cat but it felt nice to have my own space. A big part of me always felt that I couldn't properly recharge each night as I felt guilty for being in my room or obliged to entertain housemates. When we don't have the ability to recharge or check out, like mentioned we struggle to connect to what's important and that is ourselves and the accountability of reflecting on the day.

From 2014 through to 2021, I have lived alone and from 2017 through to 2021 I have worked alone. From those periods (by no coincidence) have come my biggest lessons in growing up, in personal development and learning to better understand myself, my thoughts, emotions and needs. Every so often I fall into the trap of self-isolating, removing myself from equally important aspects of life like social connection, community, exercise; all of which have led to more challenging times, but eventually I learned to identify when this eventuates and catch myself before the fall.

In the space of the last seven years, living on my own and operating solo daily I have become very close with the most important person in my life, the one person I never thought I would see eye to eye with; myself. While there is always lots more work to be done and the same thoughts that once haunted me still occasionally reappear, I now have a relationship with myself where I am proud of things I do, excited by things I am doing and grateful for the things that have got me here. No more hiding, escaping or running from the truth of who I am, or believing that I need to be around other people and their support.

I am my best support and have also become my best teacher.

While I still harass my father daily and dial his number repeatedly for advice and guidance, and need my evening video time with my mum, I have slowly regained the confidence of decision-making and the strength of who I am. It's a powerful place to be in, when you take the time to truly connect with who you are, instead of worrying about the makeup of everyone else.

Being alone is a luxury which offers everyone an array of positive outcomes. In our busy lives, it must become a priority to create those minutes in our day to find peace and solitude—to reflect, unwind, and be creative. To return to the days of almost being bored, rather than being overwhelmed.

To take those precious moments to just listen and trust in what you find. To find clarity in the chaos and comfort in the unknown.

I frequently see teachers encouraging kids who are by themselves in the schoolyard to play with other kids and join in, but I don't agree with it. I frequently hear parents complaining that their kids don't often enjoy playing with the next kid and I don't agree that it has to be something to worry about. Perhaps it is the sign from the kid that he/she understands her needs better than you do. If the kid is driven to play, they will play; if the kid doesn't want to play, they won't. It is not a sign or cause to panic, it is a sign and cause to applaud, the individuality and choices of our kids, no matter how much they don't align with you. There might be reasons to explore behind their reluctance to play, which you can connect with and work on together, but don't assume they "must" join in.

We have to allow more space for kids to just be, to carve their own path, to sit in their own silence the same way we should. We should be encouraging these young champions to slow down before it gets too fast. As a society, we should create the means for our community to know there is a place in the world for those who prefer to be on their own. To shut the world out and let it back in when they desire.

Once you taste the sweetness of silence, you realize that the best things in life are not those that we can touch or see, but instead feel with the heart and you cannot be without it. I am at my best when I am alone; it is when I organize myself spiritually, emotionally and psychologically.

Without those years in silence, I would not have discovered the uniqueness of who I am, based on my own values. I would not have realized my capacity to love and be loved the way I deserve, and I most certainly wouldn't have had the patience to write this book for you to read.

It takes no courage at all to join the crowd; bravery belongs to those who choose to sit alone. Be your own best friend, trust yourself and love yourself, the way you do so freely for others.

 ## CHANGE YOUR WORLD — TIP #40

Don't be fixated on removing that voice in your head.
That little bastard up there needs to learn some
manners, rewire his narrative with positives.
Make him raise his hand to speak.

✤ BE BEHIND ✤

Appreciate the life-miles you have already covered, the setbacks,
challenges, pain and triumphs are what makes you, YOU!
Fall in love with the life you are creating, don't fall
into tune with the walk of someone else.

In a world where every person has their mobile phone devices glued to the palm of their hand, this one is becoming increasingly tricky to navigate through and a cause of unhealthy habits and decisions. I mean you don't have to go too far to know what the next-door neighbors' auntie's brother had for dinner last night, or what Jonathon's new online business pulled in from income this month or how many bitcoins Trevor has or how many Gucci handbags Josephine bought. We live in a world of endless comparisons; a world of make-believe stories and assumptions and social media is the devil that feeds it. All the while idealizing other people's moves and simultaneously underestimating or depreciating our own value, which is catastrophic to our own self-esteem.

Don't worry, I'm right there with you. As a result of my own lack of self-worth and barrage of constrictive thoughts I too spent many years agonizing over being years and years behind where I "should be" (and occasionally still do).

I dropped out of school in Year 11, giving up my opportunity to finish school and go on to study further at university. In the same year I dropped out my first ever apprenticeship fell through. While my mates were studying and working towards their dreams, I was trying to find my first gig in the apprenticeship field. When my friends were finishing their apprenticeships, I skipped town and as a consequence had to re-sit some of the modules of my training and I fell further "behind." My mates bought houses; I was homeless. They moved house, I blew up or crashed cars. They were getting relationships; I was drunk in a mate's house. They had their first-born child, I was still trying to love myself.

The narrative of being "behind" is super unhealthy. The one that says, I am not where I should be, and other people are better than me. It serves no one. What is missing from the above is that while my friends were at high school, I was learning insurance with my dad and spending time with him. When my mates had finished their apprenticeship, I was doing it twice, gaining more skills to hold me in better stead.

I was also going through somewhat of a challenging time, something else that has led me to be in this seat right now. When they bought houses, I was starting a not-for-profit mental health charity, serving my community. When they moved property, I was traveling the world as a keynote speaker. When they had relationships, I was understanding more of who I was and when they were birthing beautiful little lives into the world, I was cheering them on and sending them gifts.

Life is not a competition. Both my friends and myself have achieved vastly different things in life, equally as beautiful. Some dream of doing things I have done, and I'd love nothing more than to have a house and kids. But I know it'll happen, for them and for me when the timing is in alignment with where I am at in the world. When the world says I am ready.

There is no roadmap or timeline that dictates the ages in which you do something.

It is very easy to get caught up believing you are behind. You are not behind anyone. That person you keep telling yourself sits above you or is doing something greater than you, would love to have many tricks, tips and learnings that you have had, and one day they'll need them and experience them their way. You are right where the world wants you to be. Those mistakes, those fuck ups, trips, falls, failures, frustrations and moments where you barely manage to keep yourself together are all part of the difficult but beautiful journey of life. It's the art of living. And it is an art form to embrace where you are.

It would be quite easy for me to get carried away and caught up in blaming and shaming parts of my life as to why I'm not where I could be, but the truth is I can't be angry at all those places and people that have caused me some sort of pain, because they have gifted me beautiful lessons or perhaps steered me towards a better direction to head in. We cannot go through life criticizing the bad pieces if we are not willing to love the good that it has created. Without loss, I am not writing this book. Without my attempts on my life there would be no Mindfull Aus. Without being homeless there would be no Aurora and Hollie, without those shit bosses, there would be a lack of empathy and compassion that I have for people today.

There's beauty in all elements of life, if we are willing to look at it.

And in those moments of beauty, we start to recognize just how magical the journey has been. Yeah, we would do it differently given the chance, but just how lucky are we to be blessed with this opportunity of life! While you read this sentence somebody has died by suicide, there is no time to sit here and be shitty with the world and the people in it because they seem ahead of the game. You have to create the game, not their game but your own. Love the bumps and bruises that come with it.

Time is of the essence. Lean into what the world is doing for you and understand no matter how hard it seems, how far behind you believe yourself to be, there are seven billion of us lunatics on the planet and if we all did things in synergy, there would be some almighty queues to stand in. Don't beat yourself up; it is your schedule and your diary to draw in: nobody else's.

I still catch my mind thinking I am a house behind, a debt out of reach and think it might be years before I catch up. But then I reconnect with myself and recognize and accept that I am comparing myself to an idea that is false. Life is full of complexities and challenges, different for everyone. The only idea that we need to follow is the one that we are always just doing our best. Life is working for us and not to us ... but only if we let it. Cheer on the journey of your closest buddies and celebrate the wins on your own path.

For we might just get to the end and recognize that our path, was the one worth living.

 CHANGE YOUR WORLD – TIP #41

When we closely inspect the shit in our lives, we find little pieces of courage and resilience we didn't know we had. Stare at failure long enough, you'll find your strength within.

⤳ BE AFRAID ⤳

This is the part that shows us that it's worth it. Bravery and courage
come from doing the things that are unknown and not guaranteed.
What doesn't kill you simply makes you stronger.

We can't selectively numb emotions we don't want to feel. Unfortunately when we numb emotions that are effectively "negative" to us, we also numb the positive emotions. For several years I turned consistently to the party lifestyle, without the partying. Not necessarily out of a weekend, rocking a smile and dancing the night away, but tucked away in somebody's backyard or house where the, "I'll just have a couple of drinks" so often became "What happened last night?"

I was unaware that this was subconsciously masking my emotion. Drugs, alcohol, gambling; I was doing whatever I could not to feel. Not because I enjoyed any of it, but to suppress something simmering below. I was petrified of the alternative, shitting myself, scared of having to feel the rip of the band-aid and watch myself bleed. I had never positively addressed any of my losses. 22 years old, raw and green dealing with the loss by this time of four mates to mind and behavioral health challenges, not to mention those I had lost to other situations. Break-ups, bullying, loss, financial stresses, all of it was sitting below, awaiting me to challenge it and look it in the eye, but I couldn't. I was afraid. A shade of the person I once was and had envisioned for myself. A failure.

The problem behind every one of these sessions where I numbed my feelings with a façade of laughter and drink in my hand, I was actually prolonging ever getting better. We can't selectively numb emotions; by numbing emotions that cause us pain we also numb the emotions that cause us joy. So I was missing out on the emotion that I needed to feel, the emotion that becomes purpose, the emotion that builds empathy, the emotion that shows us our next steps. I had fallen into an abyss, totally shut off from the world and everyone in it. I had fallen out of love for everything that I had once appreciated and felt joy for. I lost motivation and consequently wasn't a good person to myself or those around me.

NOBODY CAN SAVE ME

I was paralyzed by my own fear of myself and what I had become. It was this distorted reality that fear often presents as. You see, I was not scared of the darkness, I was used to it, I was living in it. What I was scared of was the alternative, my light. We so often see people fall into the dark where even showering is challenging, where getting up and putting one foot in front of the other feels like trying to climb Mount Everest. The smallest of tasks just so challenging. Is it a belief or a fear that prevents us from doing it?

The power of this self-talk can't be underestimated, such as:
What if I fail again?
I can't do it; I can't bare the thought of judgment.
I'm embarrassed about who I am, it's easier to stay here.

These are the subconscious thoughts and reminders that switch back and forth through our minds to create this narrative telling us all the reasons why we can't do something. We become prisoners to our own fear.

Being afraid doesn't make you stupid. It might just be that somewhere there has been an intercept in your mind that struggles to distinguish between real dangers and unreasonable dangers. This can often come from experiencing a hell of a lot of traumatic situations where things become increasingly frightening to attempt or acknowledge. But eventually the mask has to come off.

Upon my return to Victoria, I had some newfound acceptance for what I was experiencing and some life-changing moments that enabled me to decipher between what was real and what wasn't, acceptance to learn about the conscious mind. Knowing that numbing my emotions was stopping me from ever getting back to that place I desperately wanted to be, I made a decision to stop drinking—cold turkey. I wasn't an everyday drinker or partygoer, but when I did say yes, I didn't know how to pull myself up and say when it was enough.

Over the next nine months sober, I fronted up to the parts of me that were terrifying to look at. I took myself out on to cliff faces and flirted with my own fear and questioned deeply how much I wanted it, as I stared deeply into the crashing waves below. I wrote, I meditated; I did that ugly work of soul searching. I sat in the feelings of being afraid. What came up wasn't pretty but it was true.

It's okay to feel afraid and it's okay to acknowledge that you are afraid. You don't have to continue to kick back off fear and in the same way you don't have to be governed by it. Resisting or suppressing feelings of being afraid only allows it to stalk you constantly; accepting that you are where you are, takes the power out of it.

I believe a lot of good can come of being afraid. When we are afraid, we are thinking outwardly about life. Being afraid can scare us away or scare us into action when we understand that incredible things can happen when we dip our feet into the things that are not guaranteed or promised. It's an opportunity to be a little brave with our life. Subtly perhaps, being afraid is the reminder that you are actually onto something amazing.

But it takes courage and courage is not the absence of being afraid, no! It is the ability to manage the thought and overcome it, to resist letting emotion prevent you from taking that positive action. It takes true courage to turn inwards in those darkest of moments and recognize that there is something better up ahead.

And I believe that for everyone.

While it might seem hard and out of reach, when we are leading with our heart we know what we should do, rather than perhaps what we want to do, often those two answers come from two different places. Next time you have an overwhelming sense of being afraid in moments of your life, establish that your life itself is not in danger and indeed, being afraid might just be the useful tool for you to move into magic.

From being afraid of:
- That first date that turned into your remarkable relationship.
- That job interview that became the dream job.
- That sky dive that became the most exhilarating moment of your life.

- Starting that business, that now allows you to live life on your terms.
- The uniqueness of who you are …

This part is for you to finish writing, somewhere down the track.

Be afraid, but remember it's always the right time to do the right thing.

 CHANGE YOUR WORLD – TIP #42

Fear is a product of our imagination, don't confuse danger
with insanity. We all fear something, just make sure what
you fear doesn't prevent you from being you.

CONCLUSION

This is the part where I will always wonder if I have said enough. Has the message landed in the ears of the beautiful people that are waking up unsure how to make sense of each day? In the ears of the countless dedicated and selfless caregivers in their lives? Can they use the actions and ideas in this book to bridge that gap between love, belonging and connection?

There is no one-size-fits-all strategy to overcoming mental health challenges. And this book does not work alone in preventing them, I encourage you to learn all you can about other resources and services and options that you personally connect with. Is it spending more time being active, being in nature, changing your diet, being more social, spending more time alone or perhaps it's incorporating various forms of therapy when we are feeling good, rather than just when we are feeling bad.

Our brains have become overwhelmed and saturated thanks to technology and while there is a huge benefit to it when used correctly, it is my hope that we can turn to what has always existed. Our own unique strength paired with a better understanding of it.

It is not my wish for you to screw up your nose at the old model and Western ways and I am certainly not suggesting that they don't hold a place and value. Instead, cultivate an ever-greater understanding for the tools and strategies that you possess, which are often overlooked and ignored in modern psychology and certainly mainstream media.

Thanks to some incredible learning opportunities studying overseas at California State that broadened and empowered my knowledge-base, and working with some of the biggest organisations and names globally and having great support here in Australia to learn about operating in the charity sector, all of these elements enabled me to ultimately develop and deliver an evidence-based primary school program around emotional resiliency and well-being. This program has become one of **my greatest outcomes in changing the mental health playing field in early education**. It is the one sure-fire way I believe we can alter the path for a society with a growing culture of challenges. Creating new waves of young champions that are equipped, the way we were not.

People often say, "Oh aren't they too young to learn about this?" Yet about half of all lifelong mental health challenges begin by the age of 14. Early intervention, or rather education makes a huge difference in reaching children *before* they grow up and come into harsh and sudden contact with the mental health system.

This early education gives them the foundation to address their emotional and psychological state of mind firstly from an internal and holistic perspective and also within a caring, connected home environment. As they grow up these young champions can rely on their emotional skills throughout their lives, sustaining them whenever adversity strikes as it does to every one of us.

Redefining mental health and the loss of my mates have been my greatest teachers. They taught me to rewire the story in my mind from one of "torture" to one of acknowledging and giving credit to all the good things that had happened to me as a result of the pain, trauma and grief I'd been through. It formed my belief that I could in fact channel what I'd felt, seen and learned for the betterment of someone else.

The misconceptions around mental health still run deep and my work today takes me into virtually every field you can imagine; blue collar, corporate, construction, sporting environments, regional and remote communities, children and youth.

This book only represents a portion of the learnings I associate with the change society and the world desperately needs. Working towards every child, teenager and adult having the skills to be able to work through new emotions and situations, to feel their worth and feel the love and connection in their lives. Learning how to nurture your body and mind in a natural way so that we can complement professional services, therapy or medication on our quest to find our self-worth, value, true belonging and purpose.

Importantly to also know that everything that brings us pain is actually the gift of living an incredible life full of the miracle that is human emotion.

The faces of those I have lost flash before me as I bring this story to a reluctant but necessary end. There is no end however, to their memory or to my passion to keep working towards no one losing their life due to a false story they believe about themselves. I know those that have left us and those still struggling, would want the chance to talk and be heard for who—they—are, and would give anything to learn how to tap into the resilience within us all.

I hope you can rediscover hope in the kindness of others, the same way I did.

I hope that you can recognise the strength of who you are based on your own unique values, the same way I have.

I hope that you can value your emotional road map, and find the beauty in all of it.

I hope that you go on the journey of creating your own wellness by breaking negative patterns, healing from your past and creating a more self aware life. Doing this work, gives you the power to transform yourself into the person you were always meant to be. Helping you create a new and exciting narrative that you can feel energised to live by, where your emotional challenges and symptoms are messages to play in, and not run or hide from.

Most of all, I hope that you now understand that everything in life that is happening no matter how challenging or painful it has been, is carving you into the most beautiful version of you possible.

You do not need to feel stuck, overwhelmed, stressed or lost and your worth is certainly not determined by anybody or anything external to yourself.

You and you only have the power from here going forward. Rip off the band-aid and as a whole, let's start walking taller because we played in the ugly parts of life, rather than walking tall while pretending they never existed.

Once upon a time I believed that my own two hands were my way out of this world. I believed there was nothing left to be here for and that everyone in my life would be better off without me. Now I sit here and write these words with those same hands and a smile on my face, knowing it is possible for you too.

ONE LAST TIP

 # CHANGE YOUR WORLD – TIP #43

I know who I am. I am clear about that. It is not negotiable.
I belong here, perhaps I don't fit in, but I refuse to negotiate
my belonging to myself. I will continue to turn this world
upside down, until I find my place in it.
But I will not remain the same; I will evolve.

ACKNOWLEDGMENTS

To the most important people in my life, my mum and dad.

Dad, you're my best mate. None of what's written will be of any surprise to you; you know everything because you've been there every step of the way. You are my sounding board, my accountability, my kick up the ass but most importantly my comfort. No one has worn more of the punches that life has thrown at me as hard as you have and every time you do everything possible to make sure I don't fight alone.

Mum, I couldn't be more proud of being a "mother's boy" to you, no matter how many times I've yelled at you, ignored you and criticized your decisions, your love and compassion have never waivered. In critical times of suicidal ideality, you were there with all of your love and comfort just being Mum. Thank you for holding space for all of me, whichever Matt shows up. I know that all of what you do for me has only ever come from a place of love.

I wish for more people to nurture their relationship with those that brought them into the world and cared for them on their journey the same way my parents did. It is important to acknowledge that none of what went on in my life is a result or reflection of their parenting. I am and always will be one of the most fortunate people in the world to have experienced the loving relationship I have with them.

To my brother, Beau I love you mate. Thank you for being you; tenacious, competitive, unique and always true to yourself. In your own beautiful way you have taught me a hell of a lot about not conforming to suit others, about loyalty and having the confidence to just be ourselves. You are someone who lives life your way and I am the beneficiary of learning from, laughing with and witnessing all of that.

Aurora, I love and miss you. The first person who truly enabled me to feel at peace with who I was, as "weird" as I was. Your approach and warmth to life deeply engrained a desire for me to show up in the world in the same way for others. I hope that people reading this continue to ask themselves: *Who can I be Aurora for in my life?* The world would be so much more beautiful to be in with more Auroras in it.

Hollie, the one person that I could never seem to disappoint or upset. The one who chose me and stuck it out. You believed in me when I couldn't. You loved me, when I didn't. You were there, when I wasn't. All of what I do is a result of your purity in love and compassion that you have shown me. I love you, Silver & Sayte more than any words or actions combined and I always will.

To my mentors; Joe, Kev, Marg, and Heather, you all have invested and provided incredible amounts of time, effort and resources into me on my advocacy journey, each of you providing and being something uniquely important to me. Thank you for being honest with me, thank you for believing in me. Thank you for guiding me and helping me to understand the difference in the world I was born to make. I am extremely fortunate to have world-class mentors, but even more grateful for the world-class friendships I share with you all.

A VERY SPECIAL MENTION TO;

Paul Dalio, thank you for blessing my life with your unique and raw articulations of bipolar. I ran away at the fear of diagnosis and the shame of it until I met you. It is because of you that I truly believe that I live with a gift and not an illness.

Travis Marsham, the big cat. Thank you for giving me purpose and responsibility at one of the lowest points in my life. You provided me with a safe space in the most unlikely of environments to lower my walls and find acceptance. You care more about the players in your team than you do the results and that reveals your remarkable true character.

Steve, you were given the responsibility of helping me become a charity leader. You met an overwhelmed, stressed and anxious young guy who was ready to throw the towel in. With a million racing thoughts and ideas, ideas that had no other home than inside my head. You managed to capture everything I had to give and turn it into a structured game plan that has now enabled the charity to flourish and grow, creating many more beneficial impacts around the country. You are far more than a business leader to me mate, you are a great friend, a role model and someone who has helped me understand and feel more comfortable in the roles and responsibilities of a charity leader. Cheers to the importance of strategy my friend!

Griff, my best mate! I am incredibly lucky to have crossed your path on this journey mate. You're there in the shit times, holding space for my carry on and also there in the good times laughing at my carry on. Born on the same day, with all the same common interests. I'm excited about sharing the rest of the journey with you mate; don't change a thing!

I want to say a very big thank you to Susan Dean and the entire team at Dean Publishing. A massive thank you to Suzan Dalziel who worked tirelessly with me over 12 months and helped me articulate my journey in a way that I can be proud of. This process has been a beautiful catharsis of raw emotions and personal reflection. I want to acknowledge the Dean Publishing team for their ultimate professionalism and the way in which they have enabled me to express my sincere passion for this cause and topic, and their guidance in helping me become an author.

And a huge thank you to every single person, absolutely every single person I have crossed paths with. Whether it was good or bad I appreciate that it has all added up to these moments and the chair I sit in right now. Thank you to those who have inspired me, given me the energy and drive to do more and be more.

And one big final apology, to everyone that I might have caused discomfort, pain, headaches, challenges or stress on this journey—and there would be a few of you—I had to learn the hard way. We're here now and while I would love to go back and alter the course of what I have said or done to you, please know that I am using all of those fuck ups, mistakes and challenges to make it easier for others to show up in this world.

From one believer in recovery, and also in a world that looks better than the one that exists today, **you are loved, worthwhile, unique and unstoppable.**

The best is yet to come …

Matt Runnalls

Matt is sharing more in his INTERACTIVE book.

See exclusive downloads, videos, audios and photos.

DOWNLOAD it for free at deanpublishing.com/nobodycansaveme

ABOUT THE AUTHOR

Matt Runnalls works tirelessly as a mental health advocate to create awareness, acceptance, education and connection within communities to overcome the stigma and effects of suicide on a global scale. Utilizing his own lived-experience of mental illness, surviving suicide attempts, and losing too many friends to suicide, Matt is continuously creating more platforms of communication to encourage everyone to feel comfortable to talk about and manage their well-being just as he continues to do.

Through his rediscovery of hope visible in the kindness of others, Matt found his passion and purpose when he wholeheartedly pursued the creation of Mindfull Aus at the age of 24. Since devoting himself to advocacy full-time, Matt has delivered over 600 speeches and keynotes, workshops, and events across Australia, Canada, and America. Matt has facilitated right across the world for some of the world's largest Mind and Behavioral organizations, conferences and bodies.

Matt has also been a student of programs and workshops from leading experts in the field of mind and behavioral health including: Wim Hof, Tony Robbins, Dr Jordan Peterson, Dr Brené Brown, Tom Bilyeau, Deepak Chopra, Heather Yelland and Kevin Hines. Matt is trained in NLP, a certified Breathwork & Meditation Practitioner, Sciences of Wellbeing, Intro to Psychology & Counselling, EQ and Quantum Learning as Alumni at California State University.

Matt now spends his life in dedication to the loss of his mates to suicide, combined with the thought that saved his life in 2012—that of having kids one day. This understanding and passion led Matt to become a trained facilitator at the world's #1 camp for young kids (greensupercamp.com.au) where he works with young champions to improve self-esteem, equip them with accelerated development techniques and a greater understanding of emotional intelligence and relationships.

Matt's story and message have been featured in books, documentaries, songs, podcasts and films throughout many major media outlets. His dedication to change has been recognized in: *The Huffington Post*, Global Award-winning Documentary of the Year, *Suicide: the Ripple Effect*, *Guts, Grit & The Grind: a men's health manual*, and also in numerous Parliamentary sittings. Matt has also been the recipient of an Australia Day Medallion in January 2018, a finalist in the 2019 Victorian Leadership & Innovation Award, 2020 ABC Heywire Trailblazer, 2020 AMHF Best Men's Speaker Finalist, 2020 AMHF Men's Health Award Top 3 placement, 2021 Australian of the Year Nominee and 2021 Westfield Community Hero.

Matt's opportunity to ensure that the next generation doesn't walk the unknown like he did, drives him every day as he continues to make a positive impact on as many people as humanly possible.

mattrunnalls.com.au

TESTIMONIALS

"I have recently had the opportunity to talk with Matt about mindfulness. I have worked in the mental health field for a long time and I was so impressed that a person so young could be so wise. He has lots to say, much that could be life changing and certainly save lives. He is compassionate, empathetic, caring, kind, energetic, motivated, goal oriented, and he is changing dark into light for those that listen to him. Keep an eye on Matt. Read his writings. He will brighten your day. He is worth listening to and I believe he is one that will help change this world. Much success to you my friend!!"

— Cathy Cassell, Professional Mental Health Services/ Clinician

"What excites me the most is the relentless drive and compassion Matt Runnalls has for this mission. He is truly authentic in his storytelling and leaves you with the raw truth about life struggles. He provides hope and strength in humanity."

— Mel Yu, CEO & Founder MCO Events

"This young man suffered from things he didn't understand when he was younger, but he had the fortitude to find out what was going on in his body and head and bounced back to lead the pack, he is all class."

— Ricky Nixon, Former AFL Player & Manager

"If you ever get the chance to listen to this incredible man speak, don't miss it! Confronting, insightful, helpful and informative for both kids and adults. My boys and I had great conversations on the way home and will continue having them, because of this. Keep up the amazing work Matt."

—Joanne Baxter, Gippsland Umpires Association

"I listened to Matt speak in Adelaide on World Suicide Prevention Day. His ability to engage a broad audience from retirees to 12 year old school children was remarkable. He is by far the best speaker on Mental Health I've had the privilege to hear. No university degree will ever replace what can be learned from someone like Matt with his experiences. I only wish I stayed behind to tell him myself."

— Belle Barker, Director Business Solutions

"There are no words to describe the impact of what you do Matt. My brother met and heard you once and still speaks so highly of you. The words you gave him are words I see him live by every single day and there is no amount of appreciation that could compass that, you are amazing."

—Jess, Community Member

"He can reach out to a community and bring it together like nothing else I have ever seen, the way Matt can relate so easily and naturally to younger people and show them that "it's just ok to be you." He just speaks to everyone, regardless of age, gender, beliefs. He is real, he is caring, he is raw and so engaging."

— Narelle May, Catholic Care Professional Services

"Thank you for today, from the bottom of my heart you are one of if not the best public speakers I have ever heard. The work you are doing in the space of mental health is amazing. The way you are able to captivate the audience is extremely valuable. Thank you for flying into Adelaide and making this day as powerful and insightful as it was."

— Zac Mills, I Am Worthmore Ambassador

"The story Matt Runnalls shares makes you cry, it's raw and heartfelt. When you walk away you take knowledge and understanding that we didn't have before. Thank you so much for sharing your journey and heartbreak. I will be coming to more of your events, anytime."

— Erika Nickels, Event Attendee

"I've seen a lot of speakers and been involved in many confronting and unique development situations and that was hands down the best facilitation I've witnessed and experience I've been involved in, you're exceptional at what you do."

—Jaymee Sincock, Lululemon Area Manager

"Matt Runnalls is a personal hero of mine. He's also one of my greatest friends. Matt gives his absolute all in everything he does professionally, mentally, spiritually, and mindfully. He's given a lot to me personally, and has helped fuel a drive to thrive in me like none other. He's the founder and creator of Mindfull Aus, all about being mindful of those with a mind full. Matt's passion and dedication to giving back is otherwise uncharted. This young man goes above and beyond in every aspect of his life, existence, and through his passion to change not only the lives of great Australians, but those who follow him around the globe. His work ethic is impeccable, and his drive to help people find hope is absolutely breathtakingly powerful. I highly recommend Matt for your gala, school, or event. His message will change the lives of every single attendee you have."

— **Kevin Hines, Award Winning Speaker, Author And Documentary Filmmaker**

PERMISSIONS

Excerpt on page 23: from *Lost Connections: Uncovering the Real Causes of Depression and the Unexpected Solutions*, by Johann Hari (2018). Reprinted with permission of Bloomsbury Publishing Inc.

Excerpts from pages 26–29: from research by Professor Irving Kirsch, his large body of work appears in many academic journals and some are included in the endnotes of this book.

Excerpt on page 92: Paul Dalio's film *Touched with Fire* courtesy of Charlie Rose (charlierose.com). Reprinted with permission from Charlie Rose.

ENDNOTES

1. World Health Organization, News Release 17 June 2021, "One in 100 deaths is by suicide" https://www.who.int/news/item/17-06-2021-one-in-100-deaths-is-by-suicide

2. Lifeline. (n.d) "Data and Statistics." https://www.lifeline.org.au/resources/data-and-statistics

3. Suicide Prevention Australia. "Stats and Facts" [online] accessed Oct 15 2021. https://www.suicidepreventionaust.org/news/statsandfacts

4. Australian Institute of Health and Welfare, (n.d) "Suicide and self-harm monitoring"[online] https://www.aihw.gov.au/suicide-self-harm-monitoring/data/behaviours-risk-factors/psychosocial-risk-factors-suicide

5. Ibid.

PART 1

1. Hari, Johann, 11 January 2018, *Lost Connections: Uncovering the Real Causes of Depression-and the Unexpected Solutions*, Bloomsbury Publishing Inc.

2   Leo, J., Lacasse, J.R. "The Media and the Chemical Imbalance
    Theory of Depression." *Soc* **45**, 35–45 (2008). https://doi.org/10.1007/
    s12115-007-9047-3

3   Whitaker, Robert. 2010. *Anatomy of an epidemic: magic bullets, psychiatric
    drugs, and the astonishing rise of mental illness in America.* New York: Crown
    Publishers.

4   InformedHealth.org [Internet]. Cologne, Germany: Institute for
    Quality and Efficiency in Health Care (IQWiG); 2006-. "Depression:
    How effective are antidepressants?" [Updated 2020 Jun 18]. Available
    from: https://www.ncbi.nlm.nih.gov/books/NBK361016

5   Vallance, Aaron K. "Something out of Nothing: the Placebo
    Effect." *Advances in Psychiatric Treatment* 12, no. 4 (2006): 287–96.
    doi:10.1192/apt.12.4.287..

6   Kirsch, Irving. "Antidepressants and the Placebo Effect." *Zeitschrift fur
    Psychologie* vol. 222,3 (2014): 128-134. doi:10.1027/2151-2604/a000176

7   Ibid.

8   Ibid.

9   The World Health Organization. 28 September 2001. "The World
    Health Report 2001: Mental Disorders affect one in four people."
    Accessed August 2, 2021. https://www.who.int/news/item/28-09-
    2001-the-world-health-report-2001-mental-disorders-affect-one-in-
    four-people

10 Khan, A., Faucett, J., Lichtenberg, P., Kirsch, I., & Brown, W. A. "A
    systematic review of comparative efficacy of treatments and controls
    for depression." *PloS one*, 7(7), e41778. (2012) https://doi.org/10.1371/
    journal.pone.0041778

11 Kirsch, Irving. "Antidepressants and the Placebo Effect." *Zeitschrift fur
    Psychologie* vol. 222,3 (2014): 128-134. doi:10.1027/2151-2604/a000176

12 Bunce, D. M., Flens, E. A., & Neiles, K. Y. ("How Long can Students
    Pay attention in class? a Study of Student attention Decline using
    Clickers." *Journal of Chemical Education* 2010 87 (12), 1438-1443, 2010).

DOI: 10.1021/ed100409p

13 Black Dog Institute, "Facts About Suicide in Australia." [online] https://www.blackdoginstitute.org.au/resources-support/suicide-self-harm/facts-about-suicide-in-australia

PART 2

1 Harvard Medical School, 2007. "National Comorbidity Survey" (NSC). (2017, August 21). Retrieved from https://www.hcp.med.harvard.edu/ncs/index.php. Data Table 1: Lifetime prevalence DSM-IV/WMH-CIDI disorders by sex and cohort.

2 Victoria State Government, Better Health Channel, "Bipolar Disorder" accessed 14 October 2021, https://www.betterhealth.vic.gov.au/health/conditionsandtreatments/bipolar-disorder#bhc-content

3 Jones, Steve; Jones, Todd. *Andy Irons: Kissed by God*, 2 May 2018, Produced by Teton Gravity Research, Distributed by The Orchard. Dialogue cited from Dr Andrew Nierenberg, the director of Psychiatry at Harvard.

4 Charlie Rose, (charlierose.com) *Touched with Fire* [video interview of Paul Dalio] 02/04/2016, https://charlierose.com/videos/25947 (Courtesy of Charlie Rose).

5 Mental Health Foundation, "Mental Health Foundation launches 'I'm Fine' campaign," accessed online 14 October 2021. Mentalhealth.org.uk https://www.mentalhealth.org.uk/news/mental-health-foundation-launches-im-fine-campaign

6 Corey L. M. Keyes. "The Mental Health Continuum: From Languishing to Flourishing in Life." Journal of Health and Social Behavior 43, no. 2 (2002): 207-22. Accessed August 17, 2021. doi:10.2307/3090197.

7 Busy at Work, "Are you chucking it? The top industries for sickies in Australia." (August 10 2018) accessed 14 October 2021, https://www.busyatwork.com.au/chucking-top-industries-sickies-australia

8   Lally, Phillippa & Jaarsveld, Cornelia & Potts, Henry & Wardle, Jane. "How are habits formed: Modeling habit formation in the real world." *European Journal of Social Psychology*. (2010). 40. 10.1002/ ejsp.674.

9   Ware, Deann Ph.D. "Awarefulness: Neurons that Fire Together Wire Together"–But Why? Hebb's Rule and Synaptic Plasticity." http://www.awarefulness.com

10 Fredrickson, B L. "The role of positive emotions in positive psychology. The broaden-and-build theory of positive emotions." *The American psychologist* vol. 56,3 (2001): 218-26. doi:10.1037//0003- 066x.56.3.218

PART 3

1   Rapp, Charles A., and Richard J. Goscha. 2012. *The Strengths Model: a recovery-oriented approach to Mental Health Services*. New York: Oxford University Press.

2   McRaven, William H, Admiral. Commencement speech at University of Texas, Austin (May 17 2014) — known as the "Make Your Bed speech " on YouTube.

3   *The Oxford Dictionary* [online] accessed October 2 2021, https://www.lexico.com/definition/responsibility

4   Bono, G., Emmons, R.A. and Mccullough, M.E. (2004). "Gratitude in Practice and the Practice of Gratitude." In Positive Psychology in Practice (eds P.A. Linley and S. Joseph). https://doi.org/10.1002/9780470939338.ch29

5   Seppälä, Emma M et al. "Breathing-based meditation decreases posttraumatic stress disorder symptoms in U.S. military veterans: a randomized controlled longitudinal study." *Journal of traumatic stress* vol. 27,4 (2014): 397-405. doi:10.1002/jts.21936

6   Tseng, J., Poppenk, J. "Brain meta-state transitions demarcate thoughts across task contexts exposing the mental noise of trait neuroticism." *Nat Commun* 11, 3480 (2020). https://doi.org/10.1038/s41467-020-17255-9

7   The Greater Good Science Center at the University of California, Berkeley, *Greater Good Magazine*, "What Is Compassion?" accessed online October 19, 2021 https://greatergood.berkeley.edu/topic/compassion/definition

8   Resus (resus.com), (n.d) Dr Peter Has, "The 6 Human Needs," https://www.resus.com.au/the-6-human-needs

9   Mineo, Liz, April 17 2018, "With mindfulness, life's in the moment," *The Harvard Gazette*, accessed online October 2021, https://news.harvard.edu/gazette/story/2018/04/less-stress-clearer-thoughts-with-mindfulness-meditation

10 Wu, r., Liu, L. L., Zhu, H., Su, W. J., cao, Z. Y., Zhong, S. Y., Liu, X. H., & Jiang, C. L Brief "Mindfulness Meditation Improves Emotion Processing." *Frontiers in neuroscience*, 13, 1074. . (2019). https://doi.org/10.338 9/fnins.2019.01074

CONCLUSION

1   Beyond Blue is an Australian mental health and support organization.

Printed in the USA
CPSIA information can be obtained
at www.ICGtesting.com
JSHW022354121023
49865JS00004B/18